ISSUES MANAGEMENT

ISSUES MANAGEMENT

Corporate Public Policymaking in an Information Society

Robert L. Heath
Richard Alan Nelson

SAGE PUBLICATIONS
The Publishers of Professional Social Science
Newbury Park London New Delhi

For information address:

SAGE Publications, Inc.
2111 West Hillcrest Drive
Newbury Park, California 91320

SAGE Publications Ltd.
28 Banner Street
London EC1Y 8QE
England

SAGE Publications India Pvt. Ltd.
M-32 Market
Greater Kailash I
New Delhi 110 048 India

Printed in the United States of America

Library of Congress Cataloging-in-Publication Data

Heath, Robert L.
Issues management.

Bibliography: p.
1. Public relations—Corporations. 2. Advocacy advertising. 3. Corporate planning. I. Nelson, Richard Alan, 1947- II. Title.
HD59.H33 1985 659.2 85-14547
ISBN 0-8039-2535-2 (cloth)
ISBN 0-8039-3609-5 (paper)

SECOND PRINTING, 1989
FIRST PRINTING, PAPERBACK, 1989

CONTENTS

FOREWORD

This book is a major contribution to the development of issues management, the newest management profession created for the benefit of senior executives. The authors have made the first in-depth analysis of the new management technique from the standpoint of communications theory. Their work is not only timely at this stage of development but essential because of the way the field has emerged.

Issues management first emerged in the corporate world through the communications professional staff (public relations and/or public affairs). It received its name in 1976 from a veteran corporate public relations officer, W. Howard Chase, who also designed the basic issues management process model in 1977. However, because the staff work requires interdisciplinary skills from various professions (law, economics, and social sciences, as well as communications), many issues management practitioners at work today have limited knowledge of the major role communications plays in the process. Thus this book fills a widely recognized gap in many practitioners' education.

Additionally, the authors have created a new issues management communications model, which is both an important contribution to theory and an excellent guide for the practitioner.

To date, the few books from academe relating to issues management have emerged from business schools, not from communications schools. (Professors from two or three major business schools have ruefully confided to me that issues management is the first new major management technique developed where the corporate practice has outrun university theory.) However, these business school books have dwelt on their heavily reworked theories of "corporate social responsibility" rather than on the broader aspects and synergies issues management makes possible in the offices of senior corporate officers. Professors Heath and Nelson take a broad overview of the new field, identify the multiple results that can be achieved, and then focus on their field of expertise, especially advocacy advertising and other underutilized communications channels and tools.

Heath and Nelson correctly argue for greater integration of issues management into the organization's overall planning process. To date, too few corporate issues management processes are so positioned. Allstate Insurance, American Can, Monsanto, and a limited number of other large corporations have their issues management staffs located in the corporate planning department, where both business and public policy planning proposals are integrated in the CEO's office.

Finally, another major contribution the authors have made toward the advancement of issues management is their objective analysis of the Chase-Jones issues management process model. Until recently critics from the academic community have either given superficial consideration to the model or have totally lacked understanding of how the process actually works in the corporate environment. The authors have remedied this situation by reviewing past critical assessments and then making their own judgments of the model, its comprehensiveness, and its need for further supplementation. In short, they have made a contribution that truly merits the gratitude of those of us who have been practicing corporate issues management fulltime for nearly a decade.

I look forward to debating some of the points of theory and practice in this book with my fellow practitioners. We who are so close to the practice need a longer overview that reemphasizes the role of communications, which can only be supplied to us by well-grounded professionals such as Professors Heath and Nelson.

Raymond P. Ewing
Issues Management Director,
Allstate Insurance Companies
July 1985

ACKNOWLEDGMENTS

We acknowledge the assistance of the following persons in the preparation of this study: John F. Budd, Jr., Vice President, External Relations, Emhart Corporation; Raymond P. Ewing, former Director of Issues Management, Allstate Insurance Companies, President of Issues Management Consulting Group, and Chairman Emeritus, Issues Management Association; Grey Advertising, for permission to use material from *Grey Matter,* reprinted courtesy of Grey Advertising Inc.; Milton Gross, Manager, Electronic Media Bureau, Federal Communications Commission; Garth Jowett, former Director of the School of Communication, University of Houston—University Park; Joseph A. Lopez, Houston Lighting & Power; Robert W. MacDonald, Manager, Public Affairs, Exxon Chemical Americas; Patrick Maines, President, The Media Institute; Wes Pedersen, Director of Communications, Public Affairs Council; James Post, Professor of Management, Boston University; Phillip Shiffman, Manager, Media Research, ESPN; Craig R. Smith, President, Freedom of Expression Foundation; and for editorial work, Jackie Syrop, Production Editor at Sage Publications.

*If you don't manage issues,
issues will manage you.*

1

ISSUES MANAGEMENT
An Old Hat or a New Ball Game?

The importance of public opinion to the successful operation of any organization concerned with influencing controversial policy issues is not new. But sophisticated new technology options and changing social demographics are. They encourage forward-thinking organizations to pay attention as never before to the interests and needs of specified audiences.

Our bewildering information environment today offers more than a challenge—it makes possible a new dialogue, in effect demanding that key social institutions, such as corporations, vigorously speak out if they are to participate in restructuring the social agenda of the approaching twenty-first century. For business, this extends beyond mere one-way communications, marketing, advertising, public relations, government affairs, or even strategic planning efforts. Not only a matter of money, but of will, today's volatile informatic economy requires a specialized function integrating these and other disciplines into a comprehensive long-term approach to issues management.

The contemporary popularity of issues management and the forming of new infrastructures for coordinating public policy programs are the product of such ongoing societal redefinitions. As *Business Week* (1979: 47) observes, "The corporation is being politicized and has assumed another dimension in our society that it did not have as recently as 10 years ago." Consequently, "it is articulating its positions more clearly and urgently to government agencies, legislators, shareholders, employees, customers, financial institutions, and other critical audiences." This observation suggests that many business leaders are becoming more sensitive to the impact of public attitudes on the marketplace positioning of their firms.

Not until the mid-1970s, when W. Howard Chase coined the term, was "issues management" identified as a specialized and increasingly important corporate function. Closely associated and often confused with issues management, the term "advocacy advertising" probably was first used by John E. O'Toole (1975a, b), now CEO of Foote Cone & Belding. Soon after, the International Association of Advertising (IAA), in its global study of issues communication, urged adoption of the less contentious "controversy advertising" (Barnet, 1975). Making the connection between advertising and issues, Dinsmore (1978) contended that "ideas could be sold like soap," but only if their presentation was complete and truthful. In addition to these pioneering efforts, various scholars have discussed the nature, role, and strategies of issues management.

The best known and most extensive critical analysis is Sethi's (1977) *Advocacy Advertising and Large Corporations.* Critics such as Sethi ask that public communication experts guard against the tendency companies have to use issues advertising to mislead rather than inform the public. In contrast, the seminal work of J. K. Brown (1979) concentrates on the processes of issues identification, monitoring, analysis, and corporate planning. Some researchers contend that issues management is "old hat"—a function that public affairs has been performing since corporations began to manage public policy issues. As far as we know, no extended study fully integrates what seem to be the three dominant aspects of issues management: issues monitoring, corporate performance, and issues communication.

Though the evolution of issues management began at least 100 years ago, it has gradually matured into a vital corporate function. Despite lingering recessions and slow economic growth over the past decade, business continues to budget for public communication. While conclusive financial data are unavailable, total lobbying expenditures in the United States "run into the billions each year," with annual grassroots spending (including issues campaigns) exceeding $1 billion as early as the mid-1970s (U.S. Congress, 1978a: 2). Industry associations annually spend $150 to $350 million on related campaigns (Pincus, 1980: 58). Setting the goal of issues management, Robert O. Anderson, former chairman and CEO of Atlantic Richfield Company, observes: "To command significant public support, business must do more than defend itself from attack. It must learn to reach out to society and to communicate and participate effectively with outside constituencies" (Nagelschmidt, 1982: xv). Whether as a function, process, or attitude, issues management has become an energetic and increasingly sophisticated response to legislative regulation. It has taken many forms, ranging from brash counterattacks to subtle readjustments designed to accommodate public standards of corporate ethical responsibility.

At the heart of the debate is the question of whether issues management is a meaningful new strategy for monitoring social performance, readjusting corporate operating policies, and communicating on issues important to various publics. To answer this question, this chapter contrasts and compares various corporate communication, planning, and monitoring activities. As will be demonstrated, issues management is not simply public relations or affairs, nor is it a synonym for advocacy advertising. Moreover, by approaching issues management from the orientation of communication theory, we can effectively understand it as an array of activities and attitudes which are designed to adjust the company to the public and help the public understand the complexity and requirements of the company.

At the turn of the century, *publicity* was the inclusive—if imperfect—descriptor for corporate communication strategies, including what has now come to be known as issues management. Later, *public relations* was widely embraced as a euphemism by business communicators concerned about image. Unfortunately, many associate its successes with shady practices, and now both terms are often used pejoratively.

Many authors coming from public relations or advertising backgrounds overlook the importance of issues management for corporate planning, including efforts to change and implement corporate codes of social responsibility. Issues management includes the identification and monitoring of trends in public opinion which may mature into public policy and the regulation of corporations or industries. It involves the staff function, which, with technical and managerial support, can develop a corporate or industry stance to be executed in campaigns that may utilize—but are not limited to—advocacy advertising. Drawing from public relations and public affairs, issues management also includes lobbying and financial support for PACs and industry groups, corporate video presentations, internal communication, newsletters, fliers, bill stuffers, newspaper and magazine articles, public appearances by key corporate or industry representatives, and other informational strategies. No other corporate function more completely stresses the inseparability of ethical corporate behavior, public judgment, the production and delivery of goods and services, and internal and external attempts to inform targeted constituencies in order to gain their support. More than issues monitoring, whether by public opinion polling or any other means, issues management goes beyond communication with various corporate constituencies. The impact of issues management can penetrate throughout company operations (see Figure 1).

Unfavorable media coverage and legislative intrusion into industry operations often collide with a corporate desire to destroy critics, block change, or make regulation as favorable as possible. With increasing sophistication, regulators and consumers have developed standards for acceptable corporate behavior that they apply with rigor and exactness. Failures by business have resulted in the creation of numerous governmental entities such as the Environmental Protection Agency, the Occupational Safety and Health Administration, and the Food and Drug Administration to stand between the general public and what many perceive to be the corporate enemy. Corporations today must choose between complying with these norms and seeking to modify them. Corporations generally try to maximize their options, whereas special interest groups seek to limit them by directing corporate behavior toward predetermined ends. If an issues monitoring program is effective, it can identify potential changes in public policy long before legislation is formed. Much as a driver with quick reaction time has a better chance of avoiding a traffic accident, successful issues monitoring affords companies the alternative of accommodating rather than colliding with public opinion.

The growing desire to participate in the management of issues reflects a new awareness that regulatory conditions extend into the day-to-day production, marketing, and delivery of goods and services. Companies have been placed under more strict and insightful regulation than during the previous 80 or so years of their existence. Moreover, the Federal Trade Commission (FTC), the Federal Communications Commission (FCC), the Internal Revenue Service (IRS), the Securities and Exchange Commission (SEC), and other agencies influence what and how businesses may communicate.

The marketplace, whether for goods, services, or ideas, is a potent force in our capitalistic society. Corporations compete against one another for market advantage but often band together for protection against unwise regulation. In self-defense, corporations may impose self-regulation. Unfortunately, corporations' efforts to end the uncertainty that pervades regulatory struggles often run head-on into an often adversarial press and entertainment system which, despite its own corporate magnitude, has discovered that the criticism of corporations can be profitable.

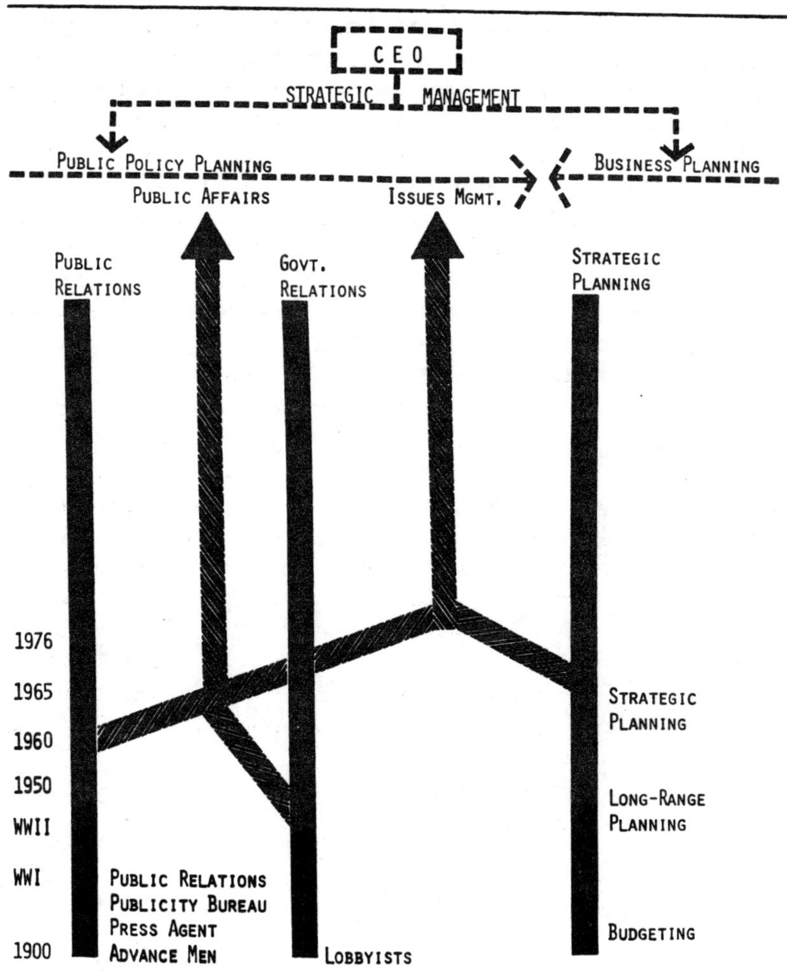

SOURCE: Ewing (1985).

Figure 1: Genealogy of Issues Management

Because they are sensitive to their image and public policy position, corporate leaders generally recognize the necessity of influencing public policy. In an address to the Issues Management Association (IMA) describing the unanticipated consequences faced by Nestlé Corporation as a result of its controversial decision to market baby formula in developing nations, Rafael D. Pagan (1983) stressed two key points he had learned: "For business, the cost of social awareness programs is great, but the cost of ignoring the outside world is greater." Continuing this line of analysis, Pagan proposed: "Issues managers can help instill social awareness into a business." As corporations realize the cost savings of monitoring and managing issues before they become explosive, issues management should gain popularity. Executives are adopting issues management teams because they want to know the public policy and communication implications of the policy changes they are contemplating.

Issues management can have many benefits, but not without risk. Issues advertising makes a company visible. As the IAA concludes in its study of controversy advertising:

> Business is subject to very careful scrutiny by several groups. Questions of factual error and omission are analyzed by the press and regulated by a wide variety of business and government bodies. Fallacious arguments are subject to a different kind of regulation: the ridicule of one's peers. The use of emotional persuasion is available to all. Such skills have served to render equal the Davids with the Goliaths [Stridsberg, 1977: 94].

Many corporate leaders opt for a low visibility response to this climate of negative public opinion. They may believe that their efforts can better be used to create more favorable public opinion toward corporations by changing corporate policy and behavior. Others are unwilling to spend the money necessary to help the public understand the operating requirements of companies. They may believe that the public is offended by advocacy campaigns. This attitude is not without merit. The 1978 House of Representatives hearings brought forth many who advocated placing regulations on advocacy campaigns. The critics proposed using a broad interpretation of what kinds of advertisements are not deductible under Internal Revenue Regulation 162-20 as necessary and ordinary operating expenses. Under the current IRS guidelines, a chilling effect has occurred: Companies have decided not to communicate with the public because the impact on the budget would be too great.

Although they are loath to criticize issues advocates in public, many corporate leaders would prefer companies such as Mobil to follow more standard corporate communication strategies. They believe that issues campaigns attract unhealthy attention, merely inviting public rejoinder and further governmental scrutiny. The risk in taking an adversary position is the likelihood that the public will be convinced that where there is smoke, there is fire. If corporations participate in public debate, their actions constitute for many an admission that some real and significant problem exists. The catch comes, however, when corporations refuse to respond, since their silence is often interpreted as guilt.

Corporations have been forced to speak out because network television and the elite press dominate the public agenda for the discussion of topical issues. Kaiser Aluminum & Chemical Corporation (1980) calls this climate "trial by television." Most corporations are not totally innocent of wrongdoing, but on the other hand, business should not continue to bear the stigma of pernicious activity without being allowed, and even encouraged, to correct the record and help shape public opinion. Constitutional free speech protections are involved here, as is the idea of fair and open debate. Much of what business does deserves praise. And although corporations must implement policy changes to conform to public expectations of ethical behavior, they should nevertheless participate in the discussion of those expectations.

During the 100 years since corporations became vital forces in American politics, economics, and society, they have enjoyed mixed reviews. Astute business leaders have realized that they cannot function effectively on the belief that corporations have no other purpose than to provide goods and services. DiBacco (1982) points out that actions taken by management traditionally have been based on economic strategies which many in the public neither understand nor appreciate. Critics of corporations have made valuable contributions to the quality of life by challenging business performance and demanding higher standards. However, some legislation has borne emotional qualities; some results from widespread misunderstanding. Big has at times been synonymous with bad; and corporate leaders are often represented as being motivated only by profit, not caring about employees nor about the quality of their goods and services.

At first corporations were timid about developing a rationale for such activities, but they are slowly evolving three lines of reasoning to justify spending corporate funds to advance their side of contested issues (Stridsberg, 1977). The first argument is that each company is an aggregate of the persons who own it. Because these shareholders have a common stake in what happens to the company, they should be willing to defend it and its industry. The second argument recognizes that employees also deserve a collective voice in the outcome of issues. The third justification grows out of companies' perception of their commitment to customers. These linkages are exemplified by the leadership of Archie Boe, CEO of Allstate Insurance Companies (1972-1982) and later President of Sears (1982-1984): "Allstate is—as are most insurance companies—in a unique position to function as a 'public interest' corporation since we literally stand in our customer's place in matters of financial loss. Very simply, their loss is our loss: What is good for them is good for us." He continues,

> When feasible, we serve as advocates or counselors for our customers, speaking and acting in their name as they would do, if they had our collective knowledge, training, experience and expertise in public matters affecting their interests. Our sense of corporate responsibility has moved us into an active role as a public interest corporation, which has a 'guidance system' concerned with human values and customer's needs. I think we've demonstrated from our efforts in securing drunk driver legislation, improved bumpers and related auto design, and modernization of the automobile insurance system, that Allstate has both the will and skill to meet its responsibilities and, at the same time, balance its public and self-interests for the benefit of all concerned.

These ideas Boe credits to General Leonard Wood of Sears, who "had a sign over the front door and it's still there. It says, 'Business must account for its stewardship, not only on the balance sheet, but also in matters of social responsibility.' We have incorporated this philosophy in our advertising efforts" (Boe, 1972).

Corporate money spent on controversy advertising and other issues management strategies can lead to constructive discussion of regulatory options, a more informed electorate, lower costs, and better customer service. As evidenced by some issues campaigns, corporations believe that certain goods and services can be made available, and at the best price, only if regulatory restrictions are lessened or removed (Stridsberg, 1977: 91-92).

A decade ago, Sethi (1974, 1977) believed that many corporations were failing to meet prevailing standards of corporate social responsibility. Moreover, they were not providing truthful and valuable information. He worried that the media would be unable to manage the space and time available so the public would have adequate access to all viewpoints. Also, he wondered whether people would have the time and patience to wade through the flood of information in order to become well informed. We share some of the same concerns, but we see the remedies in the free expression of ideas, rather than by the regulation of communication.

Corporations are not alone in their efforts to participate in the public policy debate. Nonprofit organizations are often founded on issues that have their place in the regulatory marketplace (Booth, 1978; Bates, 1982). Nonprofit agencies are developing an awareness and budgeting for their public communication functions. Many nonprofit organizations advocate issue positions that challenge corporate policies. But by taking a win-win attitude, companies often find that nonprofit organizations can be excellent allies.

Opinion Research Corporation (ORC) data gathered in 1981 indicate that 60 percent of the respondents "favored the idea of companies using paid advertising to present their points of view on controversial public policy issues." In addition, 90 percent reported having read or heard corporate advocacy advertisements within the previous two years. Of that 90 percent who had had contact with advocacy advertising, two-thirds thought the advertisements "to be at least fairly believable, and nearly the same number believed the advocacy advertisements helped them better understand the issues involved." Additionally, the survey indicated that respondents believed the advertisements had changed their minds on crucial issues. Because of what they had learned from the advertisements, 84 percent had discussed the issue with others, and 40 percent would attempt to change others' opinions on the issues. Not only did the respondents see company issues more favorably because of advocacy advertising, but they also reacted to the interest groups engaged in issue debate with particular corporations. In all, 51 percent believed that the interest groups had taken unfair advantage of the corporations because of the amount of unfavorable news the interest groups had been able to generate. By the same token, however, 60 percent indicated that while they favored corporations participating publicly in issue debate, they were concerned that the corporations had an unfair advantage because of the large amounts of money they could spend on advocacy and image advertising. Still, a substantial portion (85 percent) of the respondents believed that television companies should not exclude advocacy advertising (Ewing, 1982; Opinion Research Corporation, 1981a).

Despite this seemingly favorable reception, issues management transpires in a stormy climate. An uncertain operating climate has fostered the growing acceptance of issues management by business executives who, through trial and error, are learning that they must shape as well as respond to the regulatory and social conditions affecting their corporations (Weinstein, 1979; Divelbiss and Cullen, 1981; Buchholz, 1982). The upsurge of corporate communication has brought a sharp outcry from critics who fear that a free-market ideology presages the return to a ruthless nineteenth century robber baron mentality. These critics take their stand in defense of a public that might, they believe, too easily and significantly be swayed by the "deep pocket" spending of corporations.

TOWARD A DEFINITION OF ISSUES MANAGEMENT

Deriving a workable definition of issues management is difficult. Some treat it as a standard communication practice, an unnecessary coinage with no responsibilities beyond those served by public relations/public affairs. Because issues management is typically analyzed by studying only advocacy advertising and grassroots lobbying, many of its other functions are lost. Perhaps the greatest value in examining issues management in depth is to affirm the value of making public policy considerations a central component for corporate planning. Issues management is the one function in corporations that squarely addresses the need to adjust companies to public policy and to have public policy realistically reflect the requirements of companies.

Speaking as chairman of the Issues Management Association, Chase (1982) offered the following widely quoted definition: "Issues management is the capacity to understand, mobilize, coordinate, and direct all strategic and policy planning functions, and all public affairs/public relations skills, toward achievement of one objective: meaningful participation in creation of public policy that affects personal and institutional destiny." While Chase stressed the pro-active aspect of issues management, which "rejects the hypothesis that any institution must be the pawn of the public policy determined solely by others," he also noted its importance in helping corporate decision makers modify those institutional policies needing reevaluation once public expectations and involvement are identified (Chase, 1982: 1-2; for supplementary views, see Jones and Chase, 1979; Nagelschmidt, 1982; Chase, 1984; and Crable and Vibbert, 1985).

Taking a similar orientation, although one which more narrowly associates issues management with public affairs, the Public Affairs Council (1978) described it as "a program which a company uses to increase its knowledge of the public policy process and enhance the sophistication and effectiveness of its involvement in that process." The council also endorsed the now standard issues management model that consists of (1) monitoring the public policy arena to determine whether trends are occurring which can demand a reorientation of corporate policy and communication processes, (2) identifying those issues of greatest potential importance to the organization, (3) evaluating their operational and financial impact through issues analysis, (4) prioritizing and establishing company policy positions by coordinating and assisting senior management decision making, (5) creating the company response from among a range of issue change strategy options, and (6) implementing the plans through issue action programming.

The council and other proponents of issues management assert that it is unique in four key ways: (1) The systematic execution of the monitoring allows companies to intersect public opinion at an early formative stage atypical of most public communication efforts. (2) It is pro-active rather than reactive. (3) Issues management requires that corporations apply substantial empirical *and* qualitative analysis to solve corporate planning problems, and (4) success mandates that research and campaign targeting be supplemented by two-way strategies to reach a wider range of constituencies as part of the institutional "arena for action." Issues management is also a breakthrough because its systematic corporate matrix function demands a synergism that reaches beyond traditional departmental boundaries for establishing a platform of fact, value, and policy in corporate performance while communicating with targeted publics (including the company's senior managers). Moreover, this information approach helps both internal and external audiences understand the role of businesses in society, reorient the conditions of their operating environment, and analyze the ramifications of alternative approaches to corporate regulation.

Not everyone is as optimistic or enthusiastic about issues management. Responding to the Jones/Chase model, Ehling and Hesse (1983) doubt that it is as innovative or extraordinary as its proponents claim. Based on their own reasoning and a survey of Public Relations Society of America (PRSA) members, they argue that such activities are routine corporate communication; no new label or mandate beyond public relations/public affairs is necessary. From their survey data, Ehling and Hesse report: "Potential adopters saw 'issue management' as a kind of everyday management that any or all managers could do, . . . construed as the relatively mundane business of being cognizant of 'issues' that might have relevance to their organization or their office— and not much more." Ehling and Hesse argue that the current discussion of issues management calls for nothing beyond the effective use of survey and other issues-monitoring strategies typically employed today. If the model does nothing more than update the concept of public relations/public affairs with a new title, its revolutionary pretensions should be dismissed (Ehling and Hesse, 1983: 33). They challenge Chase and others to adopt more than social science jargon by integrating mathematically based techniques and theoretic foundations.

Generating evidence that supports *and* contradicts Ehling and Hesse's contention, Buchholz (1982) discovered that 91 percent of all Fortune 500 companies have established issues management programs. The leadership of these companies observed that issues management was extremely important (23.8 percent) or very important (50 percent).

One of the most tangible indicators of corporate support for this function is the fact that the number of personnel assigned to issues management had increased by 47.1 percent in the three years prior to Buchholz's survey. Issues managers are responsible for identifying, tracking, analyzing, and prioritizing issues, as well as formulating policy positions in response to them and implementing response strategies. A few respondents reported that issues management was vital to the long-range planning of their companies. Nearly 70 percent saw it as a function of growing importance. Approximately 40 percent believed that it would become part of corporate strategic planning, and about 20 percent believed that the future of issues management would depend on whether the coming business-government climate called for regulation. Only 13 percent believed that it is a fad.

Rather than trying to understand the role of issues management by surveying PR practitioners, we chose to look at its place in the total structure of corporations. While in theory, public relations, public affairs, and issues management overlap, the reality is that public relations/public affairs experts often are not meaningfully involved in corporate planning. Many executives, even today, fail to acknowledge the impact of public policy except in a reactive crisis situation. Post et al. (1983), in a survey of 1,001 large and medium-sized businesses, discovered no substantial evidence to confirm Ehling and Hesse's contention that practitioners routinely provide corporate planning influence. Part of this problem is due to the fact that one-half of all public affairs departments in major businesses were established in the 1970s, and at least one-third were put into place in the last decade (Post et al., 1983: 136). The level of influence exercised by public affairs depends on four factors: (1) Advice is more influential when it focuses on short-term rather than long-term issues. (2) The influence is greater in companies that are highly regulated and worry more about their operating environments. (3) In the minority of companies that genuinely use long-term planning, public affairs is more essential than in companies that plan only for the short term. (4) Large companies rely more on public affairs than do small ones (Dickie, 1984). Among the many corporate communicators who complain that strategic planning often ignores public affairs is Bergner (1982), who makes a case for blending the two functions, particularly for multinational businesses.

The internal politics of the corporate culture affect managerial willingness to redirect corporate procedures in establishing the matrix of key personnel necessary for an ongoing corporate issues management program. Failure by practitioners to be optimally involved in corporate planning will perpetuate their second-class status, particularly if they neglect the environmental monitoring of potential issues to focus on media relations or legislative lobbying. Where such individuals do not lead in convincing corporate officers to give more than lip service to issues management before a political threat or consumer controversy erupts, the door opens to capable professionals in finance, technical disciplines, and law interested in preparing their firms for the future (Bailey, 1983). Far from being an indictment against the innovativeness of issues management, the findings by Post et al., Bailey, and Ehling and Hesse loudly condemn corporate recalcitrance and the role—or the lack of one—played by many public affairs and public relations practitioners in the issues management process.

A stronger criticism of the Jones/Chase model is its lack of specificity in describing how issues management can bolster corporate planning. Once issues management is associated with corporate efforts to achieve social responsibility, it takes on the dimension that distinguishes it from routine public affairs or public relations activities.

In contrast to Ehling and Hesse is the judgment of Arrington and Sawaya (1984) of the Atlantic Richfield Company. Arrington, a lawyer by training, is the director of issues and planning, Public Affairs; Sawaya is the public affairs planning manager, Issues and Planning. They conclude that "issues management is a *process* to organize a company's expertise to enable it to participate effectively in the shaping and resolution of public issues that critically impinge upon its operations." They see this function as a complement to public affairs which is often "confined to reactive, 'fire-fighting' conduct." Because it is inseparable from basic business concerns, issues management "is simply never unrelated to bottom-line consequences" (Arrington and Sawaya, 1984: 148).

In a manner that corresponds closely to our view, Arrington and Sawaya propose that issues management should consist of "three concurrent activities: foresight, policy development, and advocacy." Foresight involves identifying, monitoring, analyzing, and prioritizing issues. But, they contend, it "is neither futurism nor forecasting; it is pragmatic, recurring judgment about external factors critical to company success" (Arrington and Sawaya, 1984: 149). Policy development, they believe, is "the routine 'heart' of issues management." It requires reconciling "conflicting internal interests on public policy issues of strategic importance in order to make a coherent external advocacy." The final function, advocacy, includes the communication efforts necessary to reach targeted audiences and achieve campaign goals.

These authors consider issues management as a subsection to strategic planning, even though the two are parallel and complementary. "Strategic planning must insure that various operating company plans are mutually consistent. Policy development in issues management must resolve differences among operating divisions on key public policy issues" (Arrington and Sawaya, 1984: 149-153).

Corporate strategic planning is the complex of goal setting and strategy selection whereby a business seeks to optimize profits. Issues management is an innovation that adds an ingredient to corporate planning. Companies are beginning to estimate the effects of public opinion on corporate decisions while adhering to standards of corporate social responsibility that marry corporate and public interests. Brown (1979) has captured the change in planning that characterizes the increased popularity of contemporary issues management. He observes: "Ten years ago, a prominent consultant has stated, 80 percent of planning was concerned with what management wanted, 20 percent with how the world affected the company; now the figures are reversed—or at least ought to be. Hyperbole perhaps; but the trend is unmistakable, and doubtless irreversible" (Brown, 1979: 3).

Being a bit timid about announcing that they are involved in "managing issues," companies often make the function nearly invisible. Because few corporations have an issues management department, the functions under that title are often handled by an ad hoc interdepartmental committee or else are located in public affairs, governmental affairs, or public relations departments. Typically, issues management is handled by a matrix of executives, staff personnel, and topic specialists. Responsibility for this activity may be a joint function of public relations and public affairs, or perhaps of one of the two in conjunction with a team consisting of management and technical experts. Alternatively, the person responsible for issues management may not be located in public relations or public affairs, but may be a member of the corporate planning team or in a department of external relations. Where issues management is located is strictly an arbitrary decision. It is the *mission* that is critical.

Drawing on the current literature and the variety of practices in companies, we prefer to treat issues management as a process *and* a state of mind. It can reside in one department which is authorized to "manage issues," or it can be diffused throughout a company and embedded in its operating and communication decisions. The models we have witnessed follow one of several patterns. If the company has a highly pyramidal structure, the primary responsibility for issues management is likely to be assigned to one major officer who works with a matrix of experts to monitor the trends in public policy, advise the corporate planning process, and communicate with constituencies. If the company has a diffused managerial system, many people may be simultaneously responsible for different aspects of issues monitoring. In both situations, a matrix management system seems to be typical, whether the activity is concentrated or dispersed (see Figure 2).

Public Affairs

Issues management overlaps with public affairs and public relations, particularly since there is no single, ideal corporate organizational structure for them, and because the terminology used by professionals in these and related business areas is circular and contradictory. Gruber and Hoewing (1980: 13) contend that public affairs is structurally responsible for helping the company relate to its *noncommercial* environment. Similarly, Nagelschmidt (1982: 290) defines public affairs as "a management function concerned with the relationship between the organization and its external environment, and involving the key tasks of intelligence gathering and analysis, internal communication, and external action programs directed at government, communities, and the general public."

Most public affairs departments are charged with monitoring legislative activities and political issue development which can adversely affect the operating climate. Public affairs concentrates on the management of governmental relations, often incorporating lobbying, shareholder, and employee information campaigns in support of public policy debate. Public affairs also has a listening function whereby it is responsible for understanding how legislative and regulative agencies are interpreting corporate responsibility. As Post et al. (1983: 139) point out, the central thrust of public affairs offices is "to narrow the gap between corporate practice and public expectations" by functioning "as a 'window out' through which management can comprehend the social and political environment and a 'window in' through which relevant external constituencies can understand the organization."

Despite the claims of management support for anticipatory solutions, CEOs often fail to integrate public affairs activities into overall corporate strategy or else bypass the department in major decisions until a crisis arises. Even when it performs effectively, public affairs is rarely

Monitoring Track	Corporate Track	Communication Track
	1. Develop corporate goals	
	2. Decide to undertake issues management	
	3. Locate issues function in corporation	
	4. Select issues personnel	
	5. Budget for function	
1. Scan/monitor public policy environment		
		1. Set communication campaign goals
	6. Apply monitoring to revise social responsibility code	
	7. Incorporate public policy issues into corporate planning	
		2. Select target audiences
		3. Design message content
		4. Select channels
		5. Implement campaign
2. Audit communication campaign		
		6. Reevaluate goals
		7. Reassess strategies
		8. Redesign campaign
		9. Select channels
		10. Execute new strategies
	8. Reevaluate corporate commitment	
	9. Reevaluate budget, personnel, and function location	

Figure 2: Issues Management Model

mandated with the chore of recommending changes in company line operations and may go unheeded in suggesting reorientations of corporate policy in response to shifts in public opinion and policy.

Public Relations

If public affairs is concerned primarily with the noncommercial aspects of corporate communication, public relations could be designated as being responsible for commercial communication, excluding paid product and service advertising. Public relations functions often include media relations, marketing publicity, investor relations, internal communication, and corporate image management. The primary purpose of this department is to place packaged information in key communication outlets. Moreover, such departments listen to public concerns and opinions. These are valuable data for corporate decision makers, but generally public relations has no power to direct corporate planning departments and other technical personnel.

Advertising

This brings us to the third major aspect of corporate communication that obscures the unique functions of issues management. Undue emphasis is often placed on advertising as the means for defining issues management, unfortunately confusing a strategic option with the broader process. Advertising can be divided into three categories: (1) product or service (brand identity) advertising; (2) corporate image advertising; and (3) issues or advocacy advertising. Because of its involvement in corporate planning, issues management can be instrumental in determining what kinds of message content should be presented in product, service, image, and advocacy.

Striving to clarify the nature of image advertising, Garbett (1981) suggests that it is "a type of corporate advertising whose prime objective is one of building basic recognition, awareness, or identity." Drawing on the research of Benson & Benson Inc. of Princeton, New Jersey, the content of image advertising typically follows several themes: diversity, productivity, energy, ecology, corporate social responsibility, consumerism, technology, major capital investment, financial performance, economics and regulation, recruiting and labor relations, acquisitions and mergers, name change or protection, and other corporate activities (Garbett, 1981: 10). Image ads have the added potential of changing unfavorable public opinion and allaying criticism while differentiating the sponsor from its competitors.

How do we know that advertising can influence people's opinions regarding corporate performance? Yankelovich et al. (1979) have demonstrated that the public is more familiar with the image of companies that advertise than of those that do not, and that people have a 34 percent better impression of corporate advertisers than of non-advertisers. Another research study produced similar results. It divided its findings into six categories: total recall, high recall, high familiarity, high association with specific traits, high favorable overall impression, and high potential supportive behavior. Corporate advertisers scored higher than non-advertisers on all six categories, and the amount of money spent was positively correlated with effectiveness. The advertising impact extended beyond the image of the company to favorably influence the public's views of quality of product, innovative research and development, good financial record, competent management, responsiveness to consumers, concern for natural resources, honest management, responsiveness of employees, truthfulness of advertising, and commitment to controlling inflation. The research found a positive connection between amounts of advertising dollars spent on corporate advertising campaigns and the public's willingness to recommend employment, buy stock, buy products without comparison shopping, read annual reports, and support the corporation's position on critical issues (Garbett, 1981: 92-95). Whether these results generalize to sponsors of issues campaigns is uncertain, but these findings clearly suggest that image advertising can affect the public's perception of corporate performance on matters prone to become issues, such as the quality of a product or responsible corporate behavior.

The subtleties of issues management are such that skilled practitioners often attempt to blend controversial positions and public service information. Companies, associations, unions and other organizations typically use the latter form to discuss salient public issues by linking their private interests to a broader public interest. In the midst of much auto safety controversy, General Motors sought to demonstrate its public service commitment by discussing drunk driving and the use of seat belts. The company even went so far as to offer a reward for the use of seat belts. Such public service statements may help the public cope with the perils of driving, but more importantly they build a political climate favorable to industry lobbying efforts to forestall the mandatory installation of expensive safety equipment.

The Mobil Oil op-ed campaign, in particular, has prompted renewed interest in the ways in which issue position and corporate image are often entwined. In 1979, Mobil stressed this connection in one of its classic advertisements, "Why Elephants Can't Live on Peanuts." Mobil argued that big corporations are needed to solve big problems, especially (during the energy crisis) the big task of finding, processing, and distributing petroleum products. Thus image advertisements can be too simplistically distinguished from issues advertisements. Even the "purest" issues advertisements reflect on the sponsoring company, suggesting that it is responsible, concerned, and "unduly restrained." (Some advertisements backfire, creating in the mind of the reader or listener a portrait of a company that is deceptive, greedy, or socially irresponsible.) If a company is attempting to communicate to targeted audiences that it is boldly willing to fight unfair criticism, and if it wants to lessen dislike for the "big" company, then such advertisements involve image.

Issues and image advertising often blend to discuss an issue once it becomes newsworthy, thus providing valuable insight into the reasons that a company is undertaking certain efforts and presenting the firm or industry as responsible and competent. Patented drugs, toys, tools, and cosmetics are only a few of the products which, once placed on the media agenda, receive in-depth scrutiny through news reporting and issues communication. Sensitivity to packaging that is either unsafe or misleading has also led to public interest attacks. For example, food additives have been criticized, particularly those used only to make the product more attractive instead of healthful. Such concerns have prompted industry representatives to make claims about safety, value, and purity which directly and indirectly attempt to allay public fears.

Overcoming negative reportage can be difficult and costly. Dow Chemical was sharply criticized during the 1960s for its production of napalm. Anti-war activists were effective in focusing on this method of warfare as indiscriminate and particularly horrifying in its killing of innocent people as well as the intended military enemy. Dow has spent a great deal of money in the years since, attempting to downplay its "mass murder" image by demonstrating its genuine concern for employees, product quality, and public safety.

Many other examples reinforce the belief that corporate image advertising is often entwined with issues management. The nuclear generating industry has attempted for over 20 years to emphasize the need for energy alternatives to fossil fuels. Booklets, press releases, films, school programs, displays, and ads all projected electrical needs and plant safety concerns well prior to the oil embargo of the 1970s. One may question their effectiveness, given the continuing belief that such efforts are mere propaganda. Nevertheless, without the willingness to continue telling their story, nuclear operators would likely face even greater difficulties. A later advertisement by American Electric Power (AEP) represented an alternative approach combining corporate image and public policy issue themes. Entitled "Nuclear Power at its Best," the 1984 advertisement extolled the success of the Donald C. Cook Nuclear Plant in Bridgman, Michigan, which had recently generated its 100 billionth kilowatt-hour of electric energy. AEP claimed that was enough energy "to serve the needs of ten million families for an entire year. Although a half dozen other U.S. nuclear plants have reached this milestone, none have done it as quickly." The plant was designed to save $1 billion, 26 million barrels of oil, and 7 million tons of coal. The conclusion of the advertisement struck a balance between image and issues: "The Cook Nuclear Plant is dramatic testimony of just how hard nuclear power can work for all of us."

THE IMAGE/ISSUE ADVERTISING CONTINUUM

Careful analysis can help avoid treating image and issues advertisements as synonymous. Drawing on Publishers Information Bureau data, Garbett (1981: 13) defines corporate image advertising by stressing several outcomes:

(1) To educate, inform, or impress the public with regard to the company's policies, functions, facilities, objectives, ideals, and standards.
(2) To build favorable opinion about the company by stressing the competence of the company's management, its scientific know-how, manufacturing skills, technological progress, product improvements, and contribution to social advancement and public welfare; and, on the other hand, to offset unfavorable publicity and negative attitudes.
(3) To build up the investment qualities of the company's securities or to improve its financial structure.
(4) To sell the company as a good place in which to work, often in a way designed to appeal to college graduates or to people with certain skills.

The IAA believes that "corporate image advertising treats the company as if it were a product, positioning it with care within its industry or industries, giving it a clear differentiation from others resembling it, and basically 'selling' it to the audiences selected. The selling objectives are usually financial, legal, and to a lesser extent governmental support, to facilitate the company's pursuit of its business objectives" (Stridsberg, 1977: 32). Some exceptionally responsible companies may suffer guilt by association. However, if the products are truly needed, the more responsible companies can gain market advantage by combining product, image, and issues advertising to communicate their responsibility and public commitment, thereby making the quality of the product and service stand out in comparison.

Trying to apply the distinction between commercial and political communication, Meadow (1981) argues for the adoption of two categories, product and nonproduct advertising. The first, by implication, falls into what some call commercial communication, while the latter is political. In his taxonomy, nonproduct advertisements range from statements in support of company images to those encouraging public support of political candidates and issues. Rather than helping to differentiate between the two kinds of communication, Meadow concentrates on the trend to treat product and nonproduct advertising as close associates.

His classification assumes that all nonproduct communication corrupts the traditional role of the company. He therefore denies it a place in the discussion of public policy issues affirmed by the Supreme Court. In the past two decades, because of the increased scrutiny of all aspects of corporate behavior, many critics in and out of government have attempted to hone in on the political implications of business activities. Nevertheless, distinctions between commercial, noncommercial, and political communication often defy attempts to dichotomize them. Two series of congressional hearings held in 1978 (U.S. Congress 1978a, b) probed the need for changes in the way issues advertising is regulated by the IRS, FTC, and FCC.

Because images and issues are closely associated, we should instead treat them as points in a circle rather than as a straight-line continuum. At one point are *direct image advertisements,* those which carefully and clearly differentiate the image of the sponsor and its products or services from those of its competitors. Other image advertisements are indirect; they discuss topics designed to help the public appreciate the company and its operating position. Only indirectly is the advertisement likely to affect the sponsoring corporation's image. These are *indirect image advertisements* that deal with social, financial, or economic issues surrounding corporate responsibility, or that feature goodwill efforts. Indirect image advertisements take informational or issues stands but do not emphasize traditional marketing concerns. Such is also the case for goodwill advertisements, which, although indicating the charitable efforts of a company or industry, are not directly associated with the company's services, products, or operating reputation. Under some circumstances, taking a policy stand can demonstrate the same kind of citizenship and image concern that Red Cross public service advertising does, and even go beyond it by looking at free enterprise and other issues basic to the national economy. By taking controversial stands, the sponsoring organization can, indirectly or directly, influence its image.

The following list suggests the variety of types of advertisements in this continuum.

(1) *Direct image,* through a favorable description of the company's products or services.
(2) *Direct image,* by providing facts about the company's or industry's operation.
(3) *Direct image,* through a favorable description of how a company's activities and policies agree with public expectations of acceptable corporate behavior.
(4) *Indirect image,* through a favorable description of the company's support of charitable and/or community service activities.
(5) *Indirect image,* by providing noncontroversial information of value to the public.
(6) *Indirect image,* through association with traditional values.
(7) *Indirect image,* through stands on social, economic, or financial issues by favoring a noncontroversial or popular point of view.
(8) *Indirect image,* through a favorable discussion of the need for corporations in general (and implying the value of the sponsoring company in specific).
(9) *Indirect image,* through a challenge of facts reported about a company or industry, attacking critics and answering criticism.
(10) *Indirect or direct image in issues idea advertisements,* by taking controversial stands on facts, values, or policy.
(11) *Indirect or direct image in issues action advertisements,* through calling for participation in the legislative and/or regulatory process.

Issues campaigns concentrate on several kinds of activities, incorporating direct and indirect image/issues appeals. In monitoring trends and providing communication related to a narrow but important range of topic areas, they call to the public to be involved in the creation, passage, or defeat of legislation; seek to blunt regulatory activities; rebut disputed facts about an industry's or a company's products, services, or operations; discuss contested norms and values of corporate behavior; and champion capitalism and free enterprise. This taxonomy is designed to discourage confusion between advertisements with issues components and those which only feature obvious marketing strategies of product, service, or corporation identity. Moreover, as will become apparent in Chapter 4, this outline is sensitive to the definitional guidelines on grassroots lobbying established by the IRS.

How have others dealt with this problem? Sethi (1977) asserts that issues advertising is a type of corporate image advertising. "It is," he argues, "concerned with the propagation of ideas and elucidation of controversial social issues of public importance in a manner that supports the position and interests of the sponsor while expressly denying the accuracy of facts and downgrading the sponsor's opponents. The managerial context of advocacy advertising is that of defending the corporation's activities and modus operandi." Sethi suggests that advocacy advertising has two other contexts as well:

> The behavioral and social context of advocacy advertising is that of changing public perception of a corporation's actions and performance from skepticism and hostility to trust and acceptance. The political context of advocacy advertising is that of the constitutional safeguards for freedom of speech where a corporation is asserting its right to speak out on issues of public importance without any regulation or censorship on the part of other private groups or government agencies [Sethi, 1977: 7].

Sethi dismisses attempts to wrap advocacy advertisements in such euphemistic terms as issues advertising, public interest advertising, or information advertising. He believes that the public simply is not fooled by labels, since such advertising constitutes advocacy. Moreover, efforts at establishing a precise taxonomy are frustrated by the fact "that most such campaigns not only may use one or more types of advocacy appeals, but may also have elements of pure corporate goodwill or image advertising, and also include some product advertising" (Sethi, 1977: 10).

To avoid arousing negative connotations, in 1977 the IAA proposed using the term controversy advertising for "any kind of paid public communication or message, from an identified source and in a conventional medium of public advertising, which presents information or a point of view bearing on a publicly recognized controversial issue." The IAA prefers this "use of advertising in the public interest" to potentially strident and contentious alternatives such as public interest advertising, public affairs advertising, cause-and-issue advertising, viewpoint advertising, strategic advertising, opinion advertising, advocacy advertising, public issue advertising, and adversary advertising. Even so, in the context of public debate, "the purpose of controversy is not to create a passively favorable climate for actions the company wants to take, but to inject the company's interests, points of view, and objectives into the outside controversy where other people are taking actions" (Stridsberg, 1977: 12-18, 33). Garbett (1981: 12, 39-41) adds the clarification that advocacy advertising commonly is in behalf of an issue, while adversary advertising is used when the sponsor takes a position opposed to an issue.

The IAA suggests that typical motivation for controversy advertising falls into three categories: "(1) Defense of an economic or social point of view. (2) Aggressive promotion of a point of view. (3) Establishment of a 'platform of fact' which entitles the advertiser to have a voice in the controversy, and to participate in its resolution." This "bears a strong resemblance to corporate image advertising. The advertisements are factual, do not present demands for action or justification of past events, and represent a selection of information intended to put the corporation in a good light." The IAA points out that defense may be necessary when corporations must respond to misrepresentation and false or distorted information. "To do so is a clear obligation of management to the owners or stockholders, and to the employees as well. Correction of fact is intended to eliminate, rather than indulge in, controversy. . . . The advertiser literally *protests* against the opposing point of view, and in so doing offers more or less specific alternatives of his own" (Stridsberg, 1977: 36-38).

The popularity of the advocacy over the adversary approach is understandable given the reality that successful persuasive campaigns typically mobilize or reinforce supporters rather than convert opponents. The IAA discovered that "most controversy advertising is not intended to confound attackers, but to reach (a) those who support (or are presumed to support) the point of view being presented, (b) those most likely to accept and communicate the point of view to others, and (c) those in the uncommitted category most inclined toward the passive acceptance of the advertised point of view." Even a casual glance at issues advertising discloses that much of it is targeted toward readers of business publications such as the *Wall Street Journal.* Nevertheless, some advocates (notably Mobil) have targeted the readers of editorial sections of major newspapers. Others use popular news magazines, specialty and opinion journals, or trade publications directed at audiences such as journalists. What is clear, however, is that issues managers do not often place their advertisements in publications most likely to confront their attackers (Stridsberg, 1977: 49).

Stridsberg (1977: 51) continues:

> If the point that controversy advertising is rarely targeted directly at an adversary audience seems unduly stressed, it is because *most of the failure of communications in controversy advertising appears to result from the fact that the creators lose sight of the basic media targets and, in the*

creative execution of the advertising message, assume that they are really speaking to their opposition.

Stridsberg, Garbett, the IAA, and Sethi are not alone in finding difficulties with definitions for advocacy and issue advertising, although Sethi later distinguished between the two by arguing that issue ads do not "carefully position" and "clearly differentiate" the sponsoring company from others. Extending this line of reasoning, Sethi (1979: 70) concludes: "Corporate image advertising is not concerned with a social problem unless it has a preferred solution. It asks no action on the part of the audience beyond a favorable attitude and passive approval conducive to successful operation in the marketplace."

By focusing on advertising, some writers overlook lobbying and other grassroots contact with prime constituencies. Often excluded from their analyses are free placement of information, such as articles written by corporate spokespersons, and other communication strategies used by issues managers to educate news writers and broadcasters. Having a corporate leader appear on a TV or radio talk show may be even more important than the design and placement of advocacy advertisements. We must not make a key mistake by failing to distinguish between a broad corporate activity (issues management) and one of its strategies (advocacy advertising).

We agree with Goodman (1983), who observes that the issues management process is complicated because "Corporations spend more time trying to label issues than they devote to managing issues. . . . [B]usiness is bombarded with too many issues—and must come up with ways to handle them." The problem is exacerbated by divisions within corporations and scholarly writing which have fractured, rather than united, issues management into three topical perspectives: (1) corporate planning and strategy, (2) corporate social responsibility, and (3) public issues management. Such structural and conceptual fragmentation often leads persons to focus on a segment, but not the total picture. As Goodman notes, these artificial subdivisions have their own publications, such as *Planning Review, Business and Society Review,* and *Public Affairs Review.* "The articles, writers and editorial boards live in the same interrelated world, but do not seem to recognize that this is the case. And business schools and corporations have failed to recognize that ambiguity and uncertainty exist."

As it has evolved in the last decade, the uniqueness of issues management is not merely its stress on communication, opinion surveying, or corporate planning. Effective issues management requires the integration of these three important activities at the corporate headquarters level: (1) issues monitoring and prioritization, (2) continuing analysis of the correspondence between public expectations of corporate behavior and the implementation of corporate codes of social responsibility, and (3) internal and external communication efforts to discuss public policy issues. All of these activities combine into the new awareness that corporations must participate as citizens in a rapidly changing political and social environment.

IMPORTANCE OF PUBLIC OPINION TO BUSINESS

The relationship between corporations and the public is often placid, but periods of contentiousness have occurred. Data on the decline in the public's confidence in corporate behavior illuminate the climate that has prompted an interest in issues management. In 1966, 55 percent of the public had "a great deal of confidence" in the capability and moral qualities of corporate leaders. By 1976, the confidence level had fallen to 16 percent, where it has remained (Kelly, 1982). (1983 Gallup research placed the figure at 18 percent.) Moreover, in the battle of credibility, corporate leaders trail TV commentators (33 percent), journalists (28 percent), and newspaper reporters (26 percent) (Gallup Report, 1983). The public is ambivalent whether government or big business is to be distrusted more. Schellhardt (1975) has reported that 56 percent of the public favored increased government regulation of corporations. Only 35 percent of the public favored less regulation. This trend continued into the 1980s. A March 23, 1981 Harris survey reports that even though 53 percent of the people feel that big government is a problem, approximately 80 percent believe that government must protect the public against corporations.

Public opinion is a misnomer to the extent that it leads us to think that at any time, on any issue, there is one public with a single dominant opinion. The most useful way to think of public opinion is to consider what segment of society has what opinion, an approach especially meaningful for issues management. In many instances, large segments of the public agree with and champion the points advanced in an issue advertisement. In contrast, other segments may have grave reservations about the same issues. The safest approach is to think of targeted audiences for which messages are designed and the channels of communication selected.

Even if the goal is not to achieve a particular corporate image, corporations must participate as citizens in a rapidly changing political and social environment. This spirit is championed by Chase (1982: 2), who writes: "The noblest aspect of freedom is that human beings and their institutions have the right to help determine their own destinies. Issue management is the systems process that maximizes self-expression and action programming for most effective participation in public policy formation."

PUBLIC POLICY ISSUES AND THE FOCUS OF ISSUES MANAGEMENT

Ehling and Hesse (1983: 24-27) challenge those who discuss issues management in order to define an issue precisely, especially a public policy issue. *An issue is a contestable question of fact, value, or policy.* These distinguishing characteristics are found, for example, when corporations become involved in discussions such as these: fact—whether oil companies control the supply of oil and create shortages?; value—what are the dimensions of corporate responsibility?; and policy—whether corporations should be required to use scrubbers to minimize emissions of sulfur dioxide? Public policy issues are those with the potential of becoming involved in governmental regulation (international, federal, state, or local).

Issues management campaigns are capable of damaging corporate images. Thus some companies avoid controversy, fearing that communicating could be more harmful than remaining silent. Backlash looms as a clear and present danger, since the antagonism inherent in contesting legislative and administrative activities can generate an increased commitment on the part of members in these governmental bodies to punish corporations. If the tone of the campaign is obnoxious, it may deter personnel recruitment and lead to resignations by valued employees. In an environment where maintaining investor relations is vital, an issues campaign can result in a loss of investor confidence. Investors may favor alternative management strategies, worrying that the cost of an issues campaign may undercut profits, market value, and dividends. Moreover, the tone of the campaign and the position on certain issues may alienate investors. Other firms may be less willing to coalesce with a company that is engaged in issues management. Faced with this list of liabilities, Garbett (1981: 50) identifies the most extreme reason for undertaking issues communication: "There can be only one valid reason for risking all these negatives. The level of pain that the corporation is experiencing from some particular public issue warrants the risk and the expense, an expense which it knows in advance will probably not be allowed as a business tax deduction." With proper pro-active issues monitoring, corporate planning, and issues communication, most companies need not experience this extreme pressure.

Some issues management campaigns are undertaken simply because corporate managements are miffed over a lack of public awareness. Similarly, corporate leaders often feel deep frustration over the ignorance of their industry on the part of those advocating new regulations. A complex problem may not be served by a simplistic answer. In contrast to the difficulties corporations have in explaining complex issues, public interest groups can often lead the public to believe that simple answers prevail which corporations are unwilling to undertake because of greed or myopia. An example involves the simplistic suggestions that the development of alternative energy sources is being held back by a conspiracy of corporations motivated only by base concerns.

For various reasons, substantial antagonism has existed between the media and corporate leaders. Entertainment industry portrayals of business people employ many negative characterizations. Many journalists, too, are deeply suspicious of industry. When business failings are uncovered, they are often played up by the press. This uneven coverage means that corporate communicators start with a disadvantage. The bad news maxim of public relations parallels Gresham's law in finance: Bad news tends to drive good news out of the public's mental marketplace.

Enjoying the protection of the fairness doctrine in choosing which issues and information they will cover, the major TV networks have cavalierly rejected most issues advertising. The electronic managers argue that the public is best served by their regular news and public affairs programming, and not by companies seeking to spread "partisan viewpoints on the basis of who is first in line . . . because of their ability to pay" (Kaiser Aluminum, 1980: 19). On the other hand, if companies will not or cannot actively communicate, they risk being criticized for their secretiveness and arrogance.

Some corporate critics further assume that companies can and will speak univocally with a monopolitical ideology. To these fears is added Sethi's (1981: 12) criticism that "a great number of advocacy campaigns contribute little or anything to the public's information base. Issues are presented with catchy headlines and simple messages which are conclusatory and deterministic. The primary emphasis is on reinforcing the sponsor's position." These serious apprehensions can be lessened by noting numerous instances where companies disagreed substantively on issues. For instance, while Allstate was campaigning for air bags, automotive industry representatives were opposing them.

It is wise to focus on the level of information used. This approach assumes that the public needs to know corporations' sides on controversial issues just as it should know the positions held by critics of industry (Gwyn, 1970). The heart of much controversy, Finn (1981: 6) believes, is that corporations, critics, and the media are "frustrated about the problem of getting the facts out to the public."

Not surprisingly, the trend in the past few years has been to decrease stridency and increase the informational content of issues advertisements and other communications. If the goal is to expand "the information pie," it does not make much sense to tie the hands of business communicators, even when they "pursue a course primarily of partisan propaganda" (Lukasik, 1981: 19). To imply that corporations should be restricted from taking stands on such issues as the free enterprise system or particular legislation, merely because they are controversial, is blatantly contrary to Supreme Court interpretations of corporate rights.

Mobil's management, in a 1982 op-ed message explaining why it chose to lead in issue advertising, succinctly put forward its position that business must speak out against the erroneous stereotypes, perpetuated by the media, which indicate that corporations do not care about anything but selling goods and services:

> Our answer is that business needs voices in the media, the same way labor unions, consumers, and other groups in our society do. Our nation functions best when economic and other concerns of the people are subjected to rigorous debate. When our messages add to the spectrum of facts and opinion available to the public, even if the decisions are contrary to our preferences, then the effort and cost are worthwhile.

Such communication is important in helping establish the "platform of fact" that we described earlier—but facts alone are not enough. How the facts are interpreted and how policies are formulated depend on the values current in public opinion. In addition to information regarding corporate operations, the public must understand the ramifications of policies. This discussion also allows various key publics to predict the liabilities and benefits of constraining or fostering admittedly complex corporate activities. Underregulation can result in irresponsibility.

Overregulation, on the other hand, can lead to a stifling operating environment that works against needed increases in productivity and job creation.

This information approach to issues communication is based on the rationale that mutual understanding can foster trust. To establish public trust, corporations must report accurate information about their operating problems and conditions. The more companies meet the public's need for information, the more likely we are to achieve a society of understanding. At a time when the public has lost much of its faith in corporations and understands less and less about their operating requirements and procedures, many corporations seem eager to play a positive role. For this reason, key publics should obtain sufficient information about corporations to help understand corporate needs and responsibility. However, the information must also have worth; it must be that which is needed and desired by the public. Taking a position such as this should challenge corporations to open the "windows of vulnerability" whereby they try to achieve public understanding instead of blind compliance. In this way, both parties have pertinent information about one another which can contribute to settling mutual differences and reaching a satisfactory solution. While conflict is not always simply a matter of misunderstanding, and while understanding does not necessarily equate with acceptance, effective issues communication can undercut the arguments of corporate critics.

COMMUNICATION THEORY AND ISSUES MANAGEMENT

Theoretical considerations are at the core of effective campaign design. Even more important, communication theory can aid our understanding of the purpose, scope, and strategies of issues management. Since the 1930s, the process of communication has been partitioned into five interrelated parts: source/sender, message, channel/media, receiver, and feedback. This standard model proposes that communication must be sensitive to contexts of time, place, social condition, ideology, culture, and other elements that prevail in the human mind. The simplest version of this model is to identify who says what through which channel to whom, and with what effect.

Hypodermic Model

Before interaction models became pervasive in communication studies, the typical approach to communication was analogous to a hypodermic injection of information into an audience. This view treats the source as active and the receiver as passive. At its extreme, this model views audiences as blank tablets upon which sources "write" messages. To illustrate this model, we can imagine a picture of a human head with a funnel inserted through the top. Into the funnel, the source (of whatever kind) pours information and influence that the receiver accepts passively. In corporate management theory terms, this view of communication assumes that authority flows from the top down or from the corporation to the community. Corporate communicators are expected to carry out policy but not help formulate it. Anti-business advocates have been somewhat successful in creating an image of public relations practitioners manipulating the press and public by "injecting" them with propagandistic information accepted (for the most part) unthinkingly. This elitist model of communication is fraught with corporate arrogance toward the passive public receivers. Researchers and theorists generally agree that it is theoretically imprecise and flawed, and many professional communicators have begun to abandon this model in the pursuit of their task.

Interactive Models

Interactional views of communication theory and research began to displace the hypodermic approach in the 1960s. An interactive model argues that a dynamic, two-way relationship exists between sender and receiver; the source-receiver relationship is thus interactive or interdependent. Communication participants can be senders as well as receivers simultaneously. Rather than merely treating the process as going from sender to receiver and looping back through the feedback stage—as was originally thought in the hypodermic model—the more contemporary model treats the receiver as active participant rather than passive vessel.

What implications does this hold in the real world? To appreciate the social and political contexts of issues management, we must acknowledge that thousands of voices are competing for attention, and that each one seeks to influence many others. We live in an era of alternative information sources, mass media clutter, and electronic devices such as computers, VCRs, and audio cassettes which allow "sovereign" viewers and readers to consciously pass up a great deal of information and refuse to yield to widespread attempts at persuasive influence. Persuasion research has become increasingly sensitive to how receivers automatically engage in refutation when they encounter messages with which they disagree. Moreover, corporations must be receivers as well as senders if they are to provide useful, "what's in it for me" information about their operating conditions to these sovereign publics. They must respond with the information the public wants; no longer can corporations survive peacefully by only telling what they want targeted receivers to know.

In this regard, corporate claims must correspond to publicly available facts or demonstrate objectively that those facts are incorrect. A truism: Lying to the public is fatal. One such incident involved a coal producers association advertisement in the *Wall Street Journal* featuring a "coal miner" as the man of the year. Rather than being a real miner, however, the spokesman was a vice president in the association's advertising agency. When this fact became known, the coal producers' image dropped dramatically (Stridsberg, 1977: 71). Such cases illustrate the dynamic influence of audiences.

Co-orientation and Symbolic Interaction

One of the most productive versions of interactive communication is co-orientation (McLeod and Chafee, 1973), which extended premises basic to symbolic interaction. This model assumes that individuals engage in bilateral communication for a purpose, with more interaction tending toward greater accuracy and satisfaction. For instance, by discussing what you think of a friend and what the friend thinks of you, you can increase the accuracy of your perceptions of one another. This in turn may lead you both to ask yourselves how satisfied each is with the other's behavior. The key to understanding other people, whether on an individual or mass society basis, is accurately knowing what they believe (Fields and Schuman, 1976-1977).

Broom (1977) adapted these co-orientation assumptions to develop a rationale for estimating the effectiveness of public relations. He proposed that we could compare the image or issue position preferred by a corporation against that held by targeted segments of the public. Broom (1977: 111) suggests that "a public relations problem exists if there is a discrepancy between the corporate definition of an issue and the views held by members of an important public. Reducing or eliminating this discrepancy then becomes the motivation for the informational and persuasive messages directed to the public."

The crucial contribution of co-orientation is that even though no standard for issue truth, corporate image, or ethical behavior exists in the abstract, we can recognize that such a standard is created through communication interaction. The key questions are: (1) What does the targeted public think of the issue? and (2) What does the corporation believe is the preferred issue position? To the extent to which these diverge, we have a result dissatisfying to the corporation, if not to the public. Conversely, if their positions converge, both parties should be satisfied. By methodological application of this analysis, we can survey the degree to which issue positions held by the corporation and the public converge or diverge. Beyond this, we can calculate the degree of satisfaction and accuracy.

Assumptions of the Jones/Chase Systems Model

One of the major innovations in communication theory was the application of systems analysis to the design and diagnosis of communication interaction. The Barrie L. Jones and W. Howard Chase model mentioned earlier assumes that issues management is a circular process starting with issues identification, leading through issues analysis to issues change strategy options and eventually to an issues action program. The model underscores the importance of the issues manager seeing management as an ongoing transaction between three dynamic parties: the corporation, power groups and others who raise issues, and the public targeted for corporate and action group communication.

A systems approach assumes the presence of input (what goes into a system), throughput or processing (how the input is handled), and output (what result the processing accomplishes). Change in one element of the system correspondingly affects other parts. For instance, corporations take in information relevant to the issues being developed. Once this information is considered, planning can lead to a change in corporate policy, or a decision can be made to undertake a communication campaign. In the latter option, information is output to be received as input by targeted audiences who process the information and decide whether to accept it or reject it. If the targeted audiences accept the information, the corporate side of the issue may prevail and the issue dies. If the information fails to be persuasive, the processing and subsequent output can be even more damaging to the efforts of the corporation. This kind of process goes on and on throughout all parts of the issues management system.

Reflecting an ever-increasing sensitivity to this orientation, the Foundation for Public Relations Research and Education, in conjunction with the Public Relations Division of the Association for Education in Journalism and Mass Communication (AEJMC), recently conducted a delphi study outlining priority questions for the decade (McElreath, 1980). The research sponsors were aware that communication practitioners cannot function effectively without serving as a liaison between management and the individuals who use and criticize corporations. They encourage research that will establish what links exist between public perceptions and the way these people act toward corporations. Such information could assist later in more accurately identifying specific audiences critical for corporate communication.

Establishing a research agenda is an important means for answering a variety of questions. For example: What techniques are best for monitoring public opinion and public reaction? How informed is the public regarding the technological and managerial requirements of corporations? Where do people get their information about companies? How can issues communicators most cost-effectively obtain and supply accurate information? How believable is the information supplied by corporations? What information do various factions *really* want as a part of their evaluation of corporate behavior? How many companies provide this information? What are the strengths and weaknesses of advocacy campaigns compared with other strategies to better inform stakeholders? At what point in an issues controversy do people stop using a corporation's goods or services or refuse to invest in it? What kinds of attitudes will lead the public to form or support special interest organizations to regulate a corporation or industry? How can companies best negotiate with activist groups or counteract them?

Perhaps no dimension of the communication process emphasizes the dynamism of the receiver more than credibility. The public is reluctant to accept claims made by sources perceived to be untrustworthy and acting out of apparent self-interest. The concerns raised by the foundation reveal a deepening recognition of the need to communicate corporate performance. Chest-beating and protestations by business communicators about being treated unfairly usually do little to reconcile the public to the plight of corporations. Such protests may even have the undesirable effect of decreasing, rather than increasing, credibility. Paradoxically, a low level of confidence in corporate behavior is evidence that the public is convinced that corporations have caused their own troubles. Many public interest groups involved in "combating the corporate giants" are creatures of the business community—arising as a response to the failed communication programs of public relations practitioners who no longer have the right to treat their function as a conduit through which management disseminates information to a willing and passive public. Issues management involves many players in an intricate dialogue that can culminate in a new understanding of the domestic and international role corporations play in economic, social, and political life.

2

ISSUES MANAGEMENT AND THE SEARCH FOR ORDER

The questioning focus on corporate behavior, prompted in the post-World War II period primarily by the civil rights movement's analysis of all institutions, blossomed during the 1960s era of multifaceted agitation. Although this challenge regenerated an awareness that boardrooms are never immune to scrutiny, issues management is not simply a contemporary phenomenon. Billions of dollars have been spent on advocacy communication during the past two decades, and yet its roots are firmly planted in the era of the robber baron. The history of issues management parallels the tumultuous growth of corporations, marked by the ongoing public contest between business critics and supporters. Business supporters generally stress the influence of corporations in creating jobs and providing products and services. They normally oppose regulation unless it stabilizes the marketplace and boosts profits. These people often believe that if interested publics understand the plight of business, they will be less willing to champion restrictions. On the other hand, business critics often argue that corporations need to comply with ever-changing public expectations of responsible behavior.

Near the end of the 19th century, few companies realized the value of courting public opinion. The regulation of business activities tended to be local; no comprehensive national policy had been formed. Federal powers were limited, and the nation was only developing a mass mentality made possible by improvements in transportation (such as rail systems) and communication (typified by the telegraph). Far-sighted business leaders, however, could see that post-Reconstruction industrialization would lead to lucrative mass markets. The modern beginnings of advertising date to this period. Even presidential campaigns of this era began to be more "national" as propaganda devices were increasingly used to magnify the impact of stump tours.

FORMATION OF CORPORATE IDEOLOGY

Crude forms of the corporation date to the Roman Empire and have evolved following the spread of commerce during the Renaissance. The growth of U. S. firms was spurred following the American Revolution by protectionist "American System" reforms promulgated by Alexander Hamilton and his ideological successors. Most corporations operate under state charters pioneered originally by New York in 1811. As a legal "person," corporations can conduct business, hold property, and even commit crimes. Corporations have the constitutionally guaranteed power to act and speak as individuals. The corporation is well suited to mass culture requiring large-scale capital formation.

At the close of the Civil War, the nation was fertile land for the growth of corporate America. The war had cost the nation dearly in money and labor force. Corporations had provided needed war matériel, and after the war they underwrote financial development for expanded industrial production. Kingpins who could generate money—sometimes by bold stock fraud schemes—were destined to shape the last years of the century.

Corporations evolved naturally rather than by calculated design. As a first step toward massive business concentrations, several manufacturing plants, small railroad companies, or oil refineries were often brought together under a committee that managed them in a trust. This system increased their efficiency and decreased competition. Slowly such committees merged into corporate giants, typified by Standard Oil. Through a process of absorption and amalgamation, 138 companies were combined into United States Steel (Kolko, 1967: 33).

In addition to capital, the nation's infrastructure began to burgeon as local markets were displaced with national ones. The slow metamorphosis from a rural-agricultural to urban-industrial society demanded that farm produce reach the urban industrial areas. This made the farmers victims of the railroads, which often charged more for local shipment than for long distance freight. Small farmers bore the brunt of the cost of shipments, which favored corporate producers.

Against rawboned and roughshod industrialization arose the voices of Populists and Progressives who believed that corporations should be constrained by energetic governmental action. These two public interest movements—made up of farmers, lawyers, small businessmen, and laborers—worked through many legislative, judicial, and administrative channels to derail the robber barons who seemed bent on creating an aristocracy of wealth. They even turned to the tactic of revising state constitutions as a means for controlling the economic giants that appeared determined to destroy their livelihoods. As reform interests gained strength in legislatures, they demanded that corporations change their operating procedures and communicate with the public.

Lacking clear historical precedent, the nation did not have established criteria by which to evaluate business performance. Because no ideology or blueprint existed for the development of policies regarding corporations and their concentrations in manufacturing, railroads, and utilities, these had to be derived through public debate. How large should a corporation be? Should the government regulate industry, or should that task be left solely to market forces? How could competition be maintained while small companies were being engulfed by larger ones or driven from the marketplace? To what extent should any one corporation be allowed to dominate the market by setting prices and establishing labor practices? The participants—corporate executives, labor leaders, government officials, and consumers—were caught in a tug of war of competing interests, values, and definitions.

The dominant philosophy of the era, Social Darwinism, championed unbridled tooth-and-fang capitalism. The face-to-face relationships that had characterized commerce were being replaced by distant corporate managements who knew little and cared less about the people who worked for the company, lived in its vicinity, bought its goods, and used its services. One characteristic of corporate policy in these robust years was the notion that the less "outsiders" knew about corporate behavior and policy, the easier it was for business leaders to arbitrarily make decisions. Armed state militia and Pinkerton agents were typical means by which corporations communicated their policies to labor. Business-to-consumer communication was hardly better; it consisted for the most part of product and service advertising fraught with factual inaccuracy and hyperbole.

This information and policy vacuum presaged the need for public relations practitioners, the pioneers in corporate communication who during the 1880s called themselves publicists. We should not underestimate their sophistication and influence. By World War I, increasing numbers of corporations employed wordsmiths to explain to key groups the importance of business in underwriting modern abundance.

The effective execution of a series of such opinion campaigns by skilled practitioners Ivy Lee, Edward Bernays, and others, notes Lippmann (1961), led to growing recognition for the field, as well as dramatically changed social attitudes. This period witnessed the shift from small, locally owned businesses to corporate America. The developing relationship between business and its critics from 1877 to 1920 has been characterized as "the search for order" (Wiebe, 1967).

The laissez-faire attitude gave way to increasingly sophisticated lobby efforts of labor leaders, middle-class Progressives, and Populist public sentiment. Moreover, federal and state government officials learned that powerful corporate leaders did not want free, unlimited competition; they too wanted order as evidenced by a variety of fundamental changes in the way they conducted business. One effort to systematize business practices resulted in the standard 4'8" railroad gauge, making possible an efficient national transportation network.

Debates over the implications of corporate size and power resulted in the Sherman Antitrust Act. While Progressive forces were successful in invoking federal and state regulation through a series of important bills passed between 1890 and 1914, such agencies have generally proved more cooperative than combative toward business. This cooperation demonstrates the widespread endorsement of capitalism even during periods of economic crisis, such as the Great Depression, or when business has failed to articulate its importance. Kolko (1967) contends that the most shrewd industry barons quickly recognized the virtue of business concentration and the use of government to protect industries; they realized that the reformist zeal of Progressivism could assist in these efforts. Part of the reason for this acceptance stemmed from the efforts of business publicists. The confidence gap and the regulatory pressures facing business have largely resulted from executives' failure to take employees and critics seriously, make needed policy reforms, and communicate their actions to key audiences.

CRITICS IN THE BUSINESS ENVIRONMENT

While not immune to criticism, corporations have become a permanent part of the social, political, and economic fabric of the country. To examine the tension between public sentiment and corporate behavior, Galambos (1975) investigated the opinions that several key occupational groups held about corporate growth. He discovered that few individuals held rigid black-and-white views. Members of these groups were not always at war with corporations; indeed, often corporations were viewed as vital to prosperity. Galambos concludes that in the early years, 1879-1892, engineers saw their economic interest as inseparable from the growth of corporations. The main gripe by engineers, especially against the railroad industry, was the miserable safety record. Engineers argued that standards should be imposed to make rail travel safer for workers and passengers (Galambos, 1975: 49-51).

During this period, Protestant ministers applauded corporate growth as evidence of the realization of a divine mission. However, they broke out of their conservatism periodically to suggest a few social welfare programs (Galambos, 1975: 53-58).

Southern farmers felt a sense of economic disparity created by corporate growth, but they appreciated the access to markets provided by large rail transportation networks (Galambos, 1975: 58-65). Midwestern farmers also appreciated this access but worried that the railroads were using government to shore up the industry (Galambos, 1975: 68). For this reason, farmers supported the Interstate Commerce Bill. Of these groups, laborers were the most concerned by the growing business concentration. They quickly realized that labor market conditions were putting them at severe disadvantage (Galambos, 1975: 69-74). Slowly, unions came to be accepted as legitimate forums for collectively representing worker views.

Passage of the Interstate Commerce Act (1887) and the Safety Appliance Act (1893) constituted landmarks in consumer regulation. The former created the Interstate Commerce Commission in an attempt to lessen the likelihood that railroad rates would be established at the caprice of distant railroad czars. Wiebe (1967: 53) observes, however, that a few railroad "executives actually welcomed it as a protective cover." At the turn of the century, Progressive small businessmen and professionals vigorously lobbied for revisions in the Interstate Commerce bill which would take even more power away from the railroads (by then deeply in debt). Railroads tended to raise rates to offset these debts, a practice resisted by middle-class Progressives who did not want to shoulder new costs at the expense of their own businesses.

Despite these trends, Galambos (1975: 78) concludes, in 1892 "few signs indicated that the concentration movement would produce a major crisis in America's middle cultures." Still, the depression of 1893 caused many to reconsider the liabilities associated with the unbridled pursuit of wealth by industrial combines. Farmers, especially, championed financial reform. In addition to their growing anger at the economic clout of bankers and other plutocrats, farmers had mixed feelings about the urban growth that corporations were causing. Young people were being lured to the big cities, far from their rural origins. "While the farmer was thus capable of conjuring up some highly abstract enemies, he lavished most of his animosity on those industries and firms with which he had direct economic relationships" (Galambos, 1975: 96). But farm groups saw their influence erode. Their role as a counterbalance to corporations was being taken over by labor organizations. A lack of finances and leadership ended most of these economic interest coalitions, culminating with William Jennings Bryan's presidential defeat in 1896.

By 1901, farmers had become less angry toward trusts than were other occupation groups, particularly engineers and laborers. Unskilled laborers realized that the battlelines had been drawn, particularly after the bloody rioting and harsh use of strikebreakers at Andrew Carnegie's Homestead steel mills near Pittsburgh in 1892. Homestead proved to labor that corporate giants such as Carnegie were determined to destroy labor unions and would kill to accomplish that end. The ensuing strikes were often extremely violent. In contrast with lower paid workers, skilled laborers looked upon corporations positively because they offered a promise of economic well-being. However, they recognized that corporations' power was not be taken lightly. By the turn of the century, Galambos (1975: 112) argues, the nation had begun to establish a coherent set of beliefs and attitudes toward corporations and their regulation. These opinions caused the regulatory measures of the later Progressive era to be more legally exact.

During the first decade of this century, corporate America lost one of its strongest supporters—the clergy. Doubts were raised whether corporations returned to the people as much as they took. Bremner (1956) observes that in contrast to other countries, the United States has never accepted the assumption that some people must live in poverty. However, he continues, one of the dramatic changes of opinion around the turn of this century was the "discovery of poverty." The Social Darwinism of the previous century argued that poverty persisted only among the lazy and spendthrift. This was no longer accepted as fact, particularly by religious reformers who observed that low wages caused laborers to suffer despite their energy and frugality. Many social evils were laid at the doorsteps of business as ministers became incensed at the poor health and living conditions typical in corporate towns. The clergy believed that whereas morality and corporate growth had been positively related before, they were now at odds (Galambos, 1975: 119-126).

Names such as J. P. Morgan and John D. Rockefeller, Sr., raised the blood pressure of many who feared that the foundations of society were being eroded because so few had so much power and wealth. The challenge of operating conditions, as evidenced by the number of regulatory measures passed in the opening decades of this century, indicated that the Progressive search for order was becoming more robust. Presidents of the United States had joined the advocates for corporate reform, sometimes out of fear of losing a valuable portion of the electorate. As he did other groups, Theodore Roosevelt encouraged farmers and other supporters of trust-busting to renew their attacks on big business. For many Progressives, passage of the Bureau of Corporations Bill in 1903, which established the Department of Commerce and Labor, marked the beginning of an important era of regulation. However, Kolko (1967: 71) concludes that the measure was enacted with strong conservative support by industrialists, who saw it as a way to lessen competition.

Many battles were fought, first over wages and working conditions and later over the quality of goods and services. Even though the debate was in its infancy, the public, along with business, was confronted with the need to formulate standards of responsible corporate behavior.

Companies often did very little to create a safe and comfortable working environment. With rare exception, wages were at a subsistence level that required long working hours. Typically, entire families—including children as young as six or seven—had to work to survive. The labor of children was favored by some employers because they could work in small and cramped quarters (particularly important to avoid unncessary evacuations in coal mines). At times, coal was stockpiled by coal companies to prevent the possibility that a strike could be effective. Railroad companies typically subjected employees to extremely dangerous working conditions.

Many shops and businesses, epitomized by Sears, Roebuck and Montgomery Ward, built a reputation on honesty and customer satisfaction. Unfortunately, others were less conscientious. Many harmful food, drug, and cosmetic products were sold. And since insurance companies, banks, and other financial institutions were unregulated, patrons risked being defrauded.

Abuses eventually sparked opposition. Muckraking journalists led by David Graham Phillips, Lincoln Steffens, Ida Tarbell, and others sought to expose the irresponsibility rampant in industry, particularly during the first two decades of this century. Books such as Frank Norris's *The Pit* (1903) and Upton Sinclair's *The Jungle* (1906) fostered discussion which helped lead to the Pure Food and Drug Act and the Federal Meat Inspection Act of 1906, two major reform victories. This latter act was the culmination of an effort to reform the meat industry which began as early as 1865 when Congress banned the importation of diseased cattle and pigs. Meat reform was supported by some of the largest packers who, unlike their cut-rate competition, maintained sanitary plants and routinely inspected their product. The bigger firms wanted to extend government inspection to all packers to establish equity of quality—and expense (Kolko, 1967: 98-101). Similarly, the Pure Food and Drug Act was endorsed by the National Pure Food and Drug Congress, which included trade groups and industry representatives such as the Creamery Butter Makers' Association, the Brewers' Association, the Confectioners' Association, the Wholesale Grocers' Association, and the Retail Grocers' Association (Kolko, 1967: 108-109).

Magazines were the major mass media vehicle by which the muckrakers reached their audience, the American middle class which was increasing in size and political importance. Steffens and Tarbell, in conjunction with Ray Stannard Baker, made *McClure's* magazine the leading outlet for reformist material. Other key journals included *Everybody's Magazine, Collier's, Arena, Success Magazine,* and *Cosmopolitan*—all joining the reform battle out of conviction and the desire to increase circulation. Influential muckrakers found much to criticize about corporate behavior. Tarbell's *History of the Standard Oil Company* (1904), first published in *McClure's*, was one of the first statements on corporate responsibility to find its way into middle-class living rooms. Steffens's *The Shame of the Cities* (also released in 1904) proved to be another landmark exposé. In the face of the challenges by muckraking journalists, Cutlip and Center (1982: 76) observe: "The corporations, the good ones along with the ruthless ones, had lost contact with their publics. For a while they sat helplessly by, inarticulate and frustrated, waiting apprehensively for the next issue of *McClure's* magazine."

In contrast to the slowly developing values needed to change labor practices, no public opinion change was necessary to condemn the consumption of tainted meat. When reformers alerted the public to the fact that meat-packing conditions were unsanitary, it was ready to demand reform. A well-informed populace can be an ally of the ethical corporate leader who fears false and deceptive practices. Such dramatic changes in public opinion underscore the fact that issues management can never ignore public opinion. The battleground is the struggle between corporations who attempt to do business for the most part in ways that coincide with accepted standards of behavior, and the public interest that is always self-interested, if fickle.

THE BIRTH OF ISSUES MANAGEMENT

Because magazines and books were the primary media used by those seeking corporate reform, they were also utilized by the public relations practitioners. Instead of advocacy advertising, public relations specialists wrote articles extolling the virtues of a company or an industry while railing against pending regulation. Each case was presented as though it resulted from objective journalistic research. For instance, George Gunton was a popular economist who championed the free enterprise system in his capacity as editor of *Gunton's* magazine. While in that position, he received a $15,000 annual retainer from Standard Oil (Kolko, 1967: 15). Industry barons sometimes entered the fray, as J. Ogden Armour (1906) did. He used *The Saturday Evening Post* to defend some of the practices of the meat industry, to invite public visits of his facilities, to describe the sanitation efforts his company was taking to ensure high quality, and to support passage of inspection legislation. Several large packing concerns, including Swift & Co., also published a series of advertisements to present a favorable image of themselves and to proclaim their commitment to healthful meat processing conditions.

Even before the turn of the century, a few corporate communicators were hired to disseminate information about their companies. As early as 1880, the railroad industry was being encouraged to recognize the value of public relations (Raucher, 1968: 33). While slow to criticize the actions of railroads and public utilities, farmers sought control, especially of the railroad rate structure. One of the earliest battlegrounds was Illinois, where the Granger-controlled legislature passed a bill in 1873 that established the rates for grain storage in railroad warehouses. This act led to the landmark case of Munn v. Illinois (1877), in which the Supreme Court ruled that state legislatures can regulate private property in the public interest.

After the turn of the century, railroad company managements worried that the public did not recognize the accomplishments and national importance of their industry. Consequently, the railroad industry hired the Publicity Bureau in 1906 to fight a move by President Theodore Roosevelt to impose regulatory legislation on it. The campaign failed when the Hepburn Act was passed, in large part because Roosevelt took his case to the people and won the battle of public opinion.

At this point the railroad industry reassessed its use of publicity, and many companies started their own public relations departments. In addition, more firms began to specialize in business communication, in what was proving a robust but difficult practice. For example, the Publicity Bureau was joined in this activity by a firm William Wolff Smith started in 1902, and by Parker and Lee, an agency that featured the talents of Ivy Lee (Cutlip and Center, 1982: 77). Lee was also hired by a railway firm in 1906—the Pennsylvania Railroad—where he proved more successful. His primary assignment was to dispute the image that railroads were heartless. The campaign began with an article in *Moody's Magazine* in November 1907. The article and follow-up propaganda proclaimed the virtues of railroads, arguing that they had expanded the West, carried goods to markets, made travel possible, and employed hundreds of workers (Lee, 1907). Later, in 1916, a group of major railroads formed the Railway Executives' Advisory Committee to manage press releases and publish articles on the industry (Wiebe, 1967: 187).

The growth of utilities was equally tumultuous. Promoters of the burgeoning electricity industry were among the first to use public relations. The battle was not against regulation but between George Westinghouse and Thomas Edison, who debated whether alternating or direct current should be the accepted technology. One of the first corporate public relations departments was established in 1889 by George Westinghouse, who wanted to promote the electricity industry by championing alternating current. Edison had started this contest of corporate and industry image building and issues management. He sponsored a booklet entitled *A Warning* to scare the public into favoring direct current because alternating current was potentially lethal. For additional substantiation, Edison was instrumental in the state of New York's decision to use alternating current to administer capital punishment. In 1889, Westinghouse countered with a booklet, *Safety of the Alternating System of Electrical Distribution,* which extolled the virtues of that technology. The debate for public acceptance was a prelude to approval by governmental agencies.

Another utility giant increased control over its industry in the last decade of the 19th century. Frederick P. Fish, who became president of the Bell Telephone System in 1900, recognized the need for his growing company to take its case to the public. His apprehension was that if the public did not understand the advantage of a monopoly, it would seek regulation and/or oppose monopolization. Either stance was contrary to the growth goals of the company. Raucher (1968) concludes "that by 1906 the American Telephone and Telegraph Company had a general policy designed to placate public hostility and had methods for broadcasting the news about that policy." That policy was aggressively continued by Theodore Newton Vail when he became AT&T president in May 1907 (Raucher, 1968: 49). He sought to insulate the communication utility from public control by convincing Americans that the phone company was operating in their best interest.

One of the first issue advertisements was put out by AT&T in 1908. It emphasized the bond between the company and its customers: "The Bell System's ideal is the same as that of the public it serves—the most telephone service and the best, at the least cost to the user. It accepts its responsibility for a nation-wide telephone service as a public trust" (Garbett, 1981: 40). By 1910, Vail had converted these ideas into a consistent, long-term campaign stressing the advantages of a privately run, publicly minded system (Schultze, 1981).

One of the first major tests of this strategy came in 1913 when the Justice Department initiated an antitrust suit. The issue behind the suit was whether AT&T, through its control of Western Union, had created an impermissible monopoly. To defend itself against the charge, another newspaper series was started under the name of Vail (*New York Times*, 1913). The case collapsed.

Part of AT&T's campaign was to avert governmental regulation, but another threat involved direct government ownership of utilities. By May 1928, AT&T Publicity Director Arthur Page could announce that their educational efforts had successfully convinced the public that the phone industry was best handled as a monopoly. But he also prudently cautioned company executives about other lingering concerns (Raucher, 1968: 76-77). Thus, even though the company was a victor in many battles over the years, the war for public confidence was never completely won by AT&T. This conclusion is best justified by its eventual breakup in the 1980s.

After initially denouncing the divestiture of local phone from long distance service, AT&T eventually accepted the political divorce in return for the opportunities afforded by expansion into new telecommunication information technology areas. In the last hours during the division of the company in October 1983, AT&T Chairman C. L. Brown issued "A Personal Appeal to Every Member of the U.S. Congress," and to shareholders and Bell System employees to oppose proposed last-minute changes in the Communications Act designed to slow implementation of the agreement. The failure to prepare not only the consumer public but also other key constituencies, such as Congress, for the dislocating after-effects of these changes led to rollbacks of proposed access revenues and continuing intervention by the FCC and lawmakers. Ruefully, even a giant such as AT&T had to learn a hard lesson on the need for continuity in issues communication. AT&T continues to suffer public scrutiny but now understands the need to once again build and maintain coalitions of internal and external stakeholders.

Public relations practices by utilities and railroads gained popularity with manufacturing companies that feared antitrust legislation. To protect the International Harvester Company, George Perkins, at the direction of Cyrus H. McCormick, fought governmental action by the Bureau of Corporations in 1906. The publicity firm of Parker and Lee again joined the fray. The argument against antitrust legislation was couched in what had become the standard theme of "the benefits of largeness," an attempt to publicize the economics of mass production. Moreover, the argument continued, corporations pay better wages than do smaller businesses. The campaign had some success because the Roosevelt administration dropped the case in 1908 (Raucher, 1968: 19-20). The Rockefellers drew heavily on public relations to protect Standard Oil against Ida Tarbell's criticisms, claims that John Sr.'s philanthropy was "tainted money," and charges of violent strikebreaking in labor relations at their Colorado Fuel and Iron Company. Despite his efforts on behalf of the Rockefellers, Ivy Lee was soundly criticized for presenting one-sided, factually inaccurate material in his bulletin entitled "Facts in Colorado's Struggle for Industrial Freedom" (Raucher, 1968: 27).

Advertising agencies, which also began to develop shortly after the turn of the century, offered their services to the beleaguered corporations. Following New York state's Armstrong Committee exposé of insurance industry corruption, the New York Mutual Life Insurance Company hired N. W. Ayer to conduct an advocacy campaign to restore confidence in the industry. Communication efforts as outlined above were never separate from the increasing attempts by the Theodore Roosevelt, William Howard Taft, and Woodrow Wilson administrations to regulate industry. Despite the best efforts of the issues managers, governmental regulatory agencies have, over the years, made many other changes in the ways that major companies do business. Many commissions were established, charged with disclosing corporate corruption, and mobilized to propose political remedies.

Generally, public relations practitioners were brought late into the fray to avert, if possible, or at least weaken the regulatory impact. Public relations practitioners contended that their efforts were aimed at correcting false information, championing traditional values, and proving the detrimental aspects of regulation. During the first decades of the century, Raucher (1968: viii) observes, corporate responsibility and ethical behavior became commonplace public relations themes.

Despite the efforts of the publicists, legislation was enacted to regulate industries, and agencies were set up to protect consumers and workers. In some instances those agencies protected corporations as much as they challenged them. Often the membership of the agencies was drawn from personnel of the industries to be regulated, a practice common today. Soon after its creation, for example, the Federal Trade Commission was headed by the avowedly pro-business Edward N. Hurley. The commission was supported and greatly influenced by the National Association of Manufacturers (Kolko, 1967: 274-277).

The discussion of the need for the Federal Trade Commission began to surface in 1911. The National Civic Federation discovered that the idea was broadly favored in an opinion poll conducted in 1911. The Progressive and Republican Parties endorsed it in 1912, and by 1914 the FTC was created to replace the Bureau of Corporations. An outgrowth of the Clayton Antitrust Act of 1914, the commission was designed to prevent large business concentrations. But like so many other aspects of the reform period, considerable discussion revolved around definitions that could be used to distinguish between "good" and "bad" business concentrations. Even today, one of the hardest parts of achieving responsible corporate performance involves deciding what it is.

TWO WARS AND THE DEPRESSION

World War I did not bring an end to reform and concern over corporate America. "The clergyman, the engineer, the farmer, the laborer—all found cause for distress in the immediate aftermath of the First World War" (Galambos, 1975: 193). Laborers' attitudes remained extremely negative throughout the 1920s. The greatest challenge facing the laborer was to protect the future of his craft, with technological change making many jobs obsolete. Although other groups started the 1920s with a sense of horror regarding the largeness of corporations, by the end of the decade they were more comfortable, convinced that corporations were bringing prosperity to all (Galambos, 1975: 220). One of the new twists in corporate issues management was the presence of Bolshevism; now, corporate representatives could claim that criticism of corporate America was unpatriotic and communistic.

Businessmen recognized that the flow of immigrants was bringing to this country many people who neither understood nor appreciated the economics of free enterprise. Clubs and leagues sprang up around the country to propagate Americanization programs (Wiebe, 1968: 184-185). Some of these efforts were aimed at combating the socialism that came with many of the immigrants. Business had no intention of letting competing economic systems gain a foothold in this country.

Often in these decades corporations were callous enough to believe that nothing more than a skilled public relations campaign was needed to erase criticism and win public confidence. Their successes by the 1920s sparked FTC interest in the manner in which public relations campaigns were conducted. The fear was that factual inaccuracy and a demogogic use of "red scare" antibolshevism would distort information received by the public.

The financial collapse evidenced by the Depression rekindled distrust of big business and raised anew questions as to whether corporations could function in the public interest. The Depression strained the love-hate relationship between the public and corporations. Because of the need to rebuild economic and industrial institutions, the public championed increased federal powers. Many in the clergy argued that one of the solutions to the Depression was to break up the corporations that had become too powerful. But rather than being totally at odds, government and business worked with surprising cooperation to return the nation to prosperity. The farmer, despite the impact on farm prices, emerged from the 1930s committed to the value of large corporations, which could buy produce and inexpensively sell the goods needed for future harvests (Galambos, 1975: 223-237).

The 1930s and 1940s witnessed a series of issue advertisements discussing the virtues of capitalism to counteract prevailing doubts as to whether corporations could be trusted to provide general prosperity. Many corporate leaders feared that the public no longer believed in the free enterprise system which had left them without work and had dashed their hopes of prosperity, even survival. It is difficult to separate the impact of particular campaigns from broad political and social developments of the period, but clearly issues communication proved of importance to business. Galambos (1975: 249) concludes:

> The values and attitudes of the new culture clearly emerged intact from the 1930s. By that time most Americans saw antitrust as a dead or dying issue. They were coming to accept—in varying degrees—a different outlook embodying modern, organizational norms and a new image of the large and postwar crisis. By 1940, corporate culture had largely supplanted the individualistic egalitarianism of the 19th century. The era of the organization man had begun.

Military intelligence operatives in Germany, Japan, and the United States developed strategies to link their information gathering and decision making. In America, Secretary of State George Marshall tabbed political specialist George Kennan to create an Office of Policy and Planning in 1946. Its staffers advised Marshall on foreign policy developments and proved influential in providing support for the Marshall Relief Plan. The success of this program spread by encouraging corporations to similarly review their planning and communication efforts (Nowlan et al., 1984: 81-82).

Among the most important long-term campaigns was that devised by Warner & Swasey. One of the firm's 1941 advertisements compared the lot of the French worker to his American counterpart. "Wonder What a Frenchman Thinks About" exemplifies how the company used the threat of Nazism to rekindle patriotic commitment to American capitalism. The piece argued that the French laborer's greed led to the plight of working "53 hours a week for 30 hours' pay." Warner & Swasey voiced the regret of the typical French worker in these words:

> "I wish I had been less greedy for myself and more anxious for my country; I wish I had realized you can't beat a determined invader by a quarreling, disunited people at home; I wish I had been willing to give in on some of my rights to other Frenchmen instead of giving up all of them

> to a foreigner; I wish I had realized other Frenchmen had rights, too; I wish I had known that patriotism is *work,* not talk, *giving* not getting" [Stridsberg, 1977: 103].

This sad plight could be interpreted as directing the U.S. worker to support the interests of a united corporate America faced with an emerging fascist danger in the midst of the Depression. The advertisement, which was circulated through many business periodicals, is replete with several of the most glaring propaganda devices identified by the Institute for Propaganda Analysis: band wagon, transfer, and card stacking.

Warner & Swasey's sponsorship of such issues communication proved durable. Although first marshaled in the face of heated debate regarding the viability of American capitalism to provide jobs and ensure the public economy, the theme of the importance of free enterprise has remained remarkably consistent over a nearly 50-year period (Garbett, 1981: 44). Such ads as "Where do your wages come from?" (1944), "To cure a headache, you don't cut off your head" (1947), "If you own a hammer, you are a capitalist" (1948), and "They don't keep feeding you cheese after the trap is sprung" (1950) discussed the problems of the welfare state. The campaign contrasted the dangers of large government and the virtues of American free enterprise exemplified in the 1970 advertisement, "What's right with America?" Other topics included the social problems created when judges are lenient on criminals. In one 1971 ad entitled "Business men are like the bashful boy who sent his girl a valentine but didn't sign it," Warner & Swasey justified the use of issue advertising. Facts were offered on how business taxes "support America's schools 1½ days every week." Business contributes to charities and provides community support. Through its research, the nation is made better. Business is cleaning up the slums, training the unemployed and unemployable. Warner & Swasey also chided other corporations to champion their contributions—speaking out so as to not let their light be smothered under the bushel basket of public ignorance (Garbett, 1981: 47).

Other notable advertisements of this era include the one by the Chesapeake & Ohio Railway—Nickel Plate Road, to dramatize the preferential treatment given transcontinental freight shipments, particularly agricultural produce. The headline of the advertisement made the point: "A Hog Can Cross the Country Without Changing Trains—But YOU can't!" This advertisement, which ran in late 1945 and 1946, was part of an internecine issue campaign waged within the railway industry (Garbett, 1981: 105).

The end of the Depression and new prosperity in the aftermath of World War II diverted attention away from the problems of corporations. Robert H. Moore (Nagelschmidt, 1982: 10-16) concludes that business during the 1950s enjoyed a public opinion honeymoon. People were thankful to have work, and the business community again seemed to offer security for the average citizen. Beneficial changes in working conditions and an apparent new level of corporate behavior seemed to indicate that corporations were indeed good community citizens. These factors combined with upbeat popular culture publicity surrounding wartime efforts (the "Riveter Annie" mystique) to help free corporations from the degree of regulatory scrutiny typical of previous decades. In the Eisenhower years, very little regulatory legislation was passed. The predictable economic recessions came and went without residual hostility or massive public interest agitation. In general, this was a period of good feeling between the public and corporations which provided jobs and supplied goods and services to a people desiring to forget the difficulties of the 1930s and 1940s.

The Cold War with the Soviet Union also blunted some corporate criticism. The argument that corporate criticism was evidence of communistic leanings returned, heightened by House Un-American Activities Committee hearings and the investigations conducted by Senator Joseph McCarthy. However, one harbinger of future nuclear regulation was the Atomic Energy Act of 1954. The public's awareness of the power and danger of nuclear energy was born when it learned of the use of atomic weaponry against Japan.

At times, corporations directed their public relations efforts against labor. For instance, Ohio Consolidated Telephone used an ad entitled "The Case of the Amputated Telephone" to discredit striking telephone workers by blaming them for damaging telephone lines. The ad read, "Since July 15, [1956] when the strike against Ohio Consolidated began, more than 50 cables have been cut, slashed, burned, hacked in half—interfering with the phone service of more than SIX THOUSAND homes and businesses!" This advertisement could alienate the public against the strikers, who were compared with dedicated employees: "Supervisors manning local and long distance telephone boards—trying desperately to keep the lines open to *you*—have been harassed, threatened, intimidated, even shot at!" The ruthlessness of the vandalistic strikers was portrayed even more dramatically: "More than ten offices have had to be closed down for short or long periods—due to vandalism or because police protection was not adequate to handle the danger to operators and equipment!" (Stridsberg, 1977: 106-107). Such advertising is a blatant labor-management power play utilizing scapegoating and fear appeals.

For the most part, however, the euphoria of the 1940s and 1950s misled corporations. Most were unprepared for the emotional outbursts and social reexamination of the 1960s and 1970s. In the face of these challenges, some companies assumed that the trouble would go away, or hoped the difficulties could be communicated out of existence. Many business leaders believed that bleeding-heart claims about the damage of regulation and the destruction of the free enterprise system would heal the wounds of agitation and criticism. Few, if any, industries were left untouched by the wind of changing standards in corporate social responsibility.

General Electric innovated in the 1950s and early 1960s by recognizing the value of keeping employees and other key constituencies informed regarding corporate plans, efforts to be responsible, and pending issues which could affect profits and employee interests. Timken Roller Bearing Company and Caterpillar Tractor were other leaders in demonstrating their good citizenship by participating in the legislative issue process. For example, Caterpillar brought to the attention of its employees and the surrounding communities the need to "hold the line on wages" in order to remain competitive—especially in foreign countries and against foreign competitors. By anticipating union attacks on the company's contentions, Caterpillar was able to mute labor's negative influence (Bateman, 1975: 3-7).

These successes are worth noting because of their singularity. Even though most national companies had public relations/affairs departments by the early 1960s, this translated as publicity, lobbying, and employee communications. Since the 1940s, for example, the number of house organs has tripled from approximately 2000 to over 6000. But questions of social responsibility had rarely been addressed, partially because few companies had networks capable of issues monitoring. Most executives simply assumed that they and their firms were acting responsibly. This lack of preparation contributed, in many cases, to the problem rather than its solution, since the issues were too complex to address in a few advertisements. Meager public relations/affairs campaigns featured newsprint advertisements written in obtuse prose and addressed the self-interest of the company more than that of the public. Corporate management could not understand how little the public knew about operations and the requirements of finance, product development, liability, and pollution control.

That an ignorant public responded with such hostility is compelling evidence that the business leadership simply failed to keep in tune with public needs by providing a platform of fact. In some obvious instances, corporations underestimated the public by believing it to be more gullible and unsophisticated than was actually the case. Rather than seeing the merits of involving critics in corporate planning, businesses tried all too often to keep them away from the company. Fortunately, many corporations at last began to reexamine themselves—but the road was not an easy one.

DISSENT FLOWERS IN THE 1960s

Even during the Depression, when the power of the corporation was substantially blunted by a government that many believed was preferable to rampant capitalism, people did not waver in their commitment to the basic business ethic. By the 1960s this had changed—underneath the good feeling was a layer of skepticism about corporate performance. During the postwar era of "good times," growing dissent in the black community and changing values publicized by the beat generation were laying a foundation for the most massive assault on corporations ever witnessed in this country. Like many other institutions—government, family life, organized religion, and education—corporations were subjected to a new scrutiny. Much of the rift between the public and corporations was unarticulated until the civil rights and antiwar activists renewed their protests. The drawn-out war in Vietnam was the forum for reexamining many aspects of corporate behavior.

The 1960s, 1970s, and 1980s witnessed a remarkable challenge to the privacy and authority that corporations had long assumed constituted their prerogatives. Coupled with the search for values that emerged from the anti-war years, reform interests pushed for a radical redefinition of corporate responsibility as part of a broader reorientation in business ethics. "Corporate citizenship" became the major public affairs theme during these decades. Quality of life—and corporations' contribution to it—took on new meanings once people (including those who had not been politically and socially aware in the 1960s) became alert that they could no longer take business for granted. Labor unions demanded higher wages and benefits even if they would eventually outpace the ability of corporations to market internationally. Accelerating the breakdown of this "social contract" were record unemployment and bankruptcies, the uncertain government response to foreign sales in the United States, the deepening trade debt, and a declining manufacturing base as America moved haltingly to a post-industrial economy devastating to the future of many traditional industries.

No longer could companies risk withholding information or declining to comment. Particularly damaging effects on images and sales resulted from public disclosures occurring while companies tried to cover up embarrassing facts. Attempting to restore credibility, a number of CEOs now personally represent their companies and are pro-actively visible on matters of public interest. Corporations became interested in applying sophisticated social science techniques not only for product sales but also in ideational marketing. Companies were forced to undertake communication campaigns to promote political education and foster participation by employees, shareholders, customers, and other allies. They became involved in grassroots programs to marshal support for issues relevant to their needs. Trade associations and political action committees (PACs) also became valuable means for expressing the corporate position without individual corporations having to be visible. The result is vigorous efforts to influence legislative activities at the local, state, federal, and international levels in ways quite different from previous decades.

One major change has been the public's increased sophistication on policy issues. Until 1971 corporations were expressly forbidden from contributing to federal candidates' campaigns or party organizations. The Federal Election Campaign Act of 1971 and its amendments in 1974 and 1976 allowed corporations, unions, and industry special interest groups to form PACs and to contribute to them so that they in turn could funnel dollars into political campaigns. PACs have become an ancillary part of most major corporations, although their existence is not without controversy. Groups such as Common Cause are troubled by corporate and special interest PAC contributions to campaigns. Of course, potential problems exist. Some employees may feel obligated to contribute to the company or union PAC despite a desire not to. And it is reasonable to believe that some companies have supplied key employees with "raises" with the express intent of that money eventually finding its way to their PAC. Most criticisms, however, lack statistical support, and a good case can be made for the contributions made by PACs to political participation in a pluralistic society (Alexander, 1983).

Uncertainty is difficult for a company, just as it is for an individual. During prior wars, the corporations that supplied matériel and armaments had been played up as having made a heroic contribution to the country's security. The agitation against the Vietnam conflict reversed the equation. Dow Chemical is a classic case of a manufacturer singled out for attack because of its production of napalm. Before Vietnam, Dow had been viewed as a very good company for which to work. College graduates once lined up for job interviews, but antiwar sentiment changed all this. By the 1970s Dow's favorable image had been replaced by that of a war-monger, indiscriminately helping to destroy nonmilitary targets. Students scorned job interviewers and made the purchase of Saran Wrap synonymous with killing innocent men, women, and children.

In addition to corporate activities directly related to Vietnam, a series of challenges broadened the range of business practices and values which felt the sting of this new criticism. In 1962 Rachel Carson stunned the nation with a series of articles in the *New Yorker* entitled "Silent Spring," later published in book form. She pointed out how insecticides and herbicides have serious side effects as silent killers. For the first time, the public learned how heavy metals such as mercury seep into the water, where they are picked up by the simplest forms of life. As each higher level of life eats each lower one, the poisonous metals are stored in fat tissues. Because bodies cannot eliminate these poisons, they are ingested in ever-concentrated amounts when little fish, which eat plankton, are devoured by larger fish. Eventually, the poison concentrates in humans who eat the larger fish.

A new level of concern for the quality of life spread throughout society; the public became aware that local concerns could multiply into problems of global proportion. Ecologists argued for a "spaceship Earth" concept in caring for our planet, because pollution is a form of suicide. Biologists and allied groups pronounced rivers and lakes dead and held national rallies to protest the destruction of the environment, which the agitators argued was a common legacy. Popular musicians and singers often participated in this effort, lending visibility to the problem and building a popular culture that rejected corporations. Image advertising slogans such as "Better Living Through Chemistry" were sarcastically used to rationalize the use of illegal drugs.

The positive contributions made by chemistry were obscured by the discovery of the impact of toxic waste and other issues. Events such as the Cuyahoga River catching fire in Cleveland dramatized the seriousness of chemical pollution. Ecologists mobilized to conduct memorial services dedicated to the past beauty of the countryside. Once, DDT had been hailed as the victory of chemistry over pests. During the 1960s, it symbolized the destruction of wildlife populations. Even the national symbol, the bald eagle, was likely to become extinct if remedies were not put into place. The legacy of the land, so deeply ingrained in the American people, had nearly been lost because of indifference, wanton waste, and corporate profits.

How business responded to these new opinions determined whether it could avoid more stringent regulation and win back public trust. When even soft drink containers became a political issue, the question shifted back to corporations. One of the most famous Advertising Council public service campaigns was the "people start pollution, people can stop it" effort financed by Keep America Beautiful, Inc. This featured an American Indian shedding a tear for the fouled landscape. By drawing attention to the need for individual (as compared to collective) responsibility in combating litter, the series adroitly sought to reposition the pollution issue by downplaying its industrial origins and deflecting efforts to punish business. This theme is not surprising, since the volunteer coordinator of the Ad Council campaign was W. Howard Chase, then with American Can Company. Board members on Keep America Beautiful also included representatives of soft drink companies, brewers, glass bottlers, and aluminum can manufacturers (Barnouw, 1978: 142, 201).

Ralph Nader helped spawn this consumerism in 1965 when he proclaimed that General Motors' Corvair compact was "unsafe at any speed." Elements of the public, ironically educated by advertising to desire high-quality products at low prices, angrily gave birth to consumer interest groups. Many critics called upon corporations to deliver all that they had promised. Rebuffed consumers formed permanent power-seeking organizations presenting a potent counterbalance to corporate interests. Consumerism and environmental protection have continued into the 1980s. Large consumer coalitions such as the Consumer Federation of America draw their financial support and membership from across the nation. In opposing sophisticated corporate lobbying efforts, consumers borrowed strategies refined by other activists who have learned to use government to control corporate performance. Their tactics have included media blitzes, class action suits, boycotts, defiant rallies, and grassroots lobbying of government agencies.

Consumerism since the 1960s has turned its attention to virtually every aspect of human life touched by business. Renfro (1982) notes that 35 major health, safety, and environmental laws have been passed, starting with the Dangerous Cargo Act in 1877. Of this number, 26 have come into being in the last 20 years. These cover tobacco and alcohol abuse, flammable fabrics, poison prevention packaging, mine and railroad protections, pollution, clean air, noise control, lead-based paint restrictions, food quality, and myriad other issues which have introduced a new vocabulary and an accompanying set of values (March, 1971). In slightly more than a decade, at least ten acts have been passed regarding endangered species (1973), safe drinking water (1974), transportation of hazardous materials (1975), toxic substances (1976), solid waste disposal and resource conservation (1976), surface mining (1977), hazardous liquid pipeline safety (1979), and environmental compensation and liability (1980).

"Biodegradable" and "returnable" became hallmarks of responsibly designed products. Housewives learned that plastic containers, which seemed so convenient, would last in unsightly landfills long after their users had died. Transplant medicine made people more recyclable than their refuse. During this period, nuclear generation and nuclear waste disposal became vital issues made even more salient by the Three Mile Island incident. The Toxic Substances Control Act and the Clean Air and Clean Water Acts created a new measure of accountability for corporate leaders. These acts made executives personally liable for ensuring that their companies complied with the standards relating to toxicity and clean air and water. In some instances the acts went so far as to state that the executives did not have to have direct information regarding the noncompliance; they would be liable for creating an environment that would *allow* noncompliance by subordinates.

Concurrently, employee rights became more clearly defined when the relationship between employer and employee became more regulated. The Occupational Safety and Health Act established an administrative agency (OSHA) charged with the responsibility of ensuring that workers are not subjected to unsafe or unhealthy working conditions. Asbestos became a major corporate political issue, particularly when it was learned that one of the pioneer companies involved in mining and processing asbestos had covered up evidence linking it with cancer.

Social and corporate hierarchies were reexamined during civil rights and antiwar agitation. Conventional notions of superiority and inferiority were rejected. Revolutionary changes in employment, hiring, salary, and promotion practices dramatically redefined corporate responsibility. Resulting from efforts by the civil and women's rights movement, corporations were required by federal law to become "equal opportunity employers." Employees' rights to speak out publicly on controversial issues were protected, as was the right to disclose illegal actions by their employers.

The love-hate relationship between corporations and their employees took a dramatic turn in the 1980s. Employees in the steel industry have seen their skills become obsolete and their jobs lost forever as steel production in the United States has declined to World War I levels. At the same time, a new assembly line of data entry operators has been born. Workers are voting to do away with their unions. Employees are buying their companies to keep them from relocating or going out of business. In several instances, such as at Rath Packing Company, new "worker" managers learn quickly that one of the first changes must be a reduction in wages and workforce. Another dramatic occurrence in the 1980s was a reduction in the number of oil companies through mergers. Very little criticism was launched against this trend, despite the fact that only a decade earlier attempts were made to break up oil companies in hopes of increasing competition and lowering gasoline prices. The fickleness of public and political opinion is easily recognized here. At the same time that oil companies have been allowed to merge with minimal public outcry, the AT&T Bell System was forceably divided into many closely interconnected, but independent, operating components.

Privacy emerged as another major employee and consumer policy issue. Fear of databanks, mailing lists, electronic banking, and computer manipulation all have played their part in pushing for government oversight of industry practices (Salvaggio, 1983). A landmark piece of legislation pertaining to potential government abuse is the Freedom of Information Act of 1966, amended in 1974, which gives public access to many federal records. This act also made public certain information that corporations have on individuals. The Privacy Act of 1974 balanced this by specifying that documents regarding employee performance must be guarded from scrutiny by unauthorized individuals. Later, the Foreign Corrupt Practices Act (1977) reflected congressional concern that information and guidelines were needed for corporate behavior overseas. The act specifies that companies operating abroad must implement adequate internal measures to prevent illegal payments being made to obtain business.

Many governmental agencies now have the power to demand information from corporations and make it public. These agencies include (but are not limited to) the Securities and Exchange Commission, the Federal Trade Commission, the Federal Communications Commission, the U. S. Postal Service, the Occupational Health and Safety Administration, the Office of Economic Opportunity, the Nuclear Regulatory Commission, the Organization for Economic Cooperation and Development, and the Environmental Protection Agency.

In the effort to regulate corporate performance, debate always centers on which criteria should be used in determining what constitutes responsible behavior. Corporations generally have much of the expertise necessary to discover the best methods for solving problems, but until pressured to do so, they are often reluctant to use this knowledge. Thus new standards of product liability and disclosure have not been easily derived.

The growth in government—still occurring despite somewhat conflicting interpretations of the "Reagan Revolution"—points to the often subtle, but profound, shifts that can occur in public opinion. Throughout its history, issues management has been expected to direct the attitudes and values of society, or to keep these from maturing into regulatory legislation. The latest surge in issues management popularity occurred in an environment of resentment, paranoia, and distrust. Many company managements have believed that the public neither can nor wants to understand their point of view. Once strong industries brought on many of their own problems by complacently avoiding the public, hiding the truth, or responding with unwarranted hostility. To solve public policy problems, companies had to realize that they could not easily change public opinion, especially with words that were contradicted by actions. In too many instances to recount, public relations practitioners were called upon to lie, and the public learned not to trust companies to tell the truth.

Although an adversarial relationship between company and agitator may be justified under some circumstances, it is usually counterproductive. Intimidation may backfire, resulting in the polarization of special interest groups. Corporations harmed their credibility when they opposed legislation without first explaining how it was unwise for the public as well as themselves. At times, corporations resorted to the most base appeals, attempting to bludgeon the public into submission. They have pitted jobs against a clean environment. They have argued that the public which does not approve nuclear generation can "damn well freeze to death in the dark." Such strategies usually fail. Corporations have ruefully discovered that changes in attitudes, values, or norms lead to the condemnation of corporate behavior that had been tolerated, and even applauded, by a previous generation. Claims that regulation causes "unnecessary" increases in the price of goods and services fell on deaf ears; the public did not believe that profits or lower-priced goods were a reasonable trade for a damaged planet. The entire chemical industry was tainted, for example, when horrors such as the toxic waste dumping at Love Canal were discovered—even when municipal agencies were later shown to have violated deed restrictions by allowing the construction of home sites on the property.

Political pressures have been effectively brought to bear by anti-industry groups. They select the issues, establish the agenda for debate, preempt "moral" arguments by convincingly couching their case in public service rather than self-serving commercial terms, and engage in relentlessly well-organized and tactically intelligent campaigns attractive to the media. Out of this test by fire, most issues managers have come to believe that the more people understand the operating conditions of corporations and the more corporations understand the expectations people have of acceptable corporate behavior, the stronger the bond beween all parties will be. Developing a platform of understanding and trust has become the heart of issues management and advocacy advertising, since having a false view of a corporation is worse than having an uninformed one.

The shrewdest companies have attempted to cooperate with moderate leaders of special interest groups, rather than destroy them and demean their efforts (Haney, 1980). One interesting case of corporate cooperation with a consumer coalition is the Food Safety Council, formed out of the mutual interest of companies and consumers to bring order to the chaos of safety standards for food ingredients (Steckmest, 1982: 21-22). Earlier, because of the uncertainties surrounding nature and toxicology, the American Industrial Health Council was formed in 1977. Approximately 200 companies and trade associations provided support for the shared interest in monitoring toxic waste and materials issues. The council represented an array of industrial concerns, including pharmaceutical and petrochemical companies. The council drew together those interested in metals, textiles, and other consumer goods which could be toxic or produce toxic wastes. The members shared the commitment to better understand the nature and control of toxic materials. Another example: To counterbalance the drive for regulation of disposable aluminum cans, Alcoa sponsored a major recycling program. Not only did this campaign succeed in abating much of the move to outlaw throwaway containers and impose returnables in their place, it also provided Alcoa and other aluminum companies with a cheaper resource, since recycled aluminum requires less electricity to process than does the refining of raw materials.

Not all contention is being eliminated by cooperation. Environmental standards for business have been hotly contested, and debates regarding safe levels of smog, noise, light, various sulfur oxides, and heavy metals have proven common (Simon, 1971). Typical of sudden radical challenges to corporate operations, E. I. Du Pont de Nemours & Company was only one of many companies caught in the fluorocarbon controversy which grew from a scientific paper published in 1974. It charged that the fluorocarbons in refrigeration, aerosol propellants, and foam-blowing agents rose into the atmosphere. There they affected the ozone layer, which in turn increased our exposure to ultraviolet wavelengths and led to a variety of other potentially serious problems.

Du Pont's campaign was managed through a steering committee chaired by the Division Manager of the Freon Products Division of the Organic Chemicals Department. The steering committee had members from marketing, research, legal, advertising, and public affairs departments. The advertising details were handled by the N. W. Ayer agency; staff assistance and counsel was obtained from Hill & Knowlton, Inc. A matrix arrangement resulted in complex approval requiring 21 different department and management clearances. The campaign discussed the facts and reasoning involved in the fluorocarbon controversy. The initial advertisement in the series appeared under the signature of Chairman of the Board Irving S. Shapiro and ran in major daily newspapers and two trade publications, *Aerosol Age* and *Editor & Publisher*. Underscoring industry concern, Du Pont indicated its willingness to fund research into the potential damage of its product to the complex chemistry of the atmosphere, since "much more experimental evidence is needed to evaluate the ozone depletion theory." Survey results indicate that the campaign helped to open the discussion rather than leaving the public with the impression that it was final. Indeed, the campaign led to many inquiries for additional information (Stridsberg, 1977: 136-139).

The Alaskan pipeline and offshore drilling controversies were also extremely volatile and denied energy industry boardrooms the freedom to disregard the environment. One does not have to be anti-business to appreciate that corporations have a responsibility for any damage they do to the land, which is the collective heritage of the people. A visit to the older oil fields in this country allows us to witness environmental devastation that is more than 60 years old. A similar visit to contemporary oil drilling and production sites offers tangible evidence of the marked improvement in social responsibility. They have not been reluctant to point to these accomplishments in attempting to restructure their tattered corporate images.

At times, companies have come off looking very bad in their efforts to explain their situation to the press and other members of the public. One example of how a company can get bad press appeared in the *Wall Street Journal* (hardly a bastion of anti-company criticism). The story surrounded Walter Peeples, Jr., whose "tiny company, Gulf Nuclear Inc., is," he claims, "the victim of onerous, nit-picking regulations made by regulators of 'questionable competency.'" One of the worst errors in handling radioactive materials occurred when a lathe operator accidentally cut in half a capsule containing Americium-241, a radioactive isotope. When this happened, the contents splattered around the workshop and nearby lunchroom. The company failed to file the state-mandated report of the accident, and employees were told not to mention the accident (Burrough, 1983). This is only one of a legion of incidents where failure to comply with approved standards of acceptable behavior was widely reported.

Two decades of energetic criticism and robust development in corporate communication, plus the prospect for future challenges in coming years, provide the context for a detailed study of issues management. In striking out in new directions, some false starts have been made. No single discussion will answer all questions or solve all controversies involved in the effort to influence targeted publics regarding corporate performance and regulation. Despite the long history of issues management, those who manage, design, or critique issue advocacy campaigns cannot always agree on which objectives the campaigns should accomplish, who they should affect, and whether they are ethical or effective.

This brief review of issues management's history reminds us of the need to bring harmony among corporations, employees, consumers, and the public. The creation of issues management units, the debate over their role, the contest over new standards of social responsibility—these and many more indicators mark the beginning of a new era in the relationship between corporations and their various publics. All in all, regardless of the interest of any one individual or organization in this social drama, the long-term result of this effort involves a search for order.

3

CASE STUDIES IN ISSUES COMMUNICATION
Mobil Sets the Stage

Corporations may use advocacy advertising as one of many issues management strategies. Even though advocacy or issue advertising accounts for less than 10 percent of corporate advertising spending, its penchant for the controversial commands attention.

Making advocacy pay off has proven a problem for some users, helping to explain its often lukewarm acceptance (Dougherty, 1983). Despite the billions spent on advocacy communication, researchers do not know the long-term impact of this effort, except anecdotally. In the midst of an earlier robust period of issues communication, Sethi (1977: 237) concluded: "Advocacy advertising, as it is being currently practiced by major corporations and industry groups, with some notable exceptions, is of largely questionable value and doubtful effectiveness." We can nevertheless speculate that such communication efforts cumulatively have helped inform and mobilize a broader public, even while skepticism about the quality of corporate leadership remains. For example, United Technologies—where a Horatio Alger spirit reigns—reports circulating 2 million reprints lauding values of freedom, innovation, thrift, common sense, and personal achievement in response to over 450,000 individual requests (Stein, 1983).

Since the mid-1970s, a decidedly conservative mood has swept the nation. How does this political trend correspond to advances in issues communication? What applications can we make to future campaigns?

Questions such as these need to be answered before the verdict is delivered on issues management, thus helping predict why some campaigns fail whereas others succeed.

The field of advocacy advertising is mostly occupied by a limited number of corporations and trade associations who feel not only a right but an obligation to speak out on public issues, "on the premise that they are being squeezed out of the public communication space by more vocal activists" (Sethi, 1977: 237). These industrial advertisers "believe that the media generally distort or ignore the business world's behavior and point of view. They are not content to let those perceived distortions, like the madman's shout, stand uncorrected, and they're willing to put their budgets behind their beliefs: seeing no other alternative, they seek a public hearing through paid advertising" (Hush, 1983: 8).

Issues advertising campaigns take many forms. Some seem designed to inform the public. Allstate Insurance, for example, participated in the automobile air bag safety controversy and helped increase public awareness of and pressure for acceptance of the device. In 1972, only 17 percent of the public viewed air bags as viable safety devices; five years later this number had risen to 55 percent, even though the bags are still unavailable on American passenger vehicles (Ewing, 1980: 16). Some opt to link themselves to general truths—during an election year (1984), Lockheed used a vague advertisement to champion "peace, liberty, and security." The closing line asserted that the preservation of these values requires ample defense spending—an obvious self-interested mixture of image and issue advertising. Still other campaigns present corporations as wounded elephants or attempt to bludgeon the opposition. The Asphalt Institute, for example, appealed to readers to let "your lawmakers know where you stand on preserving our streets and highways. The deterioration of the nation's road system must be stopped, before it stops us" (Garbett, 1981: 21). The reader could respond to this image of the institute by viewing it as caring about public transportation, or by attributing its efforts to purely self-interested grassroots lobbying.

According to a 1981 Association of National Advertisers' (ANA) corporate advertising survey, advocacy campaigns most commonly seek to:

- inform or educate target publics on subjects important to a company's future;

- advocate specific actions on matters affecting the company, its industry, and business in general; and
- communicate corporate concerns and achievements on social and environmental issues.

In general, studies indicate that advocacy advertising is most effective when it is informative, fair, nonthreatening, and direct (Kelley, 1982). Although only about 11 percent of corporate campaigns are directed at the public in general, specific demographic segments of the public—including activists, opinion leaders, financial analysts and investors, current and potential employees, plant communities, and business-to-business customers—continue to be important targets.

Handled well, advocacy advertising can produce concrete results. The best campaigns "do not seek to be all things to all people. Rather, they focus on a single important idea that can be developed over time and presented in a variety of creative executions" (Bell, 1983). Some have the effect of helping enlighten the nation as a whole about technical and operating realities. Others present a less one-sided conversation. For a number of years LTV Corporation has employed the format of a forum in expressing its point of view. Although they require greater attention and effort on the part of the reader than most other issues advertisements, those of LTV demonstrate one company's willingness to foster dialogue on controversial, vital issues.

Communication that attempts to inform rather than inflame has many benefits; it reflects a genuine public interest, improves the image of beleaguered industries, and enriches the information used to debate complex topics such as ecology. In the face of environmental protest, for example, readership recognition studies gave high marks to the American Forest Institute's "trees are the renewable resource" advertising campaign. In 1974, 34 percent of the sample thought that the forests were being managed well; by 1980 this percentage had increased to 55 (Pincus, 1980: 63). Moreover, an invitation to contact the institute for additional information produced 12,000 letters (Stridsberg, 1977: 127; Adkins, 1978). Similarly, an Opinion Research Corporation (1981a) study revealed that 62 percent of the population believed that business has helped reduce pollution.

W. R. Grace & Company's 1979 campaign against a proposed increase in the capital gains tax is another outstanding example of successful communication. As part of an all-out effort against the tax, Grace personnel compiled statistical evidence to support their belief that the tax increase would harm the economy. Those statistics became the basis for a series of ads bearing headlines such as "Taxes Up, Productivity Down; Could We Be Doing Something Wrong?" That particular execution was so convincing that it also ran as an editorial in the *Wall Street Journal* and as an article (bylined J. Peter Grace, CEO of W. R. Grace) in both the New York *Daily News* and the *Los Angeles Times.*

In addition to advertising, Grace incorporated its statistics into a 49-page memorandum delivered to every member of Congress. The results were gratifying, to say the least: Instead of increasing the tax from 49 to 52 percent, Congress reduced it to 28 percent. Grace officials believe that the company's advocacy campaign played an important role in influencing the outcome. Moreover, the campaign has been paying dividends ever since. As Stephen B. Elliot, Director of Corporate Advertising at W. R. Grace, told *Madison Avenue* magazine: "This campaign opened up relations with Congress we never had before . . . Grace suddenly became an authority in Washington." Subsequently, J. Peter Grace emerged as a celebrity by heading the Private Sector Cost Control Presidential Commission, which spotlighted practical ways to reduce government waste (Hush, 1983: 8-9).

The case studies survey that follows is not intended to be representative or comprehensive. While the tone and stylistic flavor of these issues campaigns are of interest, each accents a subtle nuance in strategic development and execution. More important, however, by examining instances where advertising has been an integral component of issues communication, we can learn about some pitfalls and strategic accomplishments that they reveal.

MOBIL: GULLIVER AND THE LILLIPUTIANS

Even though companies within the same industry share many common challenges, they may respond quite differently. At one end of the continuum is the aggressive adversarial stance of Mobil Corporation. This contrasts with the other extreme, typified by the generally innocuous comments by Getty Oil on the importance of freedom. Getty observed in one 1983 ad that "we expect it in America, "and warned that "it can be taken away, if we allow it, by the government that can assure our personal freedom. Something to think about from the people at Getty."

Mobil, too, is concerned about issues of freedom but has been much more specific in spelling out its corporate position as the "most visible—and feistiest—practitioner" of advocacy communication. Rather than having a unifying theme in the traditional sense, Mobil's advertising mission is to promote full First Amendment and free enterprise rights for corporate citizens. For better or worse, Mobil has presented itself as Gulliver in the land of the Lilliputians. The size comparison is significant, symbolizing Mobil's view that American business is artificially tied down by swarms of ill-informed bureaucrats and journalists.

In covering an array of topics, three central messages emerge: (1) bias does exist in the media; (2) protecting the integrity of free enterprise is important, with large oil companies having a particularly vital contribution to make; and (3) government is guilty of many unintentional sins, ranging from ill-conceived regulation to ineffective management. The bottom-line argument made by Mobil involves contributions made by most businesses in creating jobs, aiding prosperity, and providing other valuable services.

The company's objective, according to one Mobil spokesperson, is "to present our views and our ideas along with established facts to assist the public in making decisions." Mobil would like to achieve an alliance, an identification, with targeted audiences who also suffer from irresponsible reporting and incompetent government. *Madison Avenue* magazine reported that the publics targeted by Mobil were very special ones; not John Q, but rather print and broadcast journalists plus "all the other opinion molders and thought leaders who shape public discourse in this country" (quoted in Hush, 1983: 9).

This approach tends to provoke extreme reactions, both positive and negative. Reflecting the first decade of the program, Verne Gay (1982: 87) observes: "No other major advertising campaign has generated as much controversy or major media news coverage as Mobil's." Among respondents to a Grey Advertising corporate advertising survey of CEOs at 50 prominent U.S. companies reported in *Grey Matter,* some professed admiration for Mobil's aggressive stance and praised it for "recognizing opposing views and presenting corporate positions in a positive way," while others accused it of being "too strident" and "preaching to the converted." Examining these findings, the Grey agency concluded that, "strangely enough," divided opinions and heated debate are probably just the sort of reactions Mobil wanted (Hush, 1983: 9).

As Gay (1982: 87) notes, "Mobil's voice is distinctive and highly idiosyncratic—reflecting the personality of the company's top brass."

Mobil's campaign is the brainchild of Herbert Schmertz, Vice President for Public Affairs, but it would not have continued without support from Mobil chairman Rawleigh Warner Jr.

Conceived in 1970, Mobil's first advocacy effort was in support of improved mass transit. Although mild in terms of later issues raised by the company, highway contractors were outraged by the perceived attack on their interests. Later, Mobil expanded its communication efforts in response to questionable media statements about the oil industry during the controversy surrounding the OPEC embargo (Ross, 1976).

As petroleum costs skyrocketed in the mid-1970s and Congress sought someone to blame, Mobil centered on the critical question: Are oil companies withholding gasoline to falsely escalate prices? This proved important, since the Media Institute later demonstrated the need for an open contest of ideas in its report on news coverage during the crisis. The major problem was imbalance (Theberge and Hazlett, 1982; Fletcher, 1982). In one of its 1982 op-eds ("A Post Audit"), Mobil agreed with Media Institute findings that print and broadcast journalists failed "to properly describe the economic size of the crisis" through "overreliance on the government for information."

Early in the campaign Mobil flirted with the use of videotaped story advertisements mimicking TV journalism conventions such as authoritative stand-up framing presented as ostensibly fair coverage. Mobil also circulated at least 11 televised special reports free of charge to stations, aired mostly by licensees with small budgets seeking public service programming. Mobil's involvement in each report was indicated only by the end credit: "Produced for Mobil Oil by DWJ Associates" (MacDougall, 1981).

Limited in the use of television by network restrictions and broadcaster fears of fairness doctrine entanglements, the backbone of the Mobil campaign has focused on three kinds of print advertisements. One is a quarter-page op-ed placed periodically in business publications, national magazines, and the opinion section of major daily newspapers. A second kind of ad runs in Sunday supplements of major newspapers and some national magazines. Entitled "Observations," this series features a mix of interesting information, typically about the energy industry, capitalism, or some related theme. A light writing style and cartoon graphics enhance readability. The text often consists of a fable or story designed to reach a broad audience, whereas the op-eds are targeted at a more elite readership. The third kind of ad is of the "Red Cross" variety, which promote public service activities by the company.

These advertisements discuss some topic involved in a Mobil-sponsored artistic or civic endeavor but do not center on energy or capitalism. Mobil, for example, has long underwritten public television programs—most notably *Masterpiece Theatre.*

To supplement these advertisements, Mobil executives travel widely to address key groups, including journalists. The company also produces the Mobil Corporation Civic Action Program Newsletter, entitled *Mobil re:cap*. The newsletter series "is published periodically for active employees, annuitants, and others on request." It was founded in 1979 to provide timely information to important stakeholders regarding the gasoline shortage but has since been integrated into the total communication plan of the company. Headlines in *re:cap*'s June 1980 issue suggest how Mobil consistently presents the themes central to its advocacy campaigns: "TV: Still Pulls the Plug on Voices not Its Own," "Who Was Responsible for Gasoline Lines? Us? No, U.S.," "How States are Hampering Energy Goals," and "Governments Take More than Mobil Makes in a Year." Compare this to the June 1984 issue which discussed information relevant to these topics: "Truth vs. Freedom of the Press," "Gas Recontrol Bill Would Cut Supplies, Hurt Consumers," "Oil Company Mergers: The Healthy Result of a Changing Market," and "Study Shows 'Big Oil' Pays Higher Tax Rates."

To appreciate the effort that Mobil has expended, we can examine typical advertisements aimed at discussing the media, the oil industry, and government. In a widely discussed and reprinted five-part series, Mobil sought to answer the question, "Are the media giving us the facts?" The first ad, "The myth of the villainous businessman," starts by citing communication researcher George Gerbner of the Annenberg School of Communications at the University of Pennsylvania. Gerbner claims that television helps create a view of the world. The more television people watch, the more they adopt television's view of reality. To make this point, Mobil notes how Gerbner's studies suggest that people who watch a lot of television believe that more violence exists than is factually true. From this platform, it is a short step to argue that if television gives a distorted view of violence, it does the same for business. Here Mobil relies on Media Institute findings of anti-business television bias (Theberge, 1981).

Countering public distrust, Mobil agrees:

> To be sure, businessmen make their share of mistakes. However, business is the direct source of livelihood for millions of Americans and the indirect benefactor of many millions more. It is the producer of virtually all of the goods we as a nation consume. And if free private business is destroyed or

> threatened, all the institutions in society, including a free press and free mass communications network, would be threatened.

This statement first appeared in the *Wall Street Journal* on October 18, 1983.

Ten days later, Jan R. Van Meter (1983) published an editorial rebuttal in the *Journal*, entitled "TV Didn't Invent Evil Businessmen." Van Meter, a senior vice president of a New York City-based public relations firm, argues that long before the advent of television, novels and films used the villainous businessman as a central and recurring character. For Van Meter, the bottom line is not malicious bias but the need for television revenues. Fictional "bad guy" business executives such as J. R. Ewing are perceived by the broadcasting industry as more interesting to the viewing public than their real-life counterparts. After making this point, Van Meter responds directly to the theme of Mobil's op-ed: "What is clear is that Mobil and Accuracy in Media and The Media Institute had better find another scapegoat to blame and another hobbyhorse to ride. It's fun to attack television entertainment programming, and it may even scare some television executives. But it won't change how the culture looks at business."

In the second op-ed of the media series, Mobil continued its good guys/bad guys discussion by comparing political stereotypes prevalent in the media. The liberal politician is a "defender of consumer interests and environmental protection." In contrast, the conservative politician is "in the pocket of big business." The social activist is a public interest representative who "has unruly hair and wears folksy clothes." Finally, the business executive is "motivated by greed for more profits, unwilling to put the country's good ahead of his company's."

In the third op-ed Mobil challenged "the myth of the crusading reporter" by suggesting that in fact many media corporations are nearly pure monopolies: "The journalist has the power to shape the agenda, edit the story and place it prominently before the public eye." To demonstrate how the problem perpetuates itself, Mobil pointed out that 40 percent of Columbia School of Journalism students "advocate public ownership of corporations." So much for print media balance.

In the fourth advertisement, Mobil turned its attention to "the myth of the open airwaves." Here the villain is the FCC's fairness doctrine, with its ostensible mandate to pursue vigorous debate being undercut by programming executives seeking to prevent controversy from being aired. Indeed, as Mobil points out from its own experiences and those of other corporate communicators, broadcasters are reluctant to sell time to those wishing to respond to public affairs stories. The ad's conclusion is drawn from a 1978 Supreme Court decision: "The press does not have a monopoly on either the First Amendment or the ability to enlighten" (First National Bank of Boston v. Bellotti, 1978).

The fifth advertisement condemned the proclivity that the media have for hiding behind the First Amendment. In assuming that the Constitution protects them against irresponsibility, Mobil warned that the media may be in for a rude awakening, since there is no absolute shield preventing libel and bias actions. Mobil cautioned that "by crying 'wolf' too often, the media may well bring the wolf to their door."

In a reflective follow-up ad, Mobil concluded that "the customers always write." In this op-ed, Mobil shared excerpts from several letters by people who agreed with the media criticisms raised by the series. And, the company acknowledged, it received some "brickbats," such as one from a reader who thought Mobil dollars could be spent more productively than on advertisements criticizing the media. This reader challenged Mobil to be a more responsible steward of the economic system. But the key to the attack on the media may be revealed in Mobil's gleeful observation that it had begun a dialogue on the effectiveness of the press.

Perhaps the most explosive moment in the history of this campaign occurred when Mobil decided to boycott the *Wall Street Journal* in late 1984. While reporting on Mobil plans to build a $300 million office building in Chicago, the *Journal* implied that wrongdoing occurred when it disclosed a special arrangement between Mobil and chairman Rawleigh Warner's son-in-law, Percy R. Pyne IV, employed by the firm of Galbreath-Ruffin (leasing agents for the building). Schmertz, already angry over earlier *Journal* practices that he considered questionable, charged the paper with biased reporting because it decided to print that story while ignoring one on a Mobil refinery closing in West Germany. As he pointedly observed, "We don't believe in feeding the hand that bites us" (Schmertz, 1983a; Alter, 1984).

Undertaking its second theme, Mobil worked diligently to present the American oil industry in the most favorable light. Aside from detailed examinations of the profit picture, Mobil also sought to broaden and deepen the public's view of oil company corporate responsibility. In a 1980 op-ed, Mobil gave us pause to "count our blessings." The broad message was the effectiveness of business as both provider and creator. More specifically, the oil industry creates jobs, provides oil for other industries, "helps the little guy," and is an investor.

In a related op-ed entitled "When Golden Eagles Nest Near a Coal Mine," Mobil gave an account in 1982 of the careful effort being made to relocate nesting golden eagles so that they would be outside its Caballo Rojo coal mining property. The ad explained how the company stockpiled topsoil for the eventual reclamation of the mining site. It continued to extol Mobil's virtues as having worked closely to generate baseline data on the wildlife in the area. This discussion proclaimed: "The environment can be preserved while needed energy is produced." A cynical reader, however, could imagine that without federal and state regulations, corporations would be less "socially responsible."

To describe its efforts to increase oil field production, in other communications Mobil used the headline, "Plop, plop! Fizz, fizz!" The catchy title played on Alka-Seltzer's popular commercial jingle to attract readers to a relatively sophisticated discussion of the injection of carbon dioxide into old wells so that it will mix with crude oil, thereby thinning the oil for increased recovery. The companion "Observation" of July 17, 1983 gave a folksy version of the technical material. After describing technological advances in discovering new oil fields, the column stated: "We're also using science to squeeze more out of what we've already found. We inject carbon dioxide—the fizzy stuff that adds zip to soda pop—into 'mature' wells to increase oil recovery . . . and set fires down below to make thick, gooey oil flow to the production wells."

During the energy crisis the public believed that oil companies were using crude oil for more profitable lines of plastics rather than producing gasoline for automobiles. A whole column of "Observations" was devoted to this issue in 1983. After a brief, chatty discussion of the history of plastics, Mobil noted that plastics save energy and improve the quality of life. But, said Mobil, "in 1982 less than 1.5 percent of the oil and gas supply" in the United States was used in making plastics.

Nor has the government received high marks in Mobil's gradebook. In January 1985, Mobil's op-ed asked, "Is this any way to run a business?" The center of attention was federal waste of tax dollars through the use of obsolescent computers. The op-ed concluded: "Clearly, no private business could operate the way the government does and hope to remain in business." Regulatory agencies have also been singled out for criticism, but in a piece entitled "An Invitation Too Good To Refuse," Mobil praised EPA administrator William Ruckelhaus in 1984 for his call to scientists to assist in establishing sound guidelines. Mobil applauded his action, saying, "Too often, U.S. environmental policy has been based on political considerations or has been influenced by one-sided TV reportage." Mobil continued: "Without the guiding hand of science in environmental policy-making, the results have been predictable: confusing, contradictory, duplicative and punitive rules and regulations." In the conclusion, Mobil centered on the belief "that government officials, working together with scientists, Congress *and* industry, can forge better environmental laws that protect *both* the health and economic welfare of all the people."

This is not an isolated case of Aristotle's golden mean living in the hearts of Mobil Public Affairs personnel. Highlighting the potential for an improved business-government relationship are continuing questions over how to establish an equitable tax system, particularly when private and public interests are intertwined. Both a Congressional Joint Committee on Taxation report in 1983 and data released by the Petroleum Industry Research Foundation found that "oil companies already are among the most heavily taxed in the nation." So it is not surprising that Mobil took up taxation issues in its op-ed campaign. Mobil has also cited President Reagan, who in 1985 said: "Someday I would hope that we could arrive at a tax structure that would recognize that you can't tax things, you only tax people."

One advertisement, published after the November 1984 elections, is of particular interest in that it typifies Mobil's commitment to two-way debate rather than one-way domination. Entitled "Since You Asked, Mr. Haskell," the ad was addressed to Floyd Haskell, a former Democratic senator from Colorado who heads the Taxpayers Committee. At issue was his contention that the 1981 tax law should be repealed because it gives too many breaks to industry. Mobil built its refutation on several contentions. The first was "that *all* taxation distorts the marketplace" by robbing companies of investment capital. Second, Mobil favored the Accelerated Cost Recovery System provision that allows companies "to take deductions for plants and equipment at a faster rate than before." Moreover, Mobil challenged Haskell to advocate repeal of the windfall profit tax on oil which took $61.4 billion from oil companies between 1980 and 1983. In a letter to the editor of the Denver *Post*, Haskell (1984) responded to Mobil regarding the effects of the 1981 tax measure. He contended that instead of fostering capital investment, the opposite occurred; fewer dollars were devoted to capital investment in 1982 and 1983. He also challenged Mobil by countering that "there is no discernible correlation between corporate taxation and economic health." In closing, Haskell parried: "As a Mobil stockholder, I wonder why they [op-ed dollars] are spent at all."

Good question. Mobil continues its campaign, as it said in a 1984 op-ed, because it does not "want to be like the mother-in-law who comes to visit only when she has problems and matters to complain about. We think of a continuous presence in this space makes sense for us. And we hope, on your part, you find us informative occasionally, or entertaining, or at least infuriating. But never boring. After all, you did read this far, didn't you?" With arguments such as these, Mobil indeed wants to free the corporate Gulliver from the petty Lilliputians who would keep it from realizing its potential.

But what has resulted from more than a decade and a half of experimenting in open communication? The success of the campaign is difficult to calculate empirically. According to the IAA, "Mobil does not have a systematic program for measuring the impact of the public affairs campaign, but 'informal' measures indicate that target audiences pay close attention to the ad content." Although many admire its themes and learn from the information, "others are uneasy about the stridency and visibility of the campaign" (Stridsberg, 1977: 112).

Simons (1983) criticizes Mobil for using the metaphor of "free enterprise" without analysis or reservation. The company, he argues, merely reiterates versions of the standard theme: Things are better for everyone when the free enterprise system can work to its fullest extent. Noting Mobil's slant on the campaign, Crable and Vibbert (1983) employ the famed Prometheus story to examine the rhetorical impact of the company's "Observations." As the "bringer of fire," Mobil, by its own estimation, is often sorely misunderstood and punished for the very reason it should be applauded.

Yankelovich, Skelly, and White, in an independent 1978 survey, focused on Mobil and the American Forest Institute (Adkison, 1978). Their data indicate that Mobil ads are highly visible; 90 percent of congressional and other government leaders had read them. But 66 percent of these readers felt that the ads lacked influence and believed them to be of little value for helping people understand energy deregulation. One of the most important findings suggests that the advertisements did little to solve the energy crisis. Only 6 percent of the respondents considered the advertisements credible, whereas 53 percent believed that they lacked credibility. Hampering acceptance, the poll found, was the irritating tone of many of the ads.

In contrast, the American Forest Institute got high marks for its campaign. In all, 56 percent of the government leaders and 70 percent of the public found them valuable. The Yankelovich study concluded that the institute was most effective in winning public favor when it provided information helpful for readers' understanding of its industry; in contrast, effectiveness fell when communication became adversarial (Adkins, 1978).

Nevertheless, at least for the present, Mobil is convinced that its campaign was successful. Gay (1982) quotes Schmertz, who suggests: "If you went back over ten years you would find that many of the things that we have espoused and which were unpopular or criticized at the time have now become pretty well accepted." Schmertz believes that the willingness of the company to debate issues and performance in public has led to changes in Washington, specifically a more favorable disposition toward "big oil" as the information gap surrounding the industry has narrowed (Gay, 1982: 87-89).

THE ENERGY INDUSTRY: PROFITS, PROFITS, WHO HAS THE PROFITS?

In Kahn's futuristic study of the major issues of the latter half of this century, he made no mention of the energy crisis (Kahn and Weiner, 1967), but he didn't need a crystal ball after the OPEC embargo to feature it in a later study (Kahn et al., 1976). While industry leaders had been warning of an energy shortfall, they stuck to technical arguments and failed to foresee the long-term public opinion ramifications. This approach underscores the difficulty of predicting issues and suggests how industry and academic specialists, despite the elementary importance of energy, were unprepared for the crisis.

The United States has had a love-hate relationship with the oil industry for years. Issues management, including its advertising phase, cannot be understood fully without giving attention to the difficulties encountered by petrochemical manufacturers in attempting to explain the linkage between large profits and the availability of products such as gasoline.

Besides Mobil, examples abound. In 1977 Texaco reported that 82 percent of Americans did not know that large oil companies made as little as 1.1 cents per gallon. Continuing this campaign, Texaco noted that since "a billion dollars just doesn't go as far as it used to . . . over the next 5 years, Texaco will be spending more than $10 billion to bring you the energy you need." To do this, it would seek gas in the Baltimore Canyon, advance its coal gasification project, work to improve oil shale extraction technology, and make refineries more efficient.

Gulf explained its large profits similarly by showing how it divided the pie, claiming to have earned only 5 percent on each dollar of sales. Of the profit, 1.5 cents went to stockholders as dividends. The remaining amount was reinvested into capital programs, such as oil shale in

Colorado, tar sands in Canada, and uranium in Mount Taylor, New Mexico. To demonstrate how an oil company must remain current in its exploration program, it announced, "Thirty-five percent of its current domestic production comes from wells that didn't exist only seven years ago. In those seven years, our exploration and capital expenditures for domestic oil and natural gas amounted to $5.6 billion."

A central issue facing the industry was increased taxation. One of the most dramatic moments in this struggle was created when Jerry McAfee, Chairman of the Board of Gulf Oil Corporation, addressed an open letter to President Jimmy Carter on August 29, 1979. The arguments in his letter detailed typical concerns that imposing new tax burdens would further cut back on the ability of oil companies to cope with the energy crisis. McAfee claimed that he had "publicly committed Gulf Oil to reinvest the additional funds made available to us through decontrol in energy-related projects so long as they show promise of economic viability."

Participating in the debate over profits and windfalls, Mesa Petroleum Company gave the readers of one of its ads a bit of advice:

> When you tell your congressman how you feel about a 'windfall profits tax,' ask how many new wells the government will drill with the billions of dollars such a proposed tax would siphon out of the petroleum industry. Why don't you ask how many barrels of oil were found with the $10,800,000,000 (Billions) of *your* taxes that were allocated to the Department of Energy this year?

The ever-present Mobil also waded into the debate on the taxation of new oil. It compared four programs against nine criteria. The programs were Carter's, Mobil's, continued price control, and total decontrol. Mobil's, to no one's surprise, was found to be the only one that maximized exploration and production without new taxes and new legislation. It reduced dependency on foreign sources, avoided immediate product price increases, reduced balance of payment deficits, and maximized long-term U.S. economic health.

The taxation battle soon became obscured by the decline in the economy. Within five years of this high-profile public policy debate over the future control and direction of the oil industry, the equation of "big equals bad" was no longer chic. Public opinion has drifted to the point that not only have many mergers been allowed to happen, but they have been welcomed, in the belief that consolidation is the key to effective resource utilization. The key differences between the late 1970s and the years following are these: The price of gasoline at the pump has stabilized or fallen, while the supply has been ample, and the state of the economy has been so dismal that any hope of sustained recovery is welcomed. While one may question the quality of economic education, the producer/consumer relationship has changed markedly.

CHEMICAL COMPANIES: AN ISSUE EXPLODES

Issues become visible for many reasons. Through negative news coverage and the efforts of agitation groups, toxic chemicals have long been closely associated with environmental destruction (Freudenberg, 1984). Naturally, this link concerns the chemical industry. To revamp their image, individual companies and their trade organizations have responded by opting for a variety of public affairs approaches, notably advertising. Typical advertisements feature either a safety specialist or member of the environmental protection team who announces how safe and clean chemical facilities and procedures are. The Chemical Manufacturers Association circulated one print advertisement in 1982 that had Jerry Ivie, the manager of Environmental Operations, standing near his son and granddaughter. Ivie said: "I raised my son in this community. Now he's raising his own family in this area." By extension, the message implied, if this community is safe for my family, then the chemical industry is doing an important, socially responsive job. In 1981, for an earlier advertisement in this series, Tom Hamberger, the supervisor of the Emergency Response System, was pictured with his three daughters. Hamberger proclaimed: "Safety is my No. 1 concern. My company's too."

Such information contributes to policy discussion, but it can be ineffective when sensationalist reporting overwhelms scientific data (Media Institute, 1985; Copulos, 1985). Often the catalyst for public awareness consists of catastrophic events such as the Love Canal disclosures or the 1984 methyl isocyanate (MIC) leak in Bhopal, India, which killed more than 2000 people and resulted in nearly 100,000 injuries. Both incidents stunned the chemical industry, underscoring how smoldering issues become inflamed once they are graphically publicized. Remember Times Beach and dioxin, the derailments of chemical trains, and the ethylene dibromide (EDB) scare? Normally a story about India would receive minor play in the American press. Helping to fuel interest in Bhopal was not only the magnitude of the tragedy, but also the fact that it was a U.S. firm involved in manufacturing the same lethal chemical in this country. After Bhopal, the media naturally once again turned to "front of the book" discussions of chemical safety. Prior instances of disaster were recalled, including Texas City, Texas, in 1947; Saveso, Italy, in 1976; Beziers, France, in 1977; and the BASF factory failures in 1921 and 1979. These are classic cases of a crisis making an issue so salient that the likelihood of government intervention increases substantially. As Roth (1984) reported in the *Wall Street Journal*, because of Bhopal "the chemical industry may be facing a fresh wave of legislation to tighten controls on uses of such lethal substances."

Editorials around the country debated the value of chemicals to protecting lives and promoting food production (Boffey, 1984) versus the safety of such manufacturing facilities (Beck et al., 1984; Diamond, 1984; Grier, 1984). Activists favoring stricter regulation point out that the presence of dangerous substances in populated areas is common. Approximately 6000 facilities make hazardous chemicals, with 180,000 shipments occurring by rail and truck each day in the United States. *Newsweek* acknowledges: "The U.S. chemical industry can boast of a strong safety record. But with more than 60,000 chemicals produced and stored in America, government regulators and watchdog groups can't even tell where potential time bombs are—let alone guarantee that they won't go off" (Whitaker et al., 1984: 28). Two *Wall Street Journal* writers similarly observe: "On the inside, the chemical and refining industries maintain the most exemplary safety record in U.S. manufacturing. But outside the plants, community ignorance of chemical risk remains widespread, and preparedness for the unlikely calamity remains spotty" (Petzinger and Burrough, 1984).

A complicating factor: Authorities do not know much about the dangers posed by the chemicals already in use. The Toxic Substances Control Act, passed in 1976, requires that new chemicals be studied before they go on the market, but that requirement has been applied to only about 20 percent of all products. Chemical companies have developed internal safety rules, created their own fire departments, and established other precautions to protect workers, forestall regulation, and maintain proprietary control over various chemical products (Loddeke, 1984). Nevertheless, many of the positive steps taken by the industry are overlooked once fear enters the information equation.

Henry A. Waxman, (D-CA), veteran House subcommittee chairman holding hearings on this issue, asked on ABC TV's *This Week with David Brinkley* whether "we let the industry continue to police itself or does the government step in?" In addition to measures designed to increase safety from gas leaks, Waxman was concerned with the long-term effects of chemical exposure, particularly cancer. Underscoring his worry, the California Democrat recalled a 1981 study by Union Carbide which depicted periodic leakage of MIC and other chemicals during the manufacturing and handling processes. In the midst of this controversy, Union Carbide was fined $55,000 for nine environmental violations that it had reported as occurring since 1982 at its South Charleston Technical Center (Houston *Post*, 1984).

One of the most damaging pieces of information surrounding the disaster was Carbide's claim that it knew a runaway disaster was possible at least three months prior to the Bhopal accident. The 1984 memo had been prepared by a Carbide safety inspection team to describe a worst-case scenario and was received by the manager of the Institute, West Virginia, plant on September 19. This memo was made public by Rep. Waxman, who indicated that he did not know whether corrective action had been taken at any plants (Houston *Post*, 1985). In a later report, Carbide indicated that it had revised its operating procedures several weeks before the Bhopal incident. Jackson B. Browning, Director of Health, Safety and Environmental Affairs for Carbide, noted that company training procedures at the Institute plant had been revised and new safety measures imposed to detect the presence of water and other contaminants. But, he added, the changes in Institute were irrelevant to Bhopal because the two plants were designed differently (Winslow, 1985a). Carbide also operates an MIC facility in France, where residents assert that they are caught between working in possibly hazardous conditions and the fear of unemployment (Kamm, 1984).

Such publicity added to the fervor of those seeking to further regulate the chemical industry through the imposition of stringent national—even international—standards. In the aftermath of Bhopal, many special interest groups, including the Environmental Action Foundation, Washington Fair Share, and the Public Citizen Health Research Group, used this opportunity to voice their opinions (Solomon and Russell, 1984). Several cities and states have passed or are considering legislation to require that companies inform workers of any hazardous chemicals they are handling. An EPA study reports that current laws may be inadequate to protect the people who live around such facilities (Meier, 1985).

Just how effective has Carbide been in dealing with the press, the government, and the public at large? That is hard to prove, given the considerable international attention to the incident and the mixed news coverage Carbide has received. Bhopal was particularly tragic since the disaster was so direct and immediate, forcing the major chemical manufacturers to take a generally reactive, wait-and-see communication approach. Apparently the corporate players in this crisis believe that a low-key effort is best, since they have not mounted a major advocacy "damage control" campaign. Certainly Union Carbide has made itself available to the press and given the appearance of being interested in safety. The company continued to issue periodic media releases on legal developments, scientific finds, new safety measures, and other operating changes. But then, we would expect nothing less. It even went so far as to provide funds for medical care and to establish a research program at a university hospital in Bhopal.

Prior to embarrassing new quality-control failures at the West Virginia facility, a 1985 opinion survey conducted by the Media Institute of 16 major daily newspaper and weekly news magazine editors and 19 major chemical corporation public relations executives found Union Carbide "above average" in its responsiveness to media requests. Editors and executives were also "virtually alike" in their impression that the overall tone of media coverage toward the company had been neutral. One reason for this may have been the fact that Carbide, rather than the Indian or American governments, was able to remain the principal news source (Media Institute, 1985: 52-58).

Unfortunately, in their contacts with the media company representatives weren't always well prepared. In the face of initial questioning by reporters, for example, Carbide admitted that there were no emergency evacuation plans for Bhopal, nor did the company understand the circumstances of the accident well enough to be able to explain how it happened (Marback et al., 1984: 37). Even a month later, for better or worse, Union Carbide still was unable to clarify itself. Such information gaps raise uncertainty and assist special interest groups by sustaining reader/viewer/listener interest in their policy agenda.

Despite Union Carbide's statement that it would pursue a "total communications program" as part of its 1985 marketing strategy, company spokespersons agreed that the program's form and design were slow to emerge because of continuing uncertainty over how to approach a post-Bhopal information climate (*Business Marketing,* 1985: 136). Nevertheless, in learning from past mistakes, the industry as a whole recognizes the importance of an informed public. Much to its credit, Union Carbide volunteered to assist governmental efforts both in the United States and abroad to put into play regulatory mechanisms that could prevent a similar disaster. Moreover, it continues to work with various congressional agencies, scientific organizations, and reporters to generate information that can be used to assess the problems of producing, transporting, and storing toxic materials.

Undoubtedly much more could be said publicly if it were not for the presence of liability claims so large that the future of the company is uncertain.

The long-term effect of the Bhopal incident on the image of chemical manufacturers and their operating environment is difficult to predict. Certainly the aftershocks are not confined to Carbide. The industry has had only limited success to date in playing down the seriousness of leaks, while special interest critics and governmental regulators have proved effective in charging that any leak is unsettling. Many companies have decided to "switch rather than fight" by further conforming to public expectations. Du Pont in La Porte, Texas, for example, publicized changes in its operating procedures to limit on-site MIC storage. Company management further decided to produce MIC in a "closed-loop" system, costing $10-11 million, that will use the chemical immediately after it is produced in order to minimize the risk of large amounts escaping. Similarly, insecticide manufacturers have begun to relocate facilities closer to product sources. Surely surrounding communities are safer with production limited to several pounds rather than the estimated 45 tons that escaped in India. Such measures can result in improved and/or reinforced positive attitudes by key publics unsettled about the social responsiveness of the chemical industry.

The Bhopal incident is an excellent example of how one disaster, particularly at a time when industrial safety in the chemical industry is a hot issue, can affect many related areas. The *Wall Street Journal,* in its continuing coverage of Union Carbide's problems, noted that "the idea of applying criminal laws to corporate executives is getting increased attention world-wide" because of the mass poisoning in India. The tragedy, the *Journal* reported, "is generating demands for tougher corporate-responsibility laws." In the words of a 19th-century English judge, Edward Baron Thurlow: "Did you ever expect a corporation to have a conscience when it has no soul to be damned and no body to be kicked? . . . By God, it ought to have both." This story captured an iceberg-tip of the controversy. In addition to Union Carbide, industrial safety cases against Film Recovery Systems Inc. and General Dynamics Corporation were discussed, both involving alleged criminal negligence in employee deaths. The report also suggested that the National Association of Manufacturers actively seeks to prevent criminal penalties by claiming that civil court is the proper place for remedies. Quoted in opposition was Timothy Smith, director of the Interfaith Center on Corporate Responsibility, a coalition of church investors, who said, "Let's send people to jail" (Trost, 1985).

In this hostile atmosphere, rather than undertake an advocacy campaign, Carbide and the rest of the chemical industry have decided to change corporate procedures and communicate quietly. At times performance must change, and communication is best when it is low key and responsible.

UTILITY COMPANIES: ANOTHER LOVE-HATE ISSUES RELATIONSHIP

The benefits of electric, gas, and telephone service are largely taken for granted, yet each of these industries operates in a stormy political climate where issues involving rates and lifestyle effects are raised. No utility has been more at the focal point of this kind of controversy than the electrical generating industry. The public realizes that ultimately it pays for long and tedious rate reviews, and for safety and environmental controls. But consumers are also suspicious that shareholders of private utilities unfairly seek to profit at their expense.

The oil crisis brought renewed attention to oil and alternative fuel resources such as coal, as well as nuclear and solar generation. If the dramatic price jumps in the 1970s proved hard to explain for the petroleum companies, it was perhaps even more challenging for the electrical utilities. Equally difficult to explain were rate increases resulting from expansion improvements that the electrical industry believed were vital to meeting future power needs. Two points were highlighted by the Edison Electric Institute (EEI) in an advocacy advertisement circulated in the spring of 1981 that attempted to show "the cost of not raising utility bills": (1) Investors' belief that companies such as Commonwealth Edison will not be able to increase future rates would undercut the true value of utility stocks; and (2) financial strains can easily slow the conversion from oil to coal.

During 1981-1982, EEI brought its educational campaign to a sophisticated business audience. Using targeted financial publications such as the *Wall Street Journal*, in addition to general "opinion leader" publications like *Newsweek*, EEI had University of Wisconsin Professor of Economics Charles J. Cicchetti explain the finances of the electricity industry. Such advertisements concluded with a typical theme:

> The electric utility system is the core of this nation's industrial strength and social fabric. It is time that thoughtful people throughout the country realize the national stake in the system's health and strength. Procrastination will be more costly, and many good options will be lost. If

political expedience and inertia continue to rule the day, the ratepayer and the nation will be worse off.

Another expert used in these advertisements was Alvin L. Alm, director of the Energy Security Program at Harvard's Kennedy School of Government. He argued that "the financial integrity of investor-owned electric utilities" must be restored. Continuing into 1983, in a later version of the same kind of advertisement, the institute had Warren M. Anderson, chairman of the board at Union Carbide, ask "Will we have the power to sustain economic recovery?" The point EEI sought to make was that investor-owned utilities must be as free as possible to obtain the capital necessary to perform their role in aiding prosperity.

One of the most controversial issues management campaigns was waged by the American Electric Power Company, Inc. (AEP) in the mid-1970s. It was motivated originally by the anger of Chairman of the Board Donald Cook toward the OPEC nations which, he felt, had created the oil embargo. The campaign was also designed to promote coal as an alternative fossil fuel for generating electricity, with regular blasts at added regulatory controls over its use. Cook was eager to undertake the campaign even though, according to Garbett (1981: 51), he was aware that the controversy could bring down on his industry the wrath of federal authorities and environmental groups. The company leadership worried that without a national energy policy, America would not be able to enjoy a reliable source of electricity. Media used in this campaign consisted of national news magazines, business magazines, technical magazines, newspapers in Western coal-producing areas, and major city newspapers.

One advertising format "humorously" used cartoon depictions of Arab sheiks discussing the hold they had on the world; other advocacy ads relied heavily on text discussions of key technical, energy, and environmental issues. Often unstated in the advertising were the current technical limitations on the prevention of high coal pollution byproduct levels. Finally addressing this issue in a discussion of anti-pollutant scrubbers, AEP admitted that the technology was available "to eliminate most of the sulfur-oxide emissions" but that such devices created "horrendous problems." The reason: "Scrubber systems do remove sulfur-oxides. But in the process all of them are plagued with one or more problems that make them unreliable and impractical for a major electric utility." The company noted that ten square miles of America would be destroyed by the limestone sludge created as a part of the pollution reduction system.

The issue posed by AEP was air versus land quality. The company argued that the best solution was "to release the enormous reserves of U.S. Government-owned low sulfur coal in the West. And at the same time continue the investment of time, energy and money in the development of the technology to clean high-sulfur coal before it is burned."

A variety of fear appeals were used, such as asking readers to imagine what would happen if OPEC decided to stop the supply of oil again. Many critics felt that this theme, which amounted to little more than a xenophobic attack on Middle Eastern oil producers, damaged international relations. Both the *Washington Post* and *New York Times* editorialized against the campaign, and more than 200 letters were sent to the Environmental Protection Agency protesting the content and tone of the advertisements. One scholar who took a hard, detailed look at AEP's communication program is Sethi (1977: 126), who claims that the electric utility industry was strongly in favor of the content. AEP did not do evaluative pre- and post-testing, but, according to a 1980 Gallup & Robinson poll, theirs is one of the most successful advocacy campaigns in recent years (Hush, 1983: 8).

Subsequent analysis is necessary to determine whether AEP's efforts were cost-effective, particularly since they did not defeat the use of scrubber technology. For every action there is a reaction, and perhaps the best measure of the impact of the campaign was the resolve that environmentalists showed in fighting for increasingly rigorous protection standards. EPA staffers believed that the agency's efforts were strengthened by the AEP campaign, since the public learned more about scrubbers than it would have otherwise.

A great deal of fear and mystique surround a related utility issue, nuclear generation management. Survey results from the Opinion Research Corporation (1981b) reveal that nearly all of the sample (99 percent) believed that the control of radioactive wastes was an important issue. Almost as many respondents (94 percent) wanted close federal supervision of nuclear reactors. Demonstrating public ambivalence toward government and industry, 65 percent wanted the government to speed up the licensing of nuclear plants, while 85 percent thought the government should "require companies to give public notice of toxic substances they are making or handling." Ecology won out over energy; people wanted solutions to technical problems and shortages, but not by abandoning governmental efforts to protect the environment.

Names such as Three Mile Island, Diablo Canyon, and the Washington Public Power Supply System (also known as WHOOPS) are synonymous with some of the more sensitive aspects of nuclear power. The Diablo Canyon generating facility in California has been the object of continuing special interest protests over claims that it is not designed to withstand an earthquake. In 1983, the Washington System defaulted on several billion dollars of bonds, threatening thousands of people with the loss of their life savings. Many ratepayers in Mississippi worried that the Grand Gulf I unit (now called "Grand Goof") would increase the cost of electric service in Claiborne County by 30 percent once it went on-line. The *Wall Street Journal* gave front page attention to the struggle of one woman, Mary Sinclair, who was victorious after 15 years of battle against the Consumers Power Company. Construction of its Midland nuclear plant was abandoned despite $4 billion costs. Hardly the stereotype of the radical agitator, Sinclair is a 65-year-old mother of five and is married to a lawyer who has served as Republican county chair (Winslow, 1984). Such examples demonstrate that nuclear generation is one of the many instances where images and issues blend because of "bad press," a lack of public understanding, continuing safety fears, and corporate communication failure.

In their individual ways, many utility companies have sought to influence public opinion. One of several industry trade groups, the U.S. Committee for Energy Awareness, has undertaken a major national information campaign to help the public understand the technology and economic benefits of nuclear generation. One of the recurring complaints about issues advertisements is their inability to gain visibility because of clutter (Coe, 1983). In contrast to many advocacy campaigns which seem designed as soporifics, these are quite inviting and of particular interest because they avoid fear appeals and don't resort to technological bludgeoning. The magazine and video advertisements are unique because they use pastel colors and lively graphics to attract audience attention.

The committee is aware of public attitudes toward the dangers of nuclear generation. One of the advertisements announced that a poll conducted by Cambridge Reports, Inc. in 1984 indicated that 54 percent of adults favor nuclear energy. Of this number, 22 percent "strongly favor" and 32 percent "somewhat favor" nuclear generation. The sponsors of this campaign have tried to create a bandwagon effect by also citing technically qualified individuals; for example, in 1983 it was found that 53 percent of all scientists, 70 percent of energy experts, and 92 percent of nuclear experts believe that nuclear construction should proceed rapidly since the risks are acceptable. A 1985 advertisement by the committee cited Lynn E. Weaver, dean of the School of Engineering at Auburn University, who concluded: "Nuclear-generated electricity has become one of the basic props supporting the entire national economy." This observation, which is both an apparent truism and highly equivocal, is offered as further rationale for low-cost, reliable nuclear and coal fuel sources.

In purusing the advantages of nuclear power generation, the committee has attempted to further develop public support for its program by highlighting targeted audience self-interests. While avoiding anti-Arab propaganda stereotypes, balance of payments deficits are coupled with the apprehension of Middle Eastern energy dependence. One of the most telling comparisons is that one 1000-megawatt plant over three years would require one uranium fuel core versus 30 million barrels of oil. Moreover, cost advantages are such that nuclear power in the decade since 1974 "saved electric ratepayers an estimated $40 billion, and continues to save ratepayers $4-$6 billion each year," according to a 1984 ad. Another ad that year explained how a "blizzard of changing, costly, complex government rules and regulations" has slowed the growth rate of nuclear generation. This approach acknowledges that the construction of nuclear generating facilities is very expensive; thus the first few years' costs are much higher than those in plants using other kinds of fuels. However, over time these costs become more favorable to nuclear power because of dramatic differences in fuel costs. A January 1985 advertisement showing a nuclear plant under construction opened with this headline: "Good morning. Today and every day this year, nuclear electricity will reduce America's trade deficit by over $11 million."

Ads used in newspapers are either black-and-white versions of the magazine copy or very small insertions that contain between 150 and 200 words—rather than ponderous text—to open up white space and compensate for their size. In a few instances, several have been combined into a full-page advertisement, but each is presented separately to convey a theme, such as "Do other countries know something about nuclear energy that we don't know?"

These smaller ads, used by the U.S. Committee for Energy Awareness, are called "Energy Updates." The content is presented in a straightforward journalistic-reportorial style to provide snippets of information with minimum reader effort. Appearing in the context of the *Wall Street Journal*, the series conveys no sense of emergency or fright. Each merely briefs the reader on the "normal" progress of the nuclear generating industry. Advertisement headlines in 1984 suggest the themes discussed. Thus we find: "Without Nuclear Power, U.S. Trade Deficit Would Be Worse"; "U.S. Electric Use Hits New Peak: Coal, Nuclear Meet the Added Demand"; and "Record-Setting Plant Shows Clear Benefits of Nuclear Energy to U.S." Advocacy content such as this, targeted at an influential business readership, does help establish that platform of fact and understanding useful in making informed—if controversial—regulatory decisions.

THE WITHHOLDING TAX BATTLE: GRASSROOTS AT ITS BEST

One of the best orchestrated grassroots campaigns in recent years resulted in the repeal of part of President Reagan's 1982 tax reform measure. The provision would have required banks and other savings institutions to withhold federal income taxes on the first 10 percent of the interest earned by depositors. Then-Treasury Secretary Donald Regan estimated that approximately $20 billion of interest and dividend income was not reported. Sponsors hoped to (1) increase the likelihood of reporting, and (2) get monies to the government sooner than if they were paid only as April 15 approached. However, from the industry standpoint, if the money were sent to the IRS, it would be unavailable for loans and other investments. Moreover, individual savers would lose income on the money sent to the IRS.

In an effort to pressure Congress to overrule itself and prevent the measure from becoming effective in July 1983, a savings industry coalition was formed, spearheaded by the American Bankers Association (ABA). Surveys found that most taxpayers were uninformed about the new law but that nearly 70 percent of heads of household opposed it once the ramifications were explained to them. Some 15,000 "how to" campaign kits costing nearly $100,000 were assembled and distributed to member banks, savings associations, and credit unions. These contained camera-ready ads, monthly statement "stuffers," a poster order form, a speech, reprints, and various other editorial materials. Beginning in January 1983, grassroots appeals were made to customers earning interest or receiving dividends to write their senators and representatives. These efforts were designed to peak in March as the new session of Congress began work. The resulting lobbying avalanche (record-setting tons of mail—22 million pieces) soon had at least half of the House members and a third of the Senate co-sponsoring repeal legislation. Regan, Senate Finance Chairman Robert Dole, and House Ways and Means Chairman Dan Rostenkowski weren't used to such a popular uprising. So skillful was the campaign that bankers were able to maintain their position even though they also incurred the wrath of President Reagan, who labeled them a "selfish special interest."

Not all banks or savings associations participated (some opted for a low profile), but those that did waged a masterpiece fear campaign linked to pocketbook issues (Salamon, 1983). The outraged Dole and Regan threatened to retaliate with even stronger measures, but the constituents back home had spoken. Withholding was stayed. The lobby "had humbled some of the nation's most powerful leaders" (O'Shea, 1983). The bankers gloated in their success because they believed that pro-withholding politicians had attempted to intimidate voters for a measure wanted only by a spendthrift federal government.

An advertisement prepared in 1983 by the ABA cogently represents the types of arguments and appeals used in the campaign. Entitled "Next, the Federal Government is Going to Withhold Taxes from Your Savings and Interest," it was printed under the signature of ABA President William H. Kennedy, Jr., Chairman of the Board at the National Bank of Commerce in Pine Bluff, Arkansas. The ad's central point was this: Savers and investors would lose the use of billions of dollars each year unless the act was repealed. It was unnecessary, the ABA argued, because the taxpayer compliance rate for interest and dividends is between 85 and 90 percent. The law imposed new reporting measures on banks and savings associations that would likely increase compliance to nearly 100 percent by making them virtual collection arms of the government. This intrusion by the IRS, the ABA contended, "represents yet another attempt by the federal government to force its way into your every day life." Set against these arguments was the observation that the new regulation would create "a mountain of unproductive paperwork and an inconvenience to you—so that it will have the use of your money as an interest-free loan."

The IRS-sponsored action was also unfair, reasoned the ABA, because more than three-fourths of individual tax returns result in a refund. Consequently, if a taxpayer earned $200 dollars in interest and had $20 of it sent to the IRS, that amount would not earn additional interest because the government would be using it interest-free. Another appeal used by the ABA was equity; it asked, "Should honest taxpayers be required to give up some of their rightful income from savings and investing because the government is unwilling to use administrative procedures to find the few who cheat?" The advertisement ended with a call to action: "The government wants a piece of your savings. Instead, give Congress a piece of your mind." The nationwide ABA magazine campaign was so broad that it could hardly fail to reach stakeholders; full-page placements in *Time, Newsweek,* and *U.S. News & World Report* in January alone cost $158,000. From the resulting volume of mail, apparently the literate public agreed with the association.

While the industry broadly cooperated in opposing the original bill, no centrally designed plan could have had such impact without a groundswell of local action which increased message reach and frequency. For example, a group of savings and loan associations in the Dallas area placed a large advertisement in the *Wall Street Journal* on March 5, 1983 to ask the rhetorical question, "Do you want the IRS to withhold 10% of the interest you earn with us? . . . Neither do we." Maps showing the names and districts of local congressmen and two Texas senators were complemented by three statements that the reader could cut out and send in to appropriate officials. Other local savings and loan offices circulated sample letters by direct mail.

This straight-shooting simplicity of message and blanket constituency targeting were important building blocks to success. Appeals clearly coupling the public interest with that of the thrift institutions and, most important, pitting the strategic self-interest of stakeholders against the federal tax system provided a powerful campaign centerpiece. Those with the time and inclination to protest—the graying, responsible, middle-aged and elderly saver population segment—proved politically potent.

PERSONAL OR PUBLIC CHOICE: "BROUGHT TO YOU IN THE INTEREST OF COMMON COURTESY BY R. J. REYNOLDS TOBACCO COMPANY"

The tobacco industry is under a great deal of pressure, with major companies having reason to fear that special interest groups will continue to fight for increased restrictions on smoking. Such restraints would undoubtedly lower per capita sales of cigarettes. The following case problem exemplifies one of the starkest realities of issues management. For although many corporations are able to counteract or prevent regulation by changing their policies and operations (Post, 1978), the tobacco industry has few change options left. Because of the ban on electronic advertising, cigarette makers have tried to maintain markets by redirecting their advertising efforts to more clearly defined reader segments. Rarely is smoking characterized as "fun"; more typically, messages insinuate that smoking is part of certain adult lifestyles. Manufacturers realize that if appeals seem to encourage smoking, especially by youngsters, they will bring down public interest wrath. In fact, some product advertising capitalizes on fear motivations for those seeking to lower tar and nicotine intake.

The marketing communication strategy used by the industry includes a sophisticated public affairs lobbying effort, heavy use of print/outdoor product reminder ads, combined with an adult-oriented information program spearheaded by the Tobacco Institute. As the backbone of its legislative campaign, the industry has continued to stress tobacco's regional economic importance, get farmers involved in the battle to forestall new restrictions and taxes, and maintain a liaison with powerful congressional figures such as Senator Jesse Helms.

One goal of the Tobacco Institute has been to reopen the debate on medical findings linking smoking with a variety of health ailments, in hopes of raising doubts about earlier research. In one advertisement the institute circulated in October 1983, several "answers" were provided to the "most asked questions about cigarettes." Typical of the content was the conclusion: "A nonsmoker might have to spend 100 hours straight in a smoky bar to inhale the equivalent of a single filter cigarette."

While the institute has spearheaded advocacy communication for the industry, R. J. Reynolds Tobacco Company has undertaken its own print advertising campaign to (1) bolster its corporate image, (2) help differentiate R. J. Reynolds from its competitors while subliminally working to position the firm for diversification, and (3) display social responsibility by demonstrating concern over the smoking controversy. Reynolds offers what it believes to be factual and unbiased information to "separate fact from friction" in a pro-active attempt to open communication between smokers and nonsmokers. Since the ads complement overall industry efforts, however, a strong case can be made that the primary motivation behind them is to forestall or prevent regulation—clearly the territory of issues management.

Public interest groups have targeted an outright ban on all tobacco advertising as one major way to lessen young people's desire to smoke. Cigarette advertisements constitute nearly $900 million in revenue for magazines, newspapers, and billboards. The allegation is that advertising lures impressionable youngsters via sexually appealing and attractive advertising role models such as the Marlboro Man or the Virginia Slims Woman. Even though such behavioral linkage has never been decisively proven, marketing restrictions in other countries point to the political success of the argument.

Reynolds dealt head-on with this issue in 1984 by forthrightly acknowledging the apprehension of parents who object to the plethora of cigarette advertisements being placed where they can be seen by children. Reynolds announced: "We don't want young people to smoke. And we're running ads aimed specifically at young people advising them that we think smoking is strictly for adults." Moreover, Reynolds reports that cigarette advertising is not designed to get people to start smoking but to switch from one brand to another. "That's why we don't [product] advertise to young people." The Reynolds message to teenage readers was, "If you take up smoking just to prove you're an adult, you're really proving just the opposite." The advertisement concludes: "After all, you may not be old enough to smoke. But you're old enough to think."

Another paid message in the 1984 series disputed whether environmental tobacco smoke (ETS) is harmful to nonsmoking persons who happen to be in the vicinity of smokers. One key point made was: "There is little evidence—and certainly nothing which proves scientifically—that cigarette smoke causes disease in non-smokers." Testimony cited was from a 1983 ETS conference on lung cancer: " 'An overall evalution based upon available scientific data leads to the conclusion that an increased risk for non-smokers from ETS exposure has not been established.' " The ad quoted chief statistician of the American Cancer Society, Lawrence Garfinkel, who states: "Passive smoking may be a political matter, but it is not a main issue in terms of health policy."

With statements such as these, R. J. Reynolds has sought to weaken the commitment against ETS. Restaurants, retail stores, government offices, and airlines, among others, have realized the popularity (to say nothing of lower maintenance) associated with no-smoking restrictions. Reynolds argues that the issue really must be settled by individuals, not by "confrontation," "segregation," or "legislation." Smoking "annoyance is neither a governmental problem nor a medical problem. It's a people problem." The solution is talk, Reynolds advises. "Smokers can help by being more considerate and responsible. Non-smokers can help by being more tolerant. And both groups can help by showing more respect for each other's rights and feelings."

Reynolds's attempt to build increased public understanding by offering information that smokers can use to defend themselves against personal attack is innovative. The proposal for more civility in discourse certainly will not convince either the surgeon general or hardcore antismoking agitators to stop in their tracks. But it might blunt support for such groups if enough people are convinced that regulation is not the best way to solve this problem.

ATTACKING ANOTHER "SIN" INDUSTRY: ALCOHOL

Building on the growing concern about alcohol abuse, many public interest groups are trying to politicize drinking. Some colleges fear that student performance on tests and coursework is harmed by the high profile of beer distributors on campus. The legal drinking age has been raised in most states. Bartenders, restaurant owners, and hosts of private parties are being held responsible for the sobriety of guests, and groups such as Mothers Against Drunk Driving (MADD) continue to seek stiffer offender penalties.

Critics of alcohol advertising are attempting to imprint the same product stigma that was effective against tobacco. Out front is the Washington-based Center for Science in the Public Interest, which includes the National Council on Alcoholism, the United Methodist Church, and the 5.5-million-member National Parent-Teacher Association. Much like the early anticigarette campaign, these groups are focusing their protest on television messages that play up themes of fun and irresponsibility. And again like the tobacco interests, industry spokespersons have argued that no correlation exists between beverage advertising and product abuse; after all, alcoholism was a problem long before TV commercials were invented. Under pressure, however, the networks have tightened their standards for alcohol ad copy. NBC recently rejected a youthful wine commercial featuring break dancing and a Michael Jackson clone. Hearings considered the impact that a federal ban would have on newspaper and magazine revenues, but the FTC ruled out imposing industrywide deceptive trade regulations. So far the Supreme Court refused to clarify the issue, despite upholding interstate commerce by striking down two state laws prohibiting distant-signal alcoholic beverage TV/cable ads (Friedman, 1985).

One advertising and marketing response by the industry has been to deemphasize the "virtues" of excessive consumption. Anheuser-Busch spent over $6 million in 1984 on educational programs to combat alcohol abuse. The brewery employed baseball's Steve Garvey in 1985 to caution against product overuse in ten-second spots costing $2.5 million and seen by an estimated 90 million people. The industry also sponsors Advertising Council print and broadcast public service announcements pointing out that "friends don't let friends drive drunk." Supplemental ad copy demonstrates how motor skills deteriorate under the influence of alcohol.

Besides advertising, industry communicators offer booklets, films, speakers, and other means to enlist educator and parent support for the responsible use of alcohol. For example, the Licensed Beverage Information Council, in conjunction with the U.S. Department of the Treasury, alerted pregnant women to the effects of alcohol on unborn babies. Such campaigns helped increase awareness through information, and they have the additional persuasive potential of "proving" that the industry does indeed care about its products and the people who use them (Gavaghan, 1983).

Not all companies or industries can adapt easily to a changing social climate. Issues management proponents now have to direct their efforts to a far wider spectrum of thought leaders and nongovernmental constituencies, including outreach to adversarial groups, than they have in the past. For when regulation becomes too restrictive, businesses may be forced to close down or go underground as they did during Prohibition. Many industry representatives, at least, believe that advocacy communication helps maintain a regulatory environment where their firms can survive.

WHO CARES?

Clearly, we are talking about serious subjects in reviewing examples drawn from the last two decades, when these and other issues programs were conducted. Although a form of business propaganda, not all such communication can be dismissed merely as self-serving. Some campaigns have been very successful, while others are hard to evaluate. Many issues advertisements challenge and encourage thought rather than lull audiences into complacent acceptance of raw capitalism. Critics have argued that budgets could be better spent on other, more useful activities, but in a society where corporate performance and contemporary social standards must be in balance, communication to achieve understanding is vital. In a constitutional republic, can we be considered responsible if we refuse to "let the dialogue continue"?

4

THE REGULATORY ENVIRONMENT OF ISSUES COMMUNICATION

Despite what we believe are readily apparent advantages of issues communication, many have countered by attempting to further constrain corporate behavior, including business "speech." They seek to limit the amount of money spent on campaigns, require that all advertising and public relations claims be factual, and eventually bar issue advertisers from access to the electronic media. Anti-business advocates worry that increased corporate ad and public relations budget allocations can buy disproportionately large amounts of media print space and electronic time so as to dominate debate and distort truth.

This apprehension is to some extent justified. Most observers acknowledge that the public should have the opportunity to obtain accurate, balanced views as to the faults and strengths of corporate behavior, operating requirements, and social responsibility. Yet regulation is often problematic to implement under the best circumstances, while in matters of communication it is fraught with ambiguity, caprice, and inconsistency. Establishing public policy guidelines is complicated by the complex nature of communication and our country's commitment to keep speech as free as possible. Corporate issues managers are justifiably uncertain regarding which activities violate both federal standards and those of the 18 states that have attempted to limit corporate issue advertising. Moreover, American Civil Liberties Union Executive Director Ira Glasser (1983: 2) argues that government supporters of restrictions "see the free flow of information as a threat, and seek increasingly to insulate governmental decisions from public debate."

Those who manage corporate public affairs must keep abreast of current opportunities for as well as limitations on advocacy communication. To this end, we discuss (1) the status of relevant Federal Trade Commission (FTC), Federal Communications Commission (FCC), and Internal Revenue Service (IRS) regulations; (2) applicable Supreme Court guidelines; and (3) standards by which communication managers can calculate the effect these restraints have on their communication efforts.

While congressional appropriation guidelines now prohibit the FTC from imposing sweeping, industrywide trade regulations over commercial advertising on the grounds of unfairness, the commission is still empowered to regulate the substance of commercial communication and retains broad power to define and regulate unfair or deceptive advertising claims (Cohen, 1982; Carson et al., 1985; Section 5, FTC Act, as amended). Through the fairness doctrine, the FCC influences advertiser access to broadcast channels by overseeing media managers' performance so as to ensure ostensibly balanced presentation on controversial issues of public interest. In addition, the IRS decides which advertising campaign costs may be deducted as ordinary and necessary business expenses.

FEDERAL TRADE COMMISSION

FTC administrative problems, the nature of issues advertisements, and the increasingly blurred distinctions between political and commercial speech combine to create an ambiance of policy uncertainty. First, the FTC is undergoing review by Congress which will likely affect its regulatory agenda. Historically, the FTC has worked closely with the industries it regulates (Preston, 1975: Ch. 9; Rotfeld, 1983: 476). A more confrontational approach in the 1970s led to conflicts with advertisers and Congress, resulting in a partially successful attempt to redirect commission efforts through statutory reform in the Magnuson-Moss Warranties-Federal Trade Commission Improvement Act of 1975 and the FTC Improvements Act of 1980.

Highlighting the dilemma that communication managers face, former FTC attorney H. Robert Ronick (1983: 38) observes that even a "cursory reading of the FTC's implementing statute will show that the agency has enormous latitude and can literally use its imagination in deciding what is and is not unfair, deceptive, or unlawful." Currently, the FTC's substantiation program requires factual support for advertised claims regarding a product's safety, performance, efficacy, quality, and comparative price. Under Chairman James Miller, the FTC loosened its substantiation requirements and allowed market forces to control "unfairness" in an effort to balance both industry and consumer demands while keeping down the costs of products. This move has been much criticized by those who believe that stricter regulation must be applied to protect consumers, and that the agency should involve itself in issues advertising and continue to be confrontational in dealing with business (Saddler, 1983a, b).

Second, the nature of issue advertising is such that traditional FTC guidelines on factual verifiability are extremely difficult to apply and may be inappropriate. Issue advertisements typically involve "arguable interpretations" of fact, value, and policy. As Sethi (1977: 258) writes, "It is well nigh impossible to develop reasonably objective measures of proof of accuracy for most advocacy advertising without making them so onerous as to be unimplementable, or ad hoc and therefore capricious." In fact, it is easier to determine whether claims are unsubstantiated than to determine whether they are true, while criteria to operationalize verifiability often lag behind the need to apply them (*Regulation*, 1983).

In matters of public controversy, journalists need not submit their stories for prior governmental scrutiny to determine whether or not they are factual. Under some circumstances, libel and slander provisions are available for those seeking redress against inaccurate reporting. But under many conditions, even though a report is inaccurate, the company or industry wronged may be unable to effectively communicate its side of the case.

Applying standards of substantiation and verifiability to image advertising is problematic because of its subjectivity. In an image ad, for instance, a company may assert that it is a good neighbor by pointing to the number of pollution devices installed or various acts of community support. As values change, so do definitions of the public interest. Thus delineations between facts and values fluctuate. Such problems create uncertainty for regulators as well as business communicators.

In the debate over issue campaigns, once one gets beyond the accuracy of baseline facts, verifiability is generally irrelevant and probably impossible. Meadow (1981) has objected to companies advertising on the virtues of free enterprise, but the fact that an issue is controversial does not necessarily make it bad or unrelated to the legitimate costs of doing business. Nor have standards of factual verifiability been ignored. The point is that whereas it is easy to determine if a chain saw is rated "best" by *Consumer Reports*, it is hard to determine which oil tax policy option best serves the nation.

Public discussion of corporate behavior may thus be more important for correcting undesirable behavior or challenging image claims than litigation efforts by the FTC. In a climate of skepticism regarding corporate behavior, the burden of proof is on corporations, through arguments *and* actions. Since business cannot rely on accurate or fair reportage in the major media, supporters of issues advertising question why federal policy should not more openly support corporate communication designed to deal with social, economic, and political problems.

Image and issue advertisements elude tests of factual verifiability and demonstrate the overlap between commercial and political speech. Because of such problems, FTC guidelines have rarely been applied to either type of advertising. Not until December 1974 did the commission staff, in an FTC memorandum, take bold steps to regulate image advertisements and to differentiate between them and issue advertising. The staff began by defining corporate image advertising as that "which describes the corporation itself, its activities, or its policies, but does not explicitly describe any products or services sold by the corporation." Such advertisements would cover a range of topics, including such diverse areas as research and development and corporate "activities and programs reflecting a sense of social responsibility towards, for example, the community or the environment" (U.S. Congress, 1978b: 1450-1451).

Under the powers given it by Section 5 of the Federal Trade Commission Act, the staff urged the commission to proceed against unfair or deceptive image advertising in situations where the dominant appeal and likely effect of the advertisement was commercial. Because "claims in certain corporate issue advertisements may arguably be capable of eliciting both commercial responses and political ones" relating "to the formation of public opinion about or action on a public issue," the memorandum suggested the following six factors to determine if an advertisement fell within regulated commercial limits. These included whether:

(1) the ad claims relate to the sponsoring corporation's activities rather than assert facts, opinions, or views about general subjects or conditions;
(2) corporate logos, tag lines, etc. are present;
(3) a brand name is identifiable in the ad;
(4) the dominant purpose for disseminating the ad is economic;

(5) persons viewing the ad are likely to perceive it as an expression of facts or opinions about a public issue; and
(6) an advertisement refers to or depicts a product or service in which the sponsor has a financial interest (U.S. Congress, 1978b: 1469-1471).

Although these guidelines were not without merit, the commission stated in a news release its unwillingness to adopt the recommendations but left open the option for "such enforcement actions in the future as it deems appropriate and consistent with its understanding of its constitutional and statutory obligations" (U.S. Congress, 1978b: 1512-1513).

The FTC has subsequently treated most image and issue advertising as "protected" and thus avoided the entanglements of determining substantiation and verifiability. However, aggressive consumer-oriented leadership at the commission could reverse this trend because of the continuing lack of precise guidelines. Although the deductibility of advertisement costs will be discussed below, it is worth noting that those who would further constrain corporate speech argue that political speech costs should not be deductible as operating expenses because they do not promote products or services. Alternatively, they should be subject to FTC regulation, if they are deductible. This dichotomy is parsimonious in theory but potentially very murky in practice. Even the commission's 1974 policy proposal acknowledged a number of prior studies in which it was reported that image advertising was an effective method for bringing long-range economic benefits to the sponsoring company (U.S. Congress, 1978b: 1453-1458).

Recent Supreme Court decisions have blurred the distinctions between political and commercial communication. In *New York Times Co.* v. *Sullivan* (1964), the Court ruled that advertising which is substantial and valuable to public opinion may be protected even if it is commercial. By the mid-1970s, First Amendment protections were extended to commercial speech in *Bigelow* v. *Virginia* (1975). Commercial speech, said the Court, is protected when it discusses issues of value to society—in this case the availability of abortions. In *Bolger et al.* v. *Young Drug Products Corp.* (1981), the issue was whether a company could advertise a birth control product (commercial speech) and discuss venereal disease and family planning (political speech). The Court ruled that discussion of family planning and venereal disease made the mailing of sufficient public value to extend First Amendment protection to commercial speech. The key to such decisions is ad content and whether governmental interests are served by regulation.

Conversely, since the right of commercial speech under the First Amendment is not absolute, the courts have refused blanket protection for advocacy advertisements merely because a company considers them nondeductible political speech. Rather, the Supreme Court has followed the premise that truth and the value of information to the public are the essential criteria for the regulation and control of communication. A four-part analysis set forth in *Central Hudson Gas & Electric Corp.* v. *Public Service Commission of New York* (1980) held that (1) advertising concerning lawful activity and that is not misleading is eligible for First Amendment protection, (2) the government must demonstrate a substantial interest to restrict certain forms of advertising content, (3) the resulting regulation must directly advance the government's stated interest, and (4) regulations may not exceed the boundaries necessary to serve that interest.

In striking down a blanket ban forbidding utilities from advertising to stimulate the use of electricity, the Court concluded that "the energy conservation rationale, as important as it is, cannot justify suppressing information about electric devices or services that would cause no net increase in total energy use." However, the Court hinted that a more limited regulation might be constitutional. In *Consolidated Edison of New York* v. *Public Service Commission of New York* (1980), the justices ruled that Con Edison had a First Amendment right to send out bill stuffers advocating nuclear generation without giving equal time to its opponents. (This issue remains unresolved, as revealed by the December 1983 action of the California Public Utilities Commission which ordered Pacific Gas & Electric Company to allow Toward Utility Rate Normalization to use PG&E billing envelopes for the consumer group's fund-raising messages.) Even the casual observer will note that the issue of nuclear generation, although ostensibly political communication, has substantial commercial importance; likewise, the increased use of electricity has political implications.

The ground rules for evaluating the verifiability of advertising and the protection of commercial speech reflect the directions that the Court is likely to take. At the moment, regulatory restrictions take second place in the contest when companies are making an honest effort to accurately inform the public. Such is the case whether the advertising is ostensibly commercial or political.

FEDERAL COMMUNICATIONS COMMISSION

Although Section 326 of the Communications Act of 1934 as amended ostensibly forbids the FCC from censoring broadcast programming, Section 307 directs the commission to grant and renew licenses "based on its assessment of the licensee's ability to serve the public convenience, interest, or necessity." Through the fairness doctrine, now contained in Section 315 (a) of the Communications Act of 1934 as amended, the FCC has given electronic media managers the power to limit corporate access to the public airwaves. The fairness doctrine instructs station licensees "to devote a reasonable amount of broadcast time to the discussion of controversial issues" and "to do so fairly, in order to afford reasonable opportunity for opposing viewpoints." Despite extensive deregulation, this is still current policy (see FCC Public Notice, 1974).

Broadcasters are actually supposed to seek out balanced and contrasting views on controversial issues to air. All too often, however, controversial viewpoints are ignored by station managers concerned about profits and legal entanglements. As Henry Geller, former FCC General Counsel (1964-1970), observed: "In its post-1962 reach for perfect fairness, the Commission has lost sight of the real goal—robust, wide open debate. However well-intentioned, its actions now thwart or tend to discourage such debate" (quoted in Friendly, 1977: 223). Confronted with a lack of access to the major networks, corporations are turning to capital-starved cable companies open to issue advertising.

The chilling effect of the fairness doctrine is demonstrated statistically when reviewing the actions taken by the FCC in responding to filed inquiries and complaints. In the 1970-1982 fiscal years, for example, a total of 98,251 protests were registered with the commission. Yet during this turbulent period, with an average of 7558 complaints per year, only a relative handful of challenges proved successful. Thus the fairness doctrine is a generally ineffective remedy. When litigated, the commission overwhelmingly supports programming and editorial advertising decisions made by broadcast licensees, who at the same time often express their fear of its potential power by censoring their own ideas.

Major television networks often take stands on corporate behavior but then refuse to sell corporations advertising spots to respond, even when they offer (as did Mobil and Kaiser Aluminum & Chemical Corporation) to pay for opponents' time to reply. The major networks denied Kaiser air time for three advertisements on energy, free enterprise, and government red tape. Kaiser claimed that the broadcasters refused to accept its advertisements not because they were untrue, misleading, or inaccurate, but simply because they were controversial. Forced to go to print, samples of the filmed storyboards were reproduced so that interested readers could make up their minds whether or not the messages should have aired. Garbett (1981) reports that according to William H. Griffith, Kaiser's director of corporate advertising, the advertisement created an initial response of 2000 letters. Of these, 96 percent favored Kaiser's position (Garbett, 1981: 205). Such strategies can be helpful, as Clavier and Kalupa (1981, 1983) report. They analyzed the impact of a *60 Minutes* exposé of nuclear management problems at Illinois Power Company, as well as the feisty company rejoinder entitled *60 Minutes/Our Reply*. Subjects who witnessed both videos reported that once they had seen the Illinois Power tape, the CBS minidocumentary, narrated by Harry Reasoner, lost credibility.

The FCC is charged with the positive obligations implied in "the right of the public to be informed." In *Red Lion Broadcasting Co.* v. *FCC* (1969), the Supreme Court narrowed the rights of broadcasters when it affirmed "the right of the public to receive suitable access to social, political, esthetic, moral, and other ideas and experiences." In keeping with this mandate, the objective of the FCC has been to assure that broadcasters air both sides of controversial issues of current public interest. Nevertheless, the FCC has consistently ruled that broadcasters have great editorial latitude when deciding how an issue will be discussed and by whom.

The FCC adheres to the principle that "the sole function of the fairness doctrine is to maintain broadcasting as a medium of free speech not just for a relatively few licensees, but for all of the American people. As such it is not only consistent with the First Amendment, it promotes the underlying concept of the Amendment" (American B/casting Co., 1969). In one seminal statement of its regulatory philosophy, the FCC represented the Supreme Court as requiring the fairness doctrine "to promote robust discussion of controversial issues." Consequently, the FCC received a broad mandate for its activities:

> There is no conceivable legal reason why views should not be expressed, notwithstanding that they be distasteful, incorrect or even absurd. The burden of the licensee is to give opposing views a chance for utterance and to protect persons who might have been attacked by giving them a chance to reply [Brandywine-Main Line Radio, Inc., 1968].

On the surface, then, the FCC seems strongly committed to airing controversial discussions when it claims: "The fairness doctrine requires that each licensee afford a reasonable opportunity for the presentation of contrasting views on controversial issues of public importance." Despite this grand proclamation, the FCC quickly hedges its position and does little to support those who appeal broadcast programmers' decisions not to accept controversial statements. The FCC believes that "so long as a licensee does not deny such 'reasonable opportunity' to any competing view, it may adopt, and even vigorously support, any position it chooses on a controversial issue." Broadcasters use the following loophole to escape more active advertising participation: "The doctrine does not require equality in the opportunity afforded for the presentation of each competing view." The ruling acknowledges that "the licensee has considerable discretion in the manner and timing of achieving fairness, with the Commission's role limited to determining whether his actions have been reasonable" (Harry Lerner, 1969). Probably the most difficult task is deciding what is "reasonable" in each instance.

Special interest advocates periodically contend that they should be allowed air time to respond to product advertising when it is associated with larger political topics (Nelson and Teeter, 1982: 523-524). As we demonstrate in our review below, the FCC has found most of these complaints unpersuasive because the particular product is not the issue, but rather its use. Efforts such as these, however, evidence further the impossibility of drawing neat lines between commercial and political advertising. Continuing uncertainty may lead station managers to be less strict in accepting issue advertising or, and this is most probable, until regulators force broadcasters to be more responsive, they will remain aloof guardians of truth and opinion, saying what they wish while denying others access to the electronic channels they operate—supposedly in the public interest (Rowan, 1984). All parties in this drama have been frustrated by the imprecise definition of what constitutes a controversy of public concern.

The FCC has said that the fairness doctrine normally applies "to ballot propositions, such as referenda, initiative or recall propositions, bond proposals and constitutional amendments" (Fairness Doctrine, 1974). But while such political campaigns are typically considered to be "controversial issues of public importance within the meaning of the fairness doctrine" (Radio Station KKHI, 1980), there is a loophole. The FCC ruled that although changing the Virginia constitution was prima facie evidence of a controversy, a broadcaster could talk about the revision's constitutionality without inviting a response, since the discussion did not touch on the controversy of the issue itself (George R. Walker, 1970). Another complaint was denied, despite the presence of controversy, because it could not be concluded that statements explaining what "yes" and "no" votes meant constituted advocacy on a nuclear power issue. The licensee allegedly misrepresented the issue by over-simplification, but "as to distortion of news, absent extrinsic evidence of deliberate distortion, the FCC cannot properly investigate to determine whether an account or analysis . . . is 'biased' or 'true'" (Terrence Olesen, 1976).

Once stations allow corporations or PACs to purchase advertising on ballot issues, the fairness doctrine prescribes that free air time must be made available to responsible representatives of the opposing view. Clarifying the FCC's stance is a case involving Proposition 11, the 1982 statewide bottle-recycling bill favored by Californians Against Waste (CAW). Because of the heavy bottler/canner advertising blitz to defeat the measure, CAW was able to invoke the doctrine to gain access to public airwaves. Its own ads featured actor Eddie Albert as a spokesman explaining how the proposition, if adopted, would reduce litter. These were run throughout California at no expense to CAW (Waz, 1983).

In estimating the degree of controversy, a broadcaster must look both to the specific issue and to the larger topic of which the issue is a part. In one instance, the FCC ruled that a licensee had unreasonably denied a response to spot announcements opposing a ballot proposition relating to nuclear waste disposal. The station could not defend itself against the charge of unfairness. It could demonstrate only that broad coverage had been given to the issue of nuclear energy, not to the specific ballot issue (Radioactive Waste Policy, 1982).

In other disputes involving the fairness doctrine, advocates for controversial issues have no solid, precise guidelines—whether established by the commission or the courts—to use in determining the likelihood that certain advertisements will be aired. Those who would engage in advocacy advertising risk having to lay out production costs to prepare advertisements that may be denied air time. Consequently, we can imagine that in many instances advocates decide to say nothing rather than waste advertising dollars on messages that will never be aired. In addition, the media have monetary incentives for not willingly granting time for controversial discussion. They must defend themselves, often at substantial cost, against those who believe they have been adversely affected by the controversy.

At best, FCC rulings and a few court cases can be used to assist issue managers in understanding how to design and place their advertorials. The most important point to realize is that the Supreme Court has ruled that the First Amendment rights of advocacy advertisers are not abridged if they are denied access to electronic or print media. For electronic media, this principle was established in a complex of cases (see Columbia Broadcasting System, Inc., 1973). Basing its decision on the broadcast media's special status, the Court majority expressed its desire to avoid making the electronic media common carriers. Because the electronic media constitute a special public resource, said the Court, their regulation is best left to government and the journalistic discretion of those who prepare the programs.

The justices supported the need for the public to be informed fully and fairly, arguing that if those forces with more money to spend on advocacy advertising were also allowed to demand time, the broadcast media could become their tools. The majority opinion concluded:

> To minimize financial hardship and to comply fully with its public responsibilities a broadcaster might well be forced to make regular programming time available to those holding a view different from that expressed in an editorial advertisement; indeed, BEM [Business Executives' Move for Vietnam Peace] has suggested as much in its brief. The result would be a further erosion of the journalistic discretion of broadcasters in the coverage of public issues and a transfer of control over the treatment of public issues from the licensees who are accountable to private individuals who are not.

Siding with corporate and special interest advocates' commitment to inform the public, Justices Brennan and Marshall dissented:

> The fairness doctrine's requirement of full and fair coverage of controversial issues is, beyond doubt, a commendable and, indeed, essential tool for effective regulation of the broadcast industry. But, standing alone, it simply cannot eliminate the need for a further, complementary airing of controversial views through the limited availability of editorial advertising. Indeed, the availability of at least *some* opportunity for editorial advertising is imperative if we are ever to attain the "free and general discussion of public matters [that] seems absolutely essential to prepare the people for an intelligent exercise of their rights as citizens" [citing Grosjean v. American Press Co., 1936].

The decision pitted the fairness of journalistic discretion of licensees as regulated by the FCC against the imbalance which could result from deep pocket spending by advocacy advertisers. The decision blocked mandatory private access to the broadcast media.

A year later, in *Miami Herald Publishing Company* v. *Pat L. Tornillo* (1974), the Supreme Court granted newspapers the privilege of rejecting advocacy advertising. At issue was a Florida statute that required newspapers to print replies. The Court decided:

> Even if a newspaper would face no additional costs to comply with a compulsory access law and would not be forced to forego publication of

> news or opinion by the inclusion of a reply, the Florida statute fails to clear the barriers of the First Amendment because of its intrusion into the function of editors. A newspaper is more than a passive receptacle or conduit for news, comment, and advertising. The choice of material to go into a newspaper, and the decisions made as to limitations on the size of the paper, and content, and treatment of public issues and public officials—whether fair or unfair—constitutes the exercise of editorial control and judgment. It has yet to be demonstrated how governmental regulation of this crucial process can be exercised consistent with First Amendment guarantees of a free press as they have evolved to this time.

In its discussion, the Court acknowledged that newspapers are big business which require substantial capital; not everyone who wants to start a paper to express a personal opinion can do so. Whereas the FCC can require a response to a broadcast, the Court decided that such provision, at least under state statute, was unwise.

Exercising its mandate on electronic broadcasting, the FCC has ruled that an issue does not require response or balanced coverage unless it centers on a controversy. In an attempt to assist broadcasters and other interested parties, the FCC has broadly distinguished between controversial and newsworthy topics. The FCC has stated that even if an issue is newsworthy, it may not be "a controversial issue of public importance" (National Football League Players Association, 1973). Likewise, the FCC has consistently ruled that the licensee's freedom of speech would be infringed if the commission prescribed which persons must be invited to provide the views that balance the coverage (WCMP B/casting Co., 1973). Furthermore, the fairness doctrine does not quantify the amount of coverage and, despite popular misconceptions, does not involve equal time requirements. No attempt has been made to support those who would seek equal time "because the coverage was biased."

In implementing the fairness doctrine, one major problem involves the lack of quantifiable standards. For example, many FCC and court decisions are made on technical grounds where the commissioners and judges held that the plaintiffs had failed to document a harm. As a rule, however, there is a lack of specificity involved in examining news and public affairs journalistic judgments. Both the FCC and the courts, while retaining the weapon of intervention via the fairness doctrine and its corollaries, have been reticent to impose content criteria clarifying fairness expectations or to otherwise impinge on licensee editorial judgments. This move is ironic, because the fairness doctrine, rather than a mechanism for public access, has proved more of a shield for licensee inertia. Thus one of the primary difficulties facing advocates, whether corporate or special interest, is determining when an issue is controversial.

(1) *Issues require licensee attention whenever they are receiving extensive discussion by governmental groups, the public, and the media.*

The scale for measuring degree of controversy has three components. An issue is controversial when the relevant legislative body is discussing it, when it receives substantial media attention, and when it has major implications for public policy and mores. Although no apparent attempts have been made to develop quantifiable standards, the primary test of the degree of controversy is the extensiveness of debate in legislative, public, and media arenas (Friends of the Earth v. FCC, 1971). Once issues become widely discussed in society, and by legislatures and the media, they have reached the level of controversy whereby licensees must act responsibly to air competing views. In this regard, one licensee was found at fault because it did not treat gay activities as controversial (Council on Religion and the Homosexual, Inc., 1978). In contrast, NBC was not at fault for determining that husband-beating is not controversial. This ruling relies on the subjective estimate of the number of people involved in the discussion of an issue and its explosive effect on public policy (Roger Langley, 1978). Most observers would agree that bullfighting in Spain does not constitute a degree of controversy sufficient to warrant licensee attention (Lyn A. Sherwood, 1971). Reflecting on this and other cases, Simmons (1978: 155) contrasts the degrees of controversy involved in theories of curved space and electronic speech compression against the Vietnam war, racial integration, and sex education.

Extensiveness relates to the number of people who are discussing or who are affected by a topic at a given time. To demonstrate this point, the FCC ruled that a station which refused to carry spot announcements paid for by a union during a strike was protected by the fact that the controversy was not substantial. That the station carried advertisements for the company's products was not considered unbalanced coverage, despite the union's efforts to seek a public boycott of the products. The FCC held that the product itself was not controversial (Big Bend B/casting Corp., 1970). By contrast, a licensee was held to be unreasonable in not treating the divestiture of major oil companies as a controversial issue. It was broadly debated in the media and Congress, and was believed to be of deep public concern (Energy Action Committee, Inc., 1976).

The degree of controversy can be quantified partially by calculating the portion of the "news hole" devoted to an issue. This tactic measures the extensiveness of discussion without quantifying the depth of feeling.

Yet this latter characteristic of controversy, the FCC has claimed, is perhaps more important than the extensiveness of coverage.

> The principal test of public importance . . . is a subjective evaluation of the impact that the issue is likely to have on the community at large. The question of whether an issue is "controversial" may be determined more objectively. It is highly relevant to measure the degree of attention paid to an issue by government officials, community leaders, and the media [Fairness Doctrine, 1974].

In another instance the test was expressed in these terms: "The principal test of public importance is not the extent of media or government attention to an issue, but, rather, a subjective evaluation of whether the issue is likely to have a significant impact on the community at large or on societal institutions" (Arkansas Cable Television Association, 1976). Challenging CBS's *60 Minutes* discussion of the training and qualifications of security guards, the complainants pointed out that government officials in eight states had deliberated the issue and were considering legislation. The FCC ruled that the complainants had not shown whether other media were giving extensive coverage to the issue; moreover, they had not documented the intensity of public sentiment on the issue. The FCC required "some specific information on the degree of attention which the issue is in fact receiving from government officials and other community leaders" and "any subjective evaluation of the impact the issue is likely to have and any showing of vigorous debate with substantial elements of the community in opposition to one another" (Security World Publishing Co., 1976).

Entertainment programming is controversial only when it constitutes a discussion rather than a depiction. Thus the FCC decided that how women are presented in entertainment programming does not constitute discussion or advocacy of women's roles (National B/casting Co., Inc., 1975). Even in a distorted presentation of women's roles, mere depiction does not invoke the doctrine (American B/casting Co., 1975). The courts have supported this stand, reasoning that while the portrayal of women in entertainment programming may be biased, sufficient alternative discussions of this issue are aired. Clear parallels exist to business images in finding that news and public affairs programming had "been responsive to the needs and interests of women" (National Organization for Women v. FCC, 1977).

From these rulings we can extract the criteria that are applied when determining the degree of controversy. (1) An issue is controversial when it is being debated by relevant legislative bodies or when it concerns actions taken by them. (2) The public discussion of an issue must be extensive. This means that a substantial part of the news hole must be devoted to the issue. (3) An issue must receive careful attention when it has substantial implications for public mores and public policies. Poll data probing the depth of public sentiment, particularly by comparing the sensitivity to other issues, could provide a measure of the depth and breadth of public concern. The presence of several agitator groups may suffice as an indicator. (4) Ballot issues and political campaigns are controversial. (5) Dramatic or comic depiction does not necessarily constitute a discussion. Bias in the depiction may require licensees to develop public affairs programming to discuss the issue. In such cases, licensees have vast editorial latitude when determining who should participate in the discussion.

(2) *Along with decisions about the extent to which an issue is controversial, the FCC may also consider the controversy surrounding the solution to the problem involved in the issue.*

One relevant ruling grew out of the broadcast of a film that discussed the threat of communism and went so far as to advocate certain measures for stopping the menace. The FCC did not require the station to offer time to organizations desiring to argue that communism is no threat. However, the station "had an obligation under the fairness doctrine to afford reasonable opportunity for the broadcast of responsible contrasting viewpoints on the most effective methods of combating communism and communist infiltration" (Tri-State B/casting Co., Inc., 1962). Certain issues, according to the FCC, are not controversial, such as communism. However, aspects of those issues may be controversial and incur special attention by the licensee.

(3) *Controversy surrounding certain products and services can become sufficiently great that balanced coverage is required.*

Criteria are not well developed regarding the measure of controversy surrounding business operation issues such as industry practice, product reliability and safety, trade practices, or operating procedures. The lines needed to determine whether an issue regarding a product or business procedure is controversial or merely newsworthy are blurred. In a few instances, such as issues surrounding nuclear generation and tobacco use, the FCC has ruled that such discussion often constitutes a controversy. Typically, however, even when legislation is pending and public discussion is transpiring, the FCC is reluctant to burden broadcasters with the responsibility of a balanced treatment. In this case, claiming that an issue is newsworthy but not controversial is a broadcaster's strongest defense. Moreover, the degree of controversy is not affected by whether an issue stand by a broadcaster coincides with that of government officials or agencies such as the U.S. Attorney

General or FBI (Storer Broadcasting Co., 1968). Indeed, as in the tobacco industry, once Congress passed a law banning cigarette advertising in the electronic media, the FCC ruled and the Court agreed that the issue of the harm of smoking had been resolved and was no longer controversial (Larus & Brother Co. v. FCC, 1971).

Franklin (1981: 602) interprets the Court decision as leaving the door open to complainants to show that some aspect of the discussion is controversial, but the matter of health hazard is no longer controversial. Because of difficulties in dealing with extensions of its earlier *Banzhaf* v. *FCC* (1968) ruling, the commission's 1974 *Fairness Doctrine Report* sought to end future product advertising challenges by asserting that since such advertisements only highlight the good points of the commodity for sale, they do not make a significant contribution to public discourse. Subsequent application of the doctrine, said the commission, would be limited to commercials meaningfully involved in the discussion of public issues. As Nelson and Teeter (1982: 590) note, "The Commission simply changed its mind."

The FCC does not see as inherently controversial any programming stance which merely conflicts with the self-interest of an industry or group affected by the stance. The primary test of degree of controversy surrounding products and services seems to arise from the extensiveness of the debate leading to or surrounding their regulation. Because of the degree of controversy surrounding the nuclear generation of electricity, one licensee was required to provide time to opponents of nuclear generation. The controversy that has reached across the nation was compounded by the local controversy regarding a power company's efforts to construct a nuclear generating plant (Mary Sinclair, 1970). The FCC ruled: "Power company spot announcements which stated that nuclear power is the immediate solution to energy problems, and asserted that nuclear power is safe and environmentally clean and insurable, directly addressed the issue of the desirability of the immediate implementation of nuclear power and the interrelated issues of the safety and environmental cleanliness of nuclear power." Thus the licensee had violated the fairness doctrine (Public Media Center, 1976). In another case, however, the FCC concluded that a complainant failed to demonstrate that a licensee had touched on a controversial issue when it labeled laetrile a "phony" cancer cure (Thomas W. Lippitt, 1975).

Licensees are allowed considerable editorial latitude regarding what facts may be included when discussing controversial issues. In a case regarding food additives, the FCC decided that complainant had no basis for criticism of a broadcast merely because it did not include certain facts. "The content of the viewpoints selected for presentation is also within the licensee's reasonable, good faith discretion" (Grocery Manufacturers of America, Inc., 1977). NBC acted responsibly in a program on truck safety, according to the FCC, because "Complainants failed to show that there is a vigorous debate involving substantial elements of the community as to whether there is a serious truck safety problem (all parties agree that there is such a problem)" (Yellow Freight System, Inc., 1979). The FCC ruled that one complainant had failed to demonstrate that the conversion from oil heat to natural gas constituted a controversial issue. While it was admitted that the broadcast advocated such a switch, the FCC was not convinced that the issue was controversial "within the meaning of the fairness doctrine." Although it was proved that government debate had transpired, the complainant could not demonstrate that the issue had received vigorous debate by the public (National Oil Jobbers Council, 1980). A midwestern licensee successfully defended its documentary program on the centralization of control and unfair trade practices in the food and agricultural industries. The FCC ruled that the issue was newsworthy but not controversial, even though it had been the subject of governmental investigations and proposed legislation. In its defense, the licensee demonstrated that it had attempted to contact members of the industry, including the complainant, so they could contribute to the documentary (Iowa Beef Processors, Inc. v. Station WCCO-TV, 1982).

Because many issues involve some degree of controversy, and because not all aspects of an issue are controversial, the FCC requires that a complainant's appeal must specify the controversial part. In one such case, the FCC decided that paid advertisements used by a utility company and arguing for increased generation by nuclear and coal-fired plants did not require a response. The issue was the need to build generating plants to meet public electricity requirements, and not the safety or environmental impact of the kind of plant (Environmental Defense Fund v. KERO-TV, 1982).

No clear-cut standards exist for determining when company practice or product safety is controversial or merely newsworthy. As long as governmental debate over regulation, extensive media coverage, and widespread public discussion transpires, an issue of controversy may exist. However, from the various rulings in this matter, the FCC is unwilling to foster much balanced media coverage merely because a corporate interest is at stake. Rather, the crux of the issue seems to be the impact a product or service has on the public interest.

(4) *A controversy which is given extensive news coverage, as was the conflict in Vietnam, may not require licensees to provide balanced coverage beyond typical news programming. Even though the situation*

or issue is sufficiently controversial, news coverage alone may satisfy the public need for contrasting viewpoints.

Despite the extensive controversy surrounding the Vietnam protests of the 1960s and 1970s, the FCC did not require licensees to carry antiwar, antidraft, and antienlistment statements to counterbalance the military recruitment announcements (Alan F. Neckritz, 1970). In a related ruling, the FCC deemed news coverage of the antidraft movement sufficiently balanced so that licensees were not being arbitrary when they refused to carry antidraft statements (Albert A. Kramer, 1970). Similarly, stations were not required to carry advertisements against the draft to counter those they carried for military recruitment (Donald A. Jelinek, 1970). In all of these rulings, the stations were protected by the balance that could be demonstrated in news coverage, even though the advertisements themselves were not part of the coverage. A licensee defended itself against challenge by antiwar advocates by claiming that enlistment advertisements were only one of several factors influencing a potential recruit's decision (Citizens Communications Center, 1971).

If one of the tests of fair coverage is the public's ability to obtain information, stations can also defend themselves by arguing that their routine news coverage contains enough information so that public affairs programming is not required. Beyond the sheer informational needs of the public, the Appellate Court agreed with one broadcaster that the moral issues surrounding the Vietnam conflict had received sufficient attention in regular news coverage (Green v. FCC, 1971).

(5) *In addition to determining whether a controversy exists, the FCC is willing to adjudicate whether or not program coverage provides balanced treatment.*

This principle was established in a ruling forced by Accuracy in Media which objected to NBC's broadcast criticizing private pension plans. The FCC agreed with the complainant that the program content raised a controversy of public interest. NBC countered by demonstrating how it made a few comments at the end of the program acknowledging that private pension plans had some redeeming features. The FCC ruled: "A few statements in the program itself could be taken to present a contrasting view, but they alone could not be said to have afforded the reasonable opportunity contemplated by the fairness doctrine when compared to the views presented during the remainder of the program" (Accuracy in Media, 1973). Since balance of discussion is the crucial test of fairness, paid advertisements may cover both sides of an issue so fairly that no response is warranted. The fact that the advertisements are sponsored by one of the advocates is not prima facie evidence of bias (Georgia Power Project v. FCC, 1977).

Complainants must demonstrate that licensees have failed to provide balanced treatment of controversial issues. The fact that a licensee has taken a stand contrary to that of the complainant or has not included an issue believed relevant by the complainant does not constitute a violation by the licensee. Of all of the aspects of the fairness doctrine, proving failure to offer balanced treatment may be the most subjective and most difficult.

(6) *In the contest of degree of controversy, certain procedural and evidentiary issues are relevant.*

In addition to rudimentary substantive guidelines for arguing degree of controversy, the FCC has offered procedural guidelines. Acknowledgment by the FCC that a controversy exists does not guarantee access to those who want to participate in the public debate. Tests of significance often require that those who seek balanced coverage must demonstrate that the existing coverage is insufficient to present *their side* of the issue (Wilderness Society, 1971). In a controversy over the election of competing union officials, the complainants were charged with the responsibility of proving that the controversy extended to persons in the community beyond the union membership. Their case was not a strong one, even though the station had aired paid commercials for one of the competing officials (National Association of Government Employees, 1973). When no attention has been given to an issue, the complainant bears the full burden to prove that a controversy exists which has not received licensee attention (Public Communications, Inc., 1974). Complainants must prove that a significant issue exists by supplying a detailed demonstration of the licensee's faulty judgment. The licensee must defend itself only in light of the case presented, not on the basis of its overall programming judgment (Richard Kates, 1972).

Increasingly, the FCC has judged the specificity or narrowness of an issue as a part of the complainant's case. In making such a ruling, the FCC applies the following criteria: "A fairness complaint must include the specific issue of a controversial nature of public importance, and the burden is upon the complainant to specify the particular issue involved and substantiate its controversiality and public importance" (Saul David, 1976). The requirement that a precise issue of controversy be part of the complainant's allegation and burden of proof is set forth to prevent the "chilling effect" of sweeping regulatory interference in programming (American Security Council, 1977). The FCC has ruled:

"Public education is not a sufficient description of a controversial issue of public importance for purposes of the doctrine." (John Roscoe, 1978). When making a decision regarding a licensee's accurate ascertainment of public sentiment, the FCC charges the complainant with proving a lack of attention to "burning issues of local importance demanding program treatment" such that both sides have not been discussed fairly (Scripps-Howard B/casting Co., 1978).

When defining an issue of controversy, complainants must be quite precise; the FCC has concluded, for instance, that national security is too broad an issue to determine whether it is controversial. Issues cannot be aggregated under an umbrella topic; therefore, each individual issue must be evaluated on its own merits. The FCC takes this position because it believes "a contrary result would unduly burden broadcasters without a countervailing benefit to the public's right to be informed" (American Security Council, 1979).

> The Commission recognizes the heavy burden placed upon fairness doctrine complainants. Nevertheless, it believes the public interest is best served by avoiding governmental involvement in programming judgments whenever possible; by placing high procedural burdens on complainants, station and network inquiries initiated by the Commission are made only when the agency receives thorough, well-documented complaints [Conservative Caucus, Inc. v. CBS, 1983].

Out of this discussion of FCC rulings some vague guidelines emerge which can be used when filing a complaint against a licensee. The burden of carrying the case rests solely with complainant, who must define precisely the issue which is alleged to be controversial. The complainant is required to demonstrate that a significant amount of debate has transpired in the relevant legislative bodies and other media. The case must be based on a test of the depth of public sentiment reflected in the controversy. Finally, a complainant cannot win a case if it does not show that the licensee's coverage fails to address the controversy or that it is unbalanced. Even when the complainant is sustained, the licensee has substantial editorial discretion when deciding how the issue is to be treated and by whom. All of this suggests that the fairness doctrine has largely failed if the goal is one of expanding coverage of divergent topics chosen by combatants, not licensees. The impact, rather, has been as a coercive government weapon for limiting truly controversial views and encouraging broadcasters to engage in self-censorship. Moreover, as a counter to bias, the doctrine has shown itself to be a notably inefficient nostrum.

These facts have not been lost on the libertarian policy analysts at the FCC, and the commission now seems willing to get out of regulating programming content. Responding to requests by the National Association of Broadcasters and other media trade organizations, in 1982 and again in 1985, the FCC went to Capitol Hill to urge repeal of the fairness doctrine and political broadcasting provisions. Congress so far has failed to agree on a "Freedom of Expression Act" or approve full electronic First Amendment protections, but both the commission and the Supreme Court are independently reconsidering the regulatory premises underlying continued controls.

In May 1984, for example, the FCC requested comments on eliminating the fairness doctrine as a way of furthering electronic media First Amendment guarantees (Freedom of Expression Foundation, 1984; National Association of Broadcasters, 1984). President Reagan voiced his support for changes in the current dual system when he told the Federal Communications Bar Association that he favored constitutional protections for television and radio equal to those of print. Later, in *FCC* v. *League of Women Voters of California* (1984), the justices indicated that they would "be forced to reconsider the constitutional basis" of the fairness doctrine as decided earlier in Red Lion (1969) if it could be shown that the "doctrine has the effect of reducing rather than enhancing speech."

The FCC in 1984-85 also eliminated a number of "underbrush" regulations and other requirements which could lead to significant broadcast television deregulation along the lines of radio. The commission, which called the rulemaking proceedings "a further step toward creating an unregulated, competitive marketplace environment for the development of telecommunications," earlier had requested comments on several areas of television regulation, including programming policy and guidelines, ascertainment, and commercialization. In determining programming policy, licensees continue to have a general obligation to address issues of local community concern, but the determination of what these issues are and how they are to be covered is left to the broadcaster. No guidelines govern specified amounts or types of programming, although in the event of petitions to deny or comparative proceedings, a licensee's programming could be reviewed. These FCC actions free television stations from the obligation to allocate at least 10 percent of their time to non-entertainment programming (of which half had to be news or public affairs).

In terms of community and audience needs, broadcasters are allowed to use market conditions in determining the appropriate method for ascertainment. More directly relevant to our discussion here, the FCC lifted guidelines that formerly limited the number of commercials that TV stations could air each hour, permitting more flexibility and experimentation by licensees. Preliminary reactions to the rulemaking proceedings split along predictable lines, with criticism coming from "public interest" advocates and praise from the media industry. That debate—the government role as information arbiter of new technology options versus continuing domination of public access by the networks—is unresolved. Until these concerns move to resolution, the fairness (or as its critics would say, "unfairness") doctrine, imprecise and treacherous as it is, is still the law of the land.

INTERNAL REVENUE SERVICE

The third agency, the IRS, indirectly regulates corporate communication through its application of Federal Tax Code powers. How Tax Code provisions regarding business deductions are interpreted affects companies' participation in the public discussion of issues, since corporate communicators are reluctant to allocate nondeductible advertising dollars. For instance, Shell Oil Company decided not to engage in the windfall profits tax debate because advertisement costs on the pending piece of legislation were nondeductible. Participating in this campaign would have meant that "half of Shell's advertising budget would go for taxes" (Iverson, 1982: 18). Although willing to spend such funds, Mobil takes a conservative stance regarding the tax deductibility of its campaign expenses. Mobil Tax Legislative Counsel Thomas J. DuBos (1982) observes: "If in doubt we would decline to deduct the expenses. This position was conscientiously taken to reduce the public criticism which large companies, particularly Mobil, receive from time to time from the media and even elected officials." The ambiguity of the tax regulations and the unwillingness of many companies to challenge the IRS combine to produce great confusion and inequity in compliance with the code (U.S. Congress, 1978a: 63-150).

A substantial advantage of preventive issues management is the ability to deduct the costs of monitoring issues and communicating about them before they progress to the stage where they become pending legislation. Apparently all costs involved in monitoring issues and discussing their implications are deductible. Thus if an advertising campaign is undertaken to prove that a company is acting responsibly and should not be regulated, the costs are deductible. In any case, preventive maintenance has a good chance of being less costly than is the case once legislation is introduced.

One public policy concern is whether or not a means for attempting to achieve fairness in the competition for public opinion is best left with the IRS. Is the public interest served by companies' being unable to deduct dollars spent on issues advertising? It can be argued that if corporations are unwisely constrained, the public loses a valuable—and often unique—source of information.

Reflecting the ideological content in this position, Meadow (1981: 73) argues that nonproduct advertisements are "of questionable deductibility. Although they may not relate to a specific bill or pending legislation, it is difficult to conceive of them as other than political. Messages which purport to show the benefits of a capitalist system clearly are messages of system political support, and to the non-capitalist are debatable messages, more appropriate for legislative, electoral, or other reform." His position is that any issue surrounding corporate performance is political and therefore no longer simply a matter of image. It has become an issue.

As in regulation exercised by other federal agencies, the major public policy issue is undue influence. Efforts have been made to determine whether corporations do indeed have an undue influence. At times they spend a great deal of money, but whether they reap disproportionately large rewards remains unproven. In the 1978 hearings (U. S. Congress, 1978b: 77-78), Harvey J. Shulman, executive director of the Media Access Project, pointed out how much more money had been spent by pro-nuclear forces than by anti-nuclear generation advocates.

In retrospect, the case may be made that corporate spending does not invariably translate into undue influence. Certainly, despite large amounts of money spent, nuclear generation has not proliferated; moreover, the intensity of its regulation has increased. Gun control offers another example of an area in which undue influence may not be true. Bordua (1983; see also Schuman and Presser, 1977-1978) contends that gun control measures have been unsuccessful because public sentiment opposes them. He supports his case with a careful examination that reveals how survey data are often distorted by anti-gun advocates. In *First National Bank of Boston* v. *Bellotti* (1978: 789), Justice Powell argued that those supporting the right to regulate corporate communication had to prove that undue influence had occurred; such influence, he argued, could not be assumed merely because one side outspent the other.

The rationale behind legislative constraint is the belief that corporations have deep pockets and through grassroots lobbying can unduly influence public campaigns on referendums and/or pending legislation. In contrast, legislators believe that no such influence can prevail in direct lobbying because they have experience in dealing with such efforts (Krauskopf, 1979: 322-326). Passage of the current Tax Code provisions changed the decision in *Commarano* v. *United States* (1957), which had established the principle of tax equity by prohibiting all deductions in an attempt to place an individual seeking to influence public opinion on an equal footing with a corporation. Subsequent legislative revisions, while attempting to maintain the principle of equity, have removed that restriction, except for grassroots lobbying.

Many business critics contend that the IRS should tax the cost of advocacy campaigns to achieve tax equity. If members of the public cannot deduct expenses for advocacy advertising, then, the argument goes, companies should not enjoy this tax advantage either. In passing the current Tax Code, Congress specifically rejected some parts of the tax equity issue. For instance, direct lobbying expenses are tax deductible. Moreover, corporations enjoy other tax advantages that the general public does not. An example is that company-owned automobiles are deductible, whereas private family automobile costs are not. The former deduction is allowed because the money is spent in pursuit of profit. Of course, those who champion changing the Tax Code to allow the deduction of advocacy advertising costs can also use the argument that the money is spent in pursuit of profit, because it is designed to prevent unnecessary and costly regulation (Ehrbar, 1978).

From a public policy viewpoint, one may wonder who is being protected by the use of IRS regulations to restrict corporate communication. As noted in Chapter 1, Ewing (1982) reports data strongly suggesting that advocacy advertising is a positive force in the public discussion of vital issues. The corporate effort in this regard is important to both building the sponsor's reputation and developing public consensus.

Another public policy issue concerns the potential damage to the nation if corporations were discouraged from responsible communication. If loosely interpreted by the IRS, the Tax Code could be used to stifle such socially responsible advertising programs as General Motor's campaign on drunk driving, the National Paint and Coatings Association's campaign on urban blight, or Seagram's discussion of the alcohol content in various types of drinks.

Part of the problem in complying with the IRS Code occurs because "Section 162 (e) (2) (B) has been the subject of little litigation other than a few revenue rulings, and the scope of the section remains unclear" (Cleveland, 1981: 602). Controversy springs from the inherent conflict within IRS regulations based on the code between paragraphs (b) and (c) which prohibit grassroots lobbying and (a), which allows the deduction of expenses to present "views on economic, financial, social, or other subjects of a general nature." Grassroots lobbying is construed, in several tax rulings, to require the presence of legislation (74-407; 78-111; 78-113; 78-114; 1978-1 CB 41, 42, 43, 44; CCH IRS Letter Rulings Reports, Technical Advice Memorandums 7946009, 7951012, 8014002, and 8030102). The practice of issuing private memorandums and rulings leads to greater ambiguity, since the IRS refuses to recognize them as precedent-setting. Code Section (e) (2) (b) specifically prohibits the deduction of any amount paid or incurred "in connection with any attempt to influence the general public, or segments therefore, with respect to legislative matters, elections or referendums." This language is translated into IRS Regulation 162-20 (b) as nondeductible if "for the promotion or defeat of legislation, for political campaign purposes . . . or for carrying on propaganda (including advertising) related to any of the foregoing purposes." The regulations further provide that "no deduction shall be allowed for any expenses incurred in connection with 'grassroots' campaigns or any other attempts to urge or encourage the public to contact members of a legislative body for the purpose of proposing, supporting or opposing legislation."

Legislative matters are not defined, but "legislation or proposed legislation" is described as bills and resolutions which are the business of Congress, state, or local legislatures. Krebs (1978: 520) points out: "Oral or written proposals for legislative action submitted to a member or committee of a state or local legislature or Congress are also included within the definition" [see also Reg. Sec. 1.162-20 (c) (4) and 1.162-20 (c) (2) (ii) (a)]. In Consumers Power Company (1969, reversed on other grounds 1970), the Court of Appeals ruled that advertising costs were not deductible if the company invited the public to contact legislators, even if no legislation was pending. However, the court acknowledged that several ads possessed "borderline cases for deductibility," and if regulation 1.162-20 (b) were too broadly construed it would improperly be "capable of infinitely encompassing proportions."

The definitional dilemma because of the overlap between Sections (a) and (b) of the regulations was further highlighted by Shulman in testimony during 1978 House of Representatives Hearings on grassroots lobbying. Commenting on the deductibility of a series of ads, he focused on an ad by Crum & Foster explaining the follies and consumer costs of unwise settlements against insurance companies. Shulman concluded that an IRS determination that the ad "was grassroots lobbying could reasonably be supported, although if the corporation claimed it was not, I think that might be supported also" (U.S. Congress, 1978a: 25).

One cause of this gray area confusion is the lack of clarity as to whether advertisements that deal generally with "legislative matters," as contrasted to specific "legislation or proposed legislation," are tax deductible. Some writers assert that all ads dealing with "legislative matters" are nondeductible, but the courts have not upheld this interpretation. Applied this broadly, Section (b) would disallow issue discussion which is permitted under Section (a) (presumably not the intent of the regulation). Bostick (1981: 333) notes that such intent was central to Senate debate of Code Section 162 (e) (2) at its adoption in 1962 (citing U.S. Congress, 1962: 17,262-17,263).

One decision, this one regarding expenditures by the Association of Railway Executives, even held that issue advertising costs were deductible. These expenditures were made "to create a body of intelligent public opinion favorable to the railroads of the country and to avert the enactment of legislation unfavorable or injurious to them" (Prentice-Hall, 1982: 12,307-12,308). Nevertheless, companies whose advertisements discuss regulation are likely to find the IRS regularly claiming that such discussion of "legislative matters"—even if it only occupies a small section of the advertisement—is not deductible. If this interpretation is accurate, it could be extended to the costs of annual reports which discuss a company's position on pending legislation.

Taking a narrow interpretation, Beeken (1981) argues: "Those activities which merely encourage a viewpoint favorable to the taxpayer's concept and which do not involve a discussion of proposed legislation or are focused on nonpartisan educational activities or private conduct are acceptable." In this category he includes ads that champion the free enterprise system. Moreover, the type of audience may be more important than the message per se, for while controversial statements on legislative matters to a "grassroots" audience—including employees—are nondeductible, the same statements made to a scholarly group might be deductible. Furthermore, any discussion of tax matters is held by the IRS to be nondeductible despite the lack of case law because "solutions to tax problems are considered to be solely a legislative matter and, therefore, are construed to involve grassroots campaigning" (Beeken, 1981: 94-95).

Sethi (1979a, b; U.S. Congress, 1978a: 384-387) has made two recommendations to solve the problem. One is to make a careful distinction between political and commercial speech. Sethi interprets IRS Regulations, Section 162-20 (a) and (b) as distinguishing between deductible image ads (which he equates with "commercial speech") and nondeductible issue ads (or "political speech"). However, as noted above, such a distinction is becoming more blurred than delimited. This recommendation, moreover, rather than simply interpreting the IRS Code, would change current tax policy. This artificial distinction between commercial and political speech fails to eliminate the gray area in the Tax Code and is neither supported by code language nor tax rulings.

To eliminate this gray area, Sethi's second recommendation during the hearings was to abolish the provision that allows companies to deduct expenses incurred for the general discussion of social, economic, or financial issues even if they do not address legislation. He argued that such discussion is made by a corporation only when it thinks it has a good solution to a problem. Such issues, he continues, are "within the domain of legislative matters," which would put them into the category of grassroots lobbying. The only advertisements that should be deductible, he concludes, are those which distinguish the sponsoring company from others in the industry and goodwill advertisements, those typically called "Red Cross" (quoted in U.S. Congress, 1978a: 386).

Despite efforts such as these, overlap between image and issues ads is inevitable. Such advertisements often provide information about a company's operating procedures and requirements, facts that can lead to more informed decisions about the company or industry. Attempts by Sethi and others to differentiate between the two types seem to be based on the fact that unlike more commercially oriented image messages, issue advertisements do not *carefully position* and *clearly differentiate* the sponsoring company from others. Thus, because they are not ordinary and necessary business expenses, they should not be deductible. This rationale is contrary to Section (a), which allows the discussion of nonlegislative issues.

Somewhat confusingly, the test of whether these expenditures are directly related to profits or even the survival of the company is not at issue because the courts (as in Commarano, 1957) have consistently ruled that this defense does not protect the deductibility of expenses. Such is the case even where the legislation being opposed by grassroots lobbying would adversely affect the company (Krauskopf, 1979: 322-326; see also Reg. Sec. 1.162-20 (b) (1)). Public service advertising support groups and causes such as the Red Cross are specifically deductible, according to the code. One could argue that taking a policy stand demonstrates a similar kind of citizenship as "Red Cross" advertising does by looking at free enterprise and other issues basic to the national economy. Since "Red Cross" advertisements do not differentiate among corporations, they certainly evoke responses other than purely commercial ones—yet remain deductible.

In light of this interpretation, a more valuable conceptualization of such advertisements would include the following categories, which intertwine image and issue positions. As defined in Chapter 1, *direct image* advertisements are those which carefully and clearly differentiate a company and its products or services from its competitors', while *indirect image* advertisements deal with social, financial, or economic matters. This latter type of advertisement can demonstrate corporate responsibility or goodwill in a fashion similar to "Red Cross" advertisements, but it does not provide details about the sponsor's products, services, or reputation. The advertisement may associate the sponsor with popular causes or values but does so without identifying characteristics of the company. The advertisement is indirect because the company's services, products, or reputation cannot be identified from the content of the advertisement (Heath and Nelson, 1983a, b, 1985). This taxonomy would treat as nondeductible only those advertisements which address issues in the presence of pending legislation, encourage direct contact with legislators, or discuss taxation. This position fosters the good that can be done when companies offer opinions on issues of economic, social, and financial importance.

The future of deductibility and issues advertising is a bit uncertain. Beeken (1981: 96) claims that the IRS "is apparently attempting to define the boundaries of grassroots lobbying as broadly as possible." Starting in November 1980, the IRS sought to expand prohibitions against grassroots lobbying to include as nondeductible those advertisements which advocate a position on "the desirability of legislation" or a matter that *might become* the subject of legislation. Such ads would be nondeductible if they were distributed or made available to the general public as voters or constituents, including indirect communication with the public via news releases. The American Advertising Federation (1981) expressed concern that the proposed rules would punish corporate communication, since an almost unlimited smorgasbord of issues of vital concern *could* become matters of legislation in any given tax year. Bostick (1981: 333) postulates that such regulatory procedures would make nondeductible any ad that "discusses proposals which cannot be implemented without legislation." Widespread criticism has deterred the implementation of these provisions, and they remain in limbo.

Many federal justices and regulatory policymakers seem (within limits) increasingly willing to uphold the right of corporations to communicate on controversial issues. The underlying rationale is the necessity of having an informed citizenry while balancing between regulation, technological advances, the public interest, and the benefits from corporate participation in the emerging American information society. In the equation of protected speech, the Supreme Court is beginning to help clarify corporate issue communication rights. *Buckley* v. *Valeo* (1976) is a ruling which could have substantial effects, especially on matters of deductibility. Centering on the legitimacy of restricting contributions to political campaigns, the Court concluded that one group could not be limited as to the amount of money it spent on a campaign merely because competing groups lacked equal resources to buy advertising. It further noted that "equalizing" speech by denying some sources the right to communicate was "wholly foreign" to the First Amendment (Buckley v. Valeo, 1976: 48). The premise basic to the decision was that the need for an informed citizenry is so great that no false barricades should be put between the source and receiver of communication. Thus the Court established that equity of funding (with clear implications for the deep pockets theory) could not be used to prevent companies from informing the public. In *First National Bank* v. *Bellotti* (1978), the Court ruled that businesses could not be prevented from participating in a public debate even if the issues were not directly in the material interest of the corporation or its shareholders. As Justice Powell said, "The inherent worth of speech in terms of its capacity for informing the public does not depend on the identity of its source, whether corporation, association, union or individual" (First National, 1978: 784-785, 789).

As these issues develop, the corporate communication manager is advised to follow several simple guidelines: (1) Image and issue advertisements are not likely to be subjected to FTC standards of factual verifiability by the current administration. (2) In the near term, outside of undesirable broadcast dayparts (for example, the late overnight hours rather than prime time), advertisements discussing controversial issues face very limited acceptance by the traditional networks. However, in part because of the successful challenge to the restrictive NAB Code on antitrust grounds, individual stations, including network affiliates, have become more open to issue advertising on a spot-buy basis. (3) Costs for print or broadcast advertisements are likely to be tax deductible as long as they do not discuss tax issues, call for grassroots contact of legislators, or consider issues pending in legislatures. (4) State regulatory policies differ at times from federal standards, necessitating continual monitoring of local as well as national developments.

5

SOCIAL RESPONSIBILITY AND CORPORATE PLANNING

No company can unfailingly *manage* public policy issues, but companies can participate in the resolution process. Required are several carefully interrelated activities: integrating issues management into corporate planning, updating business codes of conduct, monitoring public opinion, and executing communication activities. This chapter concentrates on the role of issues management in corporate planning and meeting social responsibility standards. The next chapter deals with monitoring and waging a communication campaign. Although these tasks are separable for purposes of discussion, a brief review reemphasizes how carefully coordinated they are in successful issues management efforts.

One of the most important strategies for handling public policy problems does not require communicating to manage issues at all. Rather, it calls for harmonizing corporate activities with the public interest. This step is difficult because there may be no clearly defined public interest. And even when one exists, executives often find it difficult to recognize that the corporation may be wrong on some issues. Business leaders tend to become so committed to the rightness of their efforts that they have difficulty realizing the virtues (to say nothing of the power) of special interest criticism. This "public interest first" strategy is further complicated by the reluctance of management to respond to external, nonmarket forces. Many operations people fear that issues management will interfere with the orderly performance of their jobs. Because of these internal political problems, effective issues management programs require the commitment and participation of both senior and middle corporate executives.

Criticizing corporations' reluctance to make a firm commitment to issues management, Goodman (1983) observes that few companies "formally tie these programs to their corporate planning systems or include issues management in their performance appraisal systems." He believes that such is the case because executives have a hard time narrowing the number of issues down to a manageable package; moreover, the issues are not defined specifically. Their vagueness and number, Goodman argues, impede many companies from formulating specific response strategies or a firm corporate-level commitment to change. Often there is no precise position in regard to public opinion.

Top management at times believes criticism to be a "challenge to the fundamentals of free enterprise," a catch phrase that business leaders too often hide behind to justify actions not in the public interest. For issues management to work, corporate managers must realize that the question is not usually whether we should have a free enterprise system, but rather how their companies should best be managed to meet the interests of shareholders, government, select interest groups, and the public at large.

Consistent application of short-term public opinion scanning and long-range monitoring should be sensitive to what groups believe, how intensely they believe it, and how willing they are to act on their beliefs. The strength of issues management is its pro-active ability to predict and prevent public uneasiness from maturing into policy issues requiring a corporate communication response. Careful monitoring of public opinion can allow issues managers to inform management of the consequences of changing corporate operating practices versus having to wage a later issues battle in the press and legislative arenas. Once issues demand refutation, the corporate policy and budgetary support needed for a campaign may last for years.

The communication aspect of a campaign to discuss the values and policy consequences involved in changing the regulatory environment for a specific company or industry poses challenges quite different from typical advertising or public relations activities. Corporations have developed sophisticated communication strategies to associate positive concepts and motivations with products, services, and/or the company image, but issues communication is more complex. It demands that credible and relevant information concerning business operations, values, and policies be made available to important audiences in ways that do not incite antagonism. In addition, the types of topics involved in issues campaigns often resist reduction to the simplistic level found in most marketing appeals. Whereas a limited breakthrough advertising effort can quickly increase product or service visibility, issues communication generally requires longer, more complicated campaigns to gain attention and create a mental impact.

Campaigns, as we have seen, may mature into a grassroots lobbying effort soliciting governmental and public participation. Issues management is doomed to fail if it is not based on the stark reality that opinion is the foundation of laws, and that considerable media discussion transpires prior to an issue reaching legislative chambers (Hammond, 1976; Thompson, 1981). Neglect of pro-active information opportunities makes the task of the issues communicator more difficult, since statements provided during a period of controversy seem much more self-serving than they do in tranquil times. For successful campaigns, the issues discussion must be framed around the self-interest of the targeted publics rather than that of the sponsoring company or industry. One way in which forward-thinking chief executives have taken the lead in managing issues involves trying to create a mutually beneficial dialogue with employees, customers, media leaders, investors, and other special interest constituents (Nagelschmidt, 1982). If they are to become ego-involved partners in the legislative tug-of-war, these audiences should not be viewed only as potential adversaries.

Issues managers may try to either reinforce or change opinions held by targeted publics. The latter is a more difficult task for several reasons. Public opinion is at times whimsical and lacks predictability; issues arise from what are often intangible and complicated concerns shared by segments of the population. Some issues, long dormant, come to light only through the efforts of an articulate person or some event that startles the public. Agitational groups, skilled in mobilizing the media and other cooperators, can create issues where none had previously existed. Under such conditions, when one is forced to react or respond, redirecting a mindset may be impossible, since converting the unbeliever is much harder than convincing the already predisposed fellow traveler. The most vital role that issues management can play is to lessen the gap by attempting to change corporate behavior rather than public expectations (Post et al., 1983: 139).

Many issues managers are continuing the long-standing practice of forming or joining industry associations and interest groups through which several companies can collectively work to manage issues (Nagelschmidt, 1982: 45). However, the voice of any single company or even trade association is often lost in a wrangle of competing statements. Despite the negative image of big businessmen being in cahoots with one another to fix prices and buy political stooges, most firms don't cooperate to any great extent. Nevertheless, we are convinced that a long-term commitment to informing targeted publics regarding the challenges facing corporations today is a prerequisite foundation for building a stable societal understanding (Harrison, 1982). The ultimate goal of issues management is to integrate public and corporate policies so that one does not prevail at the expense of the other.

This brief review of the fundamentals of successful issues management reemphasizes our contention that it entails an executive decision to ascertain and comply with prevailing public expectations of corporate ethical responsibility, to incorporate issues monitoring into the corporate structure, to scan issues development and public interest group activity, to establish communication goals in conjunction with corporate goals, and to create contact programs targeted at various audiences. Subsequent decisions revolve around situation assessment, audience designation, campaign design, channel selection, campaign execution, evaluation, reassessing one's situation, campaign redesign, and the implementation of new strategies. The process continues with constant fine tuning.

These functions cannot be utilized in isolation; they must be treated as components of one system in order to effectively foster corporate policy. Regardless of the details of each campaign, organizational goals are central to all other activities in a company, serving as the guidelines for issues selection. Therefore, issues management must begin with a firm and clear understanding of those goals and then take a responsible and pro-active part in their formation. But corporate goals are meaningless until they are translated into action; thus a major part of issues management is to effectively maximize the outcome of corporate efforts. This realization reminds issues managers and other corporate leaders that corporate goals must be larger then merely providing goods and services and offering an employment tax base for a community.

A VARIETY OF MODELS

Even the most casual survey reveals a wide array of models that can be used in the management of issues. How each company approaches issues management depends on its structure, personnel, and culture. In some companies, issues management is more a process or an attitude than a departmental function. Others play down the activity by adopting innocuous titles such as "external affairs" or else embed the responsibilities in more established public affairs or communication departments. Still other firms have openly created departments and positions containing "issues management" in their titles. Regardless of structure or business card moniker, issues managers optimally have intimate association with the corporate planning process so that each management decision rests on public policy considerations.

Three global stages are typical of controversy campaigns: (1) development of material and plan, (2) approval at the appropriate corporate levels, and (3) measurement of impact (Stridsberg, 1977: 80-82). Offering a more comprehensive but still incomplete analysis, Garbett (1981) identifies a number of other steps also applicable for issues management. He begins with fact finding to discover who the players are, where they are located, and what they believe. On this basis, he advocates analyzing which groups subscribe to particular images of the company and identifying those that are based on reality, and then assessing the corporation's mission to discover how the company views itself. After this study, managers must develop specific objectives and establish campaign goals, assign personnel responsibilities, create agency relationships, identify targeted audiences, design messages, select media, assign reporting responsibility, and calculate the proposed budget. Based on this planning, the campaign requires corporate management review and budget commitment before actual implementation of the campaign. So that it can be fine tuned and managed in the most cost-effective manner, someone must track the campaign to see whether it is achieving the agreed-upon goals (Garbett, 1981: 145-153). Normally, this translates to short- and long-term review by upper management.

Both of these models stress those elements at the heart of an issues communication campaign, but by focusing more on the advertising component they ignore the full-range panoply of issues management. Sensitive to the cycle of issues campaigns, Raymond P. Ewing of Allstate Insurance Companies (Ewing, 1980: 16; Nagelschmidt, 1982: 47-56) developed a public policy model that features interaction among the following competing forces: public opinion, the media, governmental agencies, special interest groups, and corporations. Corporate tracking, he suggests, should monitor the way public sentiment is narrowed and framed into proposals for regulation that can eventually evolve into legislation.

As demonstrated by a major southwestern utility, the approach that each organization takes to issues management is inseparable from its conception of public policy formation and its view of how it should adapt to that process. The model used by this company is based on the belief that issues develop through five stages: (1) *Vague discontent*. The public and a few experts/agitators begin to discuss some topic that begins to receive media attention. (2) *Politicization*. Groups begin to form and agitate collectively to increase the visibility of an issue, to propagate discussion and concern, and to attract followers and money. (3) *Legislative awareness*. The key indicators here are the number and power of the legislators promoting a topic and the amount of bills generated. (4) *Regulatory guidelines*. The campaign to control a company or industry reaches a crucial stage when an existing or newly created agency is assigned the responsibility for executing regulatory guidelines. (5) *Judicial debate*. Involved are corporate efforts to obtain a court ruling for or against the regulation or law. This must be done carefully, because heavy-handed legal tactics often provide a basis to further the lack of corporate responsibility that brought about the issue in the first place. To keep on top of developments in each stage, the company seeks to monitor issues, discover allies, communicate with constituencies to lay a foundation of public and employee opinion, establish coalitions with other groups that seek to change the legislation, and implement a successful lobbying campaign. Note that this is very similar to the planning that Nabisco follows in its issues management program: (1) issue detection using opinion-based research; (2) issue analysis, using a task force; (3) corporate position development; and (4) policy articulation (Nagelschmidt, 1982: 16-18).

Many more models could be reviewed to understand how companies conceive of issues management and prepare their responses. The important point, however, is that issues management consists of monitoring public policy issues, intimately integrating the company's code of corporate social responsibility into up-to-date corporate planning, and communicating with key constituencies. Figure 2 in Chapter 1 attempts to encompass all the issues management functions and place them in order. Such a model, however, can be misleading if we fail to stress their functional interrelationship.

ISSUES MANAGEMENT AND CORPORATE SOCIAL RESPONSIBILITY

A company must begin issues management by getting its own house in order. This point was driven home vigorously during the 1960s and 1970s. Corporate leaders began to bring outsiders into the discussion so that they could obtain a more objective view of the issues and strategies involved. In this spirit, Paul Garrett, who had served as vice president of public relations at General Motors, endowed a professorship at Columbia University to foster the belief that corporations need to do more than resist negatively. Business leaders "have the knowledge and skill required" to aid in accomplishing social goals, and "they owe it to society as well as to the business system to make these contributions in a creative and forthright manner" (Anshen, 1974: ix).

In response to the turmoil surrounding corporate ethics in the 1970s, the Business Roundtable commissioned a study of corporate ethics that culminated in *Corporate Performance: The Key to Public Trust* (Steckmest, 1982). This book was developed "to provide a forum for the examination of economic issues facing the nation, to develop reasoned positions on those issues, and thereby to contribute to the formation of public policy" (Steckmest, 1982: ix). The project evidenced a willingness by corporate leaders to debate such issues as corporate performance and governance, consumer and employee rights, and the difference between legal and ethical requirements.

Through hard experience, corporations discovered the subtle but profound distinction between legal and ethical behavior. For too long, corporations had attempted to hide behind the veil of legality without realizing that the public made a real distinction between the two. Insensitive managements could claim that an action, procedure or policy was legal, even though it markedly violated public expectations of trust and morality. Even more startling was the recognition that the reputation a corporation spent a decade developing could be destroyed by a single act. Dumping toxic waste or participating in bribes and kickbacks, whether in domestic or international relations, is contrary to most standards of fair corporate practices.

Slowly, many issues managers learned the harsh reality that public opinion is the final judge of corporate behavior. In an effort to enhance their credibility, many corporations worked at becoming more "transparent." For instance, Shell Oil Company proclaimed a commitment to divulge all information upon request that did not violate the law, compromise the integrity of employees or customers, reveal proprietary secrets, or disrupt secret negotiations. Bank of America Corporation also led in the effort to regain media and public respect by championing higher standards for voluntary disclosure (Steckmest, 1982: 61-79).

Corporate ethics are complex, much more so than the public realizes. Because behavior speaks more loudly than words, corporations must estimate public standards, create a code of corporate responsibility, and use internal audit controls to implement it. One of the most difficult but fundamental steps is deciding on the content of and the amount of commitment to be made to the code. Like any regulations, these are subject to ambiguity and distortion. This fact does not excuse corporations from attempting to codify public ethics; it merely suggests that boiler-plated lists are unsatisfactory answers to complicated issues. However, even if vague at times, these codes are valuable because they espouse principles which set the tone for corporate policies and behavior. In this regard, probably the simplest standard of corporate social responsibility is captured in that timeless bit of advice: "Don't do anything that you do not want reported on the front page of the newspaper."

A statement by George Weissman (1984), former chairman and chief executive officer of Philip Morris, Inc, insightfully sets corporate responsibility into its socio-political context: "Like property, the corporation is a creation of the state. It gets its charter from the government. To survive, the corporation subjects itself to regulation by government, and to serving the needs of government and the commonwealth." The heart of this relationship is interdependence, he continues, between business and society. This "is fundamental to understanding the concept of corporate responsibility in its current context, to understanding that we are not dealing with a fad; and to understanding that we are dealing with the fundamental existence and survival of the corporation" (Weissman, 1984: 67). This interdependence constitutes the rationale for issues management, pointing to the stewardship function that businesses are now expected to perform. The experience of the past two decades suggests that the role of the corporation has changed, with business becoming more involved in community activities and areas formerly assumed to be the responsibility of government (Chrisman and Carroll, 1984).

Hathaway (1984), asserting that companies need to speak out about their societal accomplishments, offers some advice to issues managers. They should select salient problems and concentrate their efforts where they can gain the greatest impact and visibility. Particularly if a corporation is committed to participating in the development of a platform of fact, it can continually generate information that the public finds valuable for understanding the exigencies of corporate behavior. Using effective communication techniques, this information can counterbalance the public view that corporate activities are purely self-serving.

But communication alone usually cannot solve problems where corporate behavior differs significantly from public standards. Sethi (1977: 58) argues that corporate performance is all too often on one end of a continuum with public expectation on the other. The extent to which they differ from one another is a measure of the "legitimacy gap." One cost-benefit reason for becoming more sensitive to public standards is to avoid the nuisance and expense of dealing with regulatory agencies. Despite the belief of Weissman and of Chrisman and Carroll that corporate social responsibility pays for itself, Cochran and Wood (1984) discovered a low correlation between corporate social responsibility and financial performance. Cochran and Wood also indicate their dismay that the degree of social responsibility exhibited by many companies corresponds to the age of the manufacturing facilities. For instance, those factories built before the 1960s are more likely to pollute and to cost more to bring them within federal and state standards.

Another reason for increased sophistication in monitoring public standards is the growing number of court awards against companies. Twenty-five years ago, a $1 million settlement was news. In 1980, 130 multimillion dollar awards were made; this figure jumped to 235 in 1981 (Foote, 1984: 217). The huge cost to industry in the 1984 Agent Orange case added a new dimension to the analysis of social responsibility costs.

Other environmental and diagnostic studies are essential to determine the opinion environment and to use it to reconsider a corporation's performance strengths and weaknesses. Rowe and Schlacter (1978: 10) claim that unless social responsibility is integrated into the corporate structure, an issues campaign will surely flounder because of hypocrisy. They propose the use of a social audit which can "identify those social responsibilities which a company thinks it ought to be discharging." It may be used "to examine what the company is doing in these areas and to determine how satisfactory is the performance." If a performance gap is discovered, the audit can effectively "determine how far the company should go in filling it" and "whether a company is vulnerable to potential criticism or attack." The ultimate goal of the audit is to bring together "the thinking of managers at all levels of a social point of view."

Codes are of minimal value until they are disseminated to employees and become part of the rewards and punishments in the appraisal process. Although many companies allege to be increasing their commitment to issues management, Goodman (1983) concludes that few have married their standards of corporate performance to employee appraisal systems. As leaders in this effort, he points to General Electric,

Norton-Simon, Bank of America, General Mills, Ciba-Geigy, Connecticut General, Union Carbide, AT&T, International Paper, Eaton Corporation, Allied Chemical, Standard Oil of California, and Standard Oil of Indiana. Periodic internal audits performed objectively and without regard to an individual's corporate rank can impress upon employees the seriousness of executive management's commitment to the intent and principles of the codes.

ISSUES MANAGEMENT AND CORPORATE STRUCTURE

No matter where the function is located, it cannot succeed without executive-level authority and budgetary support (Lukasik, 1981; Zraket, 1981; Spitzer, 1979). One of the most comprehensive statements on the relationship between corporate structure, issues management, and issues planning is that developed by J. K. Brown (1979). Establishing several simple guidelines for the issues monitoring process, Brown suggests that the initial phase "must be comprehensive," "have broad internal participation" and "be integrated with other key functions." Criteria, including deadlines, need "to be articulated in general and specific terms." Issues management loses effectiveness if it lacks a "foundation for specific priorities and strategies." To prevent being unduly myopic, it "must include external validation." Throughout, everyone involved must hold "the process in perspective." In framing issues, they should first be stated in relatively neutral language; no attempt should be made to cast them in terms of right and wrong. Company lingo, including technical jargon, may be incorporated, but the explosive language of special interest groups seeking legislative remedies is best avoided (Brown, 1979: 34-36, 59).

Brown says that the issues process may be handled by making one of several people responsible, with these alternatives:

(1) Allow the chief executives to specify issues.
(2) Conduct informal discussions among a small group of executives. Typically this could be done by a planning committee. ARCO, for example, uses a strategic planning council which meets each fall to identify the key issues the company will face in the next 18-24 months.
(3) Use questionnaires to solicit input by middle as well as top managers, or the process can be narrowed to division leaders and profit center heads.
(5) Create a cadre of volunteers to scan a wide array of publications looking for issues trends. Some companies use various outsiders, including trade associations, issue trend consultants, and academic advisers.

However gathered, the information can be placed into a matrix with one axis estimating the probability that the issue will mature into legislation; the other axis measures the likely impact of the issue on corporate operations.

Most corporations use some form of matrix management to bring together operating managers and other specialists for planning and executing issues campaigns (Buchholz, 1982). Offering other examples of typical matrices, Thompson (1981) reports on Sperry Corporation, Rexnord, and Union Carbide. Sperry has a group that combines information received from managers into a summary considered at annual communication conferences involving executives from both domestic and international divisions. Out of the process comes a report identifying and listing issues by priority. Finally, executive management selects the specific issues to be managed and helps set goals for those actually conducting the campaign. Sperry campaigns typically include congressional action components. The issues team prepares position papers, circulates monthly legislative newsletters and issues books, and sends "actiongrams" asking managers to provide timely information to targeted legislators. In close coordination with these activities, internal communication keeps employees abreast of issue developments and the corporate position.

Rexnord implemented an issues matrix consisting of operations, staff, and midmanagement personnel. At Union Carbide, issues management is similarly tied to corporate strategic planning. Once an issue is isolated, research and analysis are performed from three perspectives: public attitudes, political and regulatory actions, and the impact on the company. Key-issues communication managers, who work in conjunction with traditional public affairs specialists, prepare position papers on these vital Carbide activities. This information is then made available to plant managers around the country.

Issues management matrices are typically headed by a communication specialist or a person with technical, financial, corporate planning, or legislative experience. In many instances, issues management is a responsibility of public affairs/public relations departments. Regardless of the education and experience of the person heading the matrix, he or she should report directly to a senior member of management. In a survey of companies, Post et al. (1983: 137, 144) discovered that most public affairs departments were headed by a vice president, while 60 percent reported to a chairman, president, or CEO. The survey revealed that "many companies are experimenting with new organizational arrangements such as issue managers, public policy committees, public issue task forces, and various forms of formalized public affair/corporate planning coordination. These experiments are an effort to find improved ways of integrating staff activities and business operations to achieve corporate objectives" (Post et al., 1983: 147).

In addition to having a close working relationship with executive management, the matrix must bring together needed experts with authority to perform their function in a timely manner. Whether members of the company or outside consultants, these experts should be balanced to draw on a vital range of expertise: (1) *managerial*—finance, economic forecasting, marketing, product liability, and personnel aspects of the company, (2) *technical*—production and handling of company products and services, including engineering (or its technical equivalent, such as pharmaceutics or medicine), (3) *public policy*—formation of issues, (4) *governmental affairs*—ways in which public sentiment becomes legislation, and (5) *corporate ethical behavior*—strategies for auditing corporate social performance. Every effort should be made to involve people whose collective understanding of the company represents all of the major decision points and departmental/product/plant operating activities. Although each matrix is responsible for monitoring and selecting issues, as well as developing the corporate stance and preparing position papers, an external advertising or public relations agency is often hired to execute an advocacy campaign (Stridsberg, 1977: 78-79).

Early in the development of the matrix, executive management must specify how approvals will be granted for major operating decisions in the campaign. Who decides the final priority of the issues to be managed? How will information about public sentiment be used to reevaluate corporate performance standards? Does each controversy advertisement need approval? In the face of a crisis, what mechanism exists to ensure that the response meets management expectations? Can each response be approved quickly enough to maintain accuracy while satisfying journalistic demands for timely information? Questions such as these must be answered for the effective management of the campaign. If too many people are involved in the approval process, valuable time and advantange can be wasted. On the other hand, faulty screening may result in grave errors of fact or false estimations of issue impacts on corporate survival.

Offering advice to corporations relevant to the climate necessary for successful handling of issues, Nowlan and associates (1984) advise against the pitfalls of not appropriately rewarding those involved, permitting value systems to obstruct the process, having ill-defined committee priorities, allowing information-gathering systems to be poorly organized, and overloading people so that they cannot function systematically. Even more important advice centers on the use of an issues committee. One of the first steps in forming such a committee is to examine the "corporation's culture—the methods, attitudes, and practices of its corporate and division managements." Reflecting on the importance of climate, the authors observe: "Those companies whose cultures have provided the most hospitable environment for the group process in the past will also be successful in their efforts to create consensus-building and awareness-building committees on a wide range of corporate problems" (Nowlan et al., 1984: 13).

ISSUES MANAGEMENT AND CORPORATE PLANNING

Corporate planning, as Hax and Majluf (1984) note, consists of identifying three kinds of hierarchical decisions: corporate, business, and functional. At the corporate level, a "vision of the firm" is created by identifying the corporate philosophy or mission. How this mission is achieved depends on the ability of corporate and business planners to formulate strategies. At the corporate level, these strategies are relatively broad and conceptual, becoming more specific at the business and functional levels. Consequently, in conjunction with the formulation of a corporate mission and action plan, a corresponding plan is needed at the business and functional levels. Lower level plans are designed to support the upper level ones. The higher level plans in turn provide guidance for the lower level plans. Each set of plans is budgeted based on its cost in support of the total hierarchy of plans and objectives.

Although strategic corporate planning may be organized in various ways, most systems incorporate several steps, such as "goal formation, environmental analysis, strategy formulation, strategy evaluation, strategy implementation and strategy control" (Thomas, 1984: 56). Thomas's model assumes that management always exists in a problem-solving environment fraught with ambiguity and uncertainty. To be successful, a manager should have a planning model which is founded on problem identification and solution implementation. Thomas (1984: 68-69) argues that the "top manager needs to first build his strategic agenda through careful inquiry and examination of his problems in terms of alternative . . . 'theories.' " Problem-solving strategy should begin by examining the degree to which "strategy choice would be consistent with the pressures of the external environment, the corporation's goals and resources, the risk-taking propensities of the corporation and the culture and value systems embedded within the organisation."

Not all issue identification and strategic planning stages lend themselves to the kinds of concerns addressed by issues managers, but many do. For this reason, corporations should be sensitive to the kinds of issues in corporate planning that have public policy implications. Rather than being hostile ground for issues management influence, traditional corporate planning models stress the need for environmental scanning, part of which suggests the need to be sensitive to public policy trends. Thus the key to understanding corporate planning is recognizing how it is supported by cognitive skills basic to decision analysis (Thomas and Schwenk, 1984).

Because issues management is vital to the conceptualization of problems, the formulation of solutions, and the monitoring of performance, a formal liaison should exist between it and company strategic planning. According to Arrington and Sawaya (1984), each can be treated as separate departmental functions, but the people from each department should work together. The corporate planning side is most interested in the business environment, whereas issues management people concentrate on public policy events that may impinge on the business. In coordination with long-range corporate planning scenarios, issues management foresight analysis includes issue identification, monitoring, and priority setting. Out of this grow decisions for long-range strategic planning and the issues process. All of this detail is eventually analyzed to assure its best fit with the business and public policy environments (Arrington and Sawaya, 1984: 153-155).

As an advocate for making planning skills more systematic, McGinnis (1984) observes: "Intelligence is the firm's ability to simultaneously scan and interpret its external environments, monitor itself, and communicate effectively with itself." To achieve balance, a company should "be centralized and decentralized simultaneously." Issues management can aid this goal by helping various departments concentrate on the internal and external policy implications of their activities. A common set of operating standards and an awareness of public policy implications offer managers in diverse parts of a company a singular sense of their operating environment constraints.

So far, so good. But theory and reality do not always mesh. We hear again the theme which comes up time and again: Corporate planning too often does not carefully consider public affairs advice on policy issues unless the company is involved in a controversy (Post et al., 1983: 137). Half of all companies fail to utilize public affairs expertise in defining issues or prioritizing their importance. About one-quarter of public affairs departments actually provide long-term sociopolitical forecasts and planning scenarios (Post et al., 1983: 148). These figures are heartening if they demonstrate a trend toward more involvement by public affairs, but if they do not, they are a bit bleak. Case studies suggest that the impact of public affairs departments on planning is low in utility companies and banks, high in computer companies, and moderate in the chemical industry. These differences in the extent to which issues management is used in corporate planning seem to coincide with the personality of the CEO more than any other factor.

As the Post et al. (1983) survey reveals, public affairs has its greatest influence on short-term problems faced by corporations rather than on long-range planning. In fact, "the influence wanes unless great care is taken to interpret the long term to line managers so that it has immediate relevance." This limitation seems predictable given the tendency that companies have to follow a quarterly planning mentality. The survey also disclosed that public affairs is more likely to be influential on corporate strategic planning in highly centralized companies. The authors conclude: "Companies using long range, strategic planning of a qualitative nature are far more likely to have influential public affairs offices." This seems "intuitively logical because strategic planning tends to examine the environment more broadly and systematically than do operationally focused and/or less formal planning systems" (Post et al., 1983: 147).

The authors of this book found evidence that helps balance this picture. For example, corporate planning is highly sensitive to the operational plans of various product lines in the quiet but very successful issues management program at Exxon Chemical Americas. The system requires that each major department develop an issues planning book reviewing highlights of the previous year and identifying the key challenges it will face in the coming 12 months. The next step is to specify how these challenges will be met in conjunction with all other departments. Since it is primarily a business-to-business producer, Exxon Chemical is less directly involved with consumer concerns than governmental relations.

Putting this series of books together required a great deal of internal discussion and coordination. At the end of the effort, a master activities plan summarizes how each department can count on specific actions from other departments. Documented are product line activities as well as communication, monitoring, and lobbying efforts. By sharing information in this manner, issues managers can have pro-active input into operating activities early enough to matter. Moreover, communication support can be realistically budgeted, with operations and financial managers having a ground floor opportunity to consider and authorize the funding of any issues campaign (s).

Although time-consuming, these activities make issues management central to corporate planning. With this procedure there is time to pause and consider what the prevailing standards of corporate social responsibility are and how they apply to operations and support activities. Such planning makes operations people aware of the public policy consequences of their business decisions and alerts communication experts to the possible dangers of corporate efforts. Finally, the total campaign—whether operations or communication—becomes the product of the collective wisdom of major department managers. In this way, issues management is infused into corporate planning and evaluation. By continuing careful coordination, line and staff executives have the opportunity to make adjustments during the year by monitoring how well the plan is working and whether it continues to coincide with management thought, business opportunities, and public expectations.

Because information is crucial to the formation and execution of corporate goals, issues management should fit comfortably with management by objectives (Nager and Allen, 1984). Part of the planning process can include estimates of the kinds of groups that will have a positive or negative reaction to company and industry policies and actions. Such estimates can be made issue by issue and group by group. Each group can be placed on a pro-con, committed-uncommitted continuum ranging from strongly ego-involved stakeholder to committed special interest advocate. Some groups are valuable because they are willing to buy products or services. Other groups are important because they are willing to take sides on public policy debates. Sometimes sizable groups of individuals fall into both categories. By identifying each issue by group, the company can determine what information each has and what the attitudinal impact of the information is. By dissecting the audiences this way, the company can better determine whether to wage a communication campaign or solve the problem by adjusting its corporate performance.

Typical corporate planning models explicitly or implicitly rely on "what if" considerations to estimate probabilities in formulating contingency plans (Shim and McGlade, 1984). Attempting to identify those conceptual variables that impinge on corporate decision making, Schwenk (1984) argues that the process follows three distinct stages: goal formulation/problem identification, strategic alternatives generation, and evaluation and selection. Issues management has its strategic corporate planning role at each of these three stages. At the first stage, issues managers can help corporate planners determine the public policy implications related to corporate goals. Attempts are then made to isolate and weigh input/output variables that may impinge on operations. The goal of bringing issues management into the corporate planning arena is to clarify the likely effect of public policy expectations on specific corporate practices.

The third stage requires that the cost/benefit analysis of the first and second stages be resolved so that strategies can be selected to foster corporate profit and image goals. Planners estimate the complex of variables, which includes marketplace competition, production costs and schedules, transportation, acquisition of materials, capital improvement, labor conditions, and financing costs. The standard equation sometimes goes like this: *What* will public opinion be *if* plant operations allow periodic discharges of noxious fumes? *What* changes will occur in capital costs *if* legislation matures into new environmental regulatory standards requiring improved pollution control? *What* public opinion cries will be heard *if* a toxic materials procedure failure kills several thousand people? Or the issues management team might consider the probability that new legislation will be voted into law to increase the tax burden on oil companies already "reaping windfall profits."

NESTLÉ—SOCIAL RESPONSIBILITY AND CORPORATE PLANNING

We can examine the delicate balance between public standards of social responsibility and corporate planning by studying how Nestlé handled the hotly contested battle centered on infant formula marketing in less developed nations. October 1984 marked a milestone in corporate/special interest cooperation with the official end of the seven-year International Nestlé Boycott Committee struggle to improve Third World health care. This controversy exemplified the true meaning of issues management as it brought together into one arena activists, industry members, the media, federal authorities, foreign governments, and World Health Organization (WHO) officials.

As early as the 1930s, medical experts recognized the risk of bottlefeeding babies in poverty areas. Once a mother stops natural nursing, she soon loses her ability to produce milk. Without proper sanitation and clean water, bottlefeeding introduces children to health and nutrition problems that breastfeeding does not. Despite these problems, by the 1960s milk substitutes became increasingly popular in less developed nations. Extensive industrywide product advertising showed only healthy, robust children. These images complemented marketing programs conducted by local nurses on company payrolls.

Critical attention was directed to this situation by Dr. Derrick Jelliffe, who persuaded the United Nations Protein-Calorie Advisory Group to investigate. But the public did not learn about the problem until Mike Muller published a series of articles in the *New Internationalist*, followed by a stark pamphlet entitled *The Baby Killer* in 1974. In Switzerland, home of Nestlé, the title was changed to *Nestlé Kills Babies*.

The resulting trial in 1975 engendered substantial publicity and spurred the formation of numerous pressure groups. The crucial moment occurred in mid-1977 when the Infant Formula Action Coalition (INFACT) began its boycott of Nestlé products. Organizers were successful in promoting their cause by creating an alliance with the National Council of Churches' Interfaith Center on Corporate Responsibility. INFACT also began to work with staff members for Edward Kennedy, chairman of the Senate Subcommittee on Health and Human Resources. Hearings were held and foreign aid purse strings were manipulated to involve other governments in combating the overseas sales effort, with Nestlé as the major target. Eventually the coalition involved the highly respected WHO by pushing for comprehensive social responsibility standards in infant formula marketing. The Carter administration fully supported the boycott, but the Reagan administration did not. Once President Reagan's pro-industry position became public, a protest erupted. Opposition congressional leaders seized this opportunity to picture the president as insensitive, and coalition members renewed their mobilization efforts.

The boycott targeted Nestlé's U. S. operations, even though the company did not produce or market infant formula in this country. The prolonged challenge had an impact: Nestlé executives began to develop a seige mentality. Although the company tried conventional public affairs programs "to neutralize one of the most pervasive, vicious, scurrilous and morale-wrecking attacks in modern times against one of the world's largest and most prestigious corporations," management recognized that the cost in morale and public image was high. By 1981 Nestlé had retained and dismissed two of America's largest public relations agencies (Pagan, 1983: 2-4). Clearly, some new approach was called for—issues management.

In handling its problems, Nestlé drew five conclusions early in the campaign. (1) It decided to solve the issue of its corporate performance rather than combating the critics. (2) The campaign received the attention of top management and drew its authority from it. (3) The issues management team and corporate management decided that some changes in corporate policy were needed before the campaign could succeed. (4) All levels of management were instructed to support the campaign, and issues managers were willing to rely on the advice and receive the information that operations managers provided. (5) The issues management team drew on the expertise of several of its company's disciplines: technical, scientific, nutritional, political, and sociological.

Rafael D. Pagan, Jr. (1983: 4), president of the Nestlé Coordination Center for Nutrition, recalls: "The essential first step in resolving the infant feeding dilemma was for Nestlé to recognize that it was a political, as well as a nutritional, issue and therefore to recognize the legitimacy of some of our critics' concerns and to listen to them carefully." One of the most difficult tasks of issues management is convincing management that policies must be changed because they are at odds with public opinion. As Pagan (1983: 8) concludes, "A primary task of issues management, then, must be to reach beyond our profession and work with senior executives to instill attitudes of awareness and openness in our business firms."

Born from the fire of public criticism and special interest agitation, Nestlé, in conjunction with the WHO, undertook to produce a code of ethics. One of the first responses to this controversy was the creation of an industrywide umbrella organization, the International Council of Infant Food Industries. This group quickly banned commission payments to milk nurses. Company members also agreed to reduce mass media advertising. This effort by the industry was initiated in the truest sense of what Wiebe (1967) means by "a search for order."

Nestlé recognized the dangers in assuming that it could continue doing business as usual, since here was a classic case of power resources being effectively managed by special interest groups. One of the lessons demonstrated by the Nestlé campaign is the importance of working to defuse the adversary's cause by making meaningful change once the lines of social responsibility become blurred. Much to its credit, and with the assistance of its critics, Nestlé drafted a "Recommended UN Code for Marketing Infant Formula" in 1981. Once the code was adopted, the company worked for more than two years to translate it into company activities. During this implementation stage, the Nestlé Infant Formula Audit Commission (NIFAC) played a vital role. On several points the Nestle code differs from the one created by the WHO. Although an imperfect document, it has helped clarify the standards of acceptable behavior. To remedy problems of vagueness and inconsistency, NIFAC scientists, clergy, and ethicists review specific instances where the Nestlé and WHO codes may have been violated. Through this mechanism, Nestlé attempts to ensure that it complies with the spirit of the WHO code and that it translates its own code into specific employee behavior. Created with the assistance of former Senator Edmund Muskie, the commission is testament to what can be done once a corporation decides that the temper of the times demands a new and honest standard of social policy (Post, 1985).

Once Nestlé convinced others of its sincerity, the boycott eased. After considering Nestlé's side of the case, a United Methodist Church Task Force voted not to boycott Nestlé products. Today the company stands as a model of corporate responsibility, setting an example for an industry that moved vigorously to put its house in order. Despite the earlier controversy, the industry now works regularly with Third World physicians and foreign government representatives. Not only is much of the tarnish removed from its image but industry product sales have rebounded. Even so, the Nestlé instance was also one of the first victories for agitators working against the actions of a multinational corporation abroad (Baker, 1985; Barovick, 1982). The company's struggle to reform itself coincided with the much larger task of formulating *The OECD Guidelines for Multinational Enterprises,* portending the growing need to have a workable set of corporate ethics for operations abroad as well as in the United States.

In sharing its experiences, Nestlé Corporation contributed substantially to our understanding of how to manage issues. Only as the issues campaign progressed did many of those involved realize the difficulty of achieving compatibility between the long-term commitment necessary to change opinions and short-term management constraints for returns on investments. At this point, management realized that it could not operate in a public policy vacuum and woke up to the full meaning of special interest agitation and corporate social responsibility. The company leadership quickly learned through trial and error that issues management must be incorporated into all other corporate functions, no matter how painful the task or divisive the atmosphere. In a highly diversified company, issues managers must monitor a wide array of issues and be expert on a variety of topics while understanding their public policy and regulatory implications.

Pagan (1983: 9) argues that one of the most important issues management responsibilities is to obtain and disseminate accurate information in a timely fashion:

> Good information must be developed through an ongoing process and it must be periodically screened and evaluated. It is only then that trends can be discerned and the issue screening process can work. We cannot fight all possible future trends we don't agree with, but we must be able to determine which ones are important and which must be addressed at the earliest moment. An effective issue screening process is at the heart of our efforts.

Since all members of a company are potential public relations advocates, they must be briefed on the details and goals of the campaign.

MUCH REMAINS TO BE DONE

Even though the corporate planning role of issues management is apparent, its involvement has not reached the level desired by writers such as Post, Arrington, Sawaya, Ehling, Hesse, Ewing, Chase, and Jones. The task confronting issues managers in specific, and public relations/public affairs practitioners in general, is to win the credibility necessary to influence corporate planning. Modern issues management is still in its infancy, both in terms of its role in corporate policy development and its place in organizational structure. To optimize success, an internal as well as external marketing job is called for, since advocating change increases uncertainty and encourages possible co-worker resistance from other departments and from corporate power centers (Coch and French, 1948; Katz and Kahn, 1978).

Issues managers must provide useful information to the leadership cadre of their organizations as a result of their intelligence gathering and communication expertise. In addition, they must continually marshal their persuasive skills to articulately legitimize the continuance of their function. They must recognize that the more risk and complexity perceived in their recommendations, the less likely they are to be successfully implemented (Fidler and Johnson, 1984). Unfortunately, the tools for strategic implementation have not kept in sync with planning, as evidenced by many failed plans and abandoned planning efforts. As Brodwin and Bourgeois (1984) observe in their study of strategic action, research demonstrates that few executives get beyond their short-range problems to articulate long-term projections. The politics of corporate culture may also mean that compromise is an essential component of success, even if it means abandoning optimal plans. Unwilling "cooperation" by managers coerced into supporting projects they do not really believe in generally leads to failure, even when there is underlying merit to the proposal. Issues management is simply a buzzword unless its role in the corporation is accompanied by the active encouragement of a participative atmosphere tolerant of different views, an opening up of the decision-making process to encourage the involvement of subordinates in providing unbiased information, and integrative planning between the central corporate staff and line organizational levels.

6

ISSUES MONITORING AND THE ISSUES COMMUNICATION CAMPAIGN

Issues analysis rests on the ability to understand what issues are becoming salient. According to the late Herman Kahn, a complete technological revolution has occurred every five years since the end of World War II. It took this social upheaval, plus continuing blunders such as the SST fiasco, aftershocks from the energy and import crises, and hard-nosed competition from Asia and Europe, to prod U.S. corporations into once again taking futures monitoring seriously. American business no longer dominates international markets, and today's executive is caught up in the "future shock" that is already here. But much of the resistance to change was the fault of the so-called "futurists" themselves. Early research predictions made in the 1950s were oversold to progressive companies such as Monsanto, Sears, and General Electric. The resulting emphasis on questionable long-range, pie-in-the-sky projections led the whole field of futures studies, except for a few major think tanks, to fall into disrepute.

Unlike earlier fortune-teller generalists, today's issues managers concentrate on tangible short-term (one to five years) social and political trend studies. Following is one example from a recent *Grey Matter* survey (reprinted courtesy of Grey Advertising, Inc.): While most businessmen were dancing at Ronald Reagan's inauguration in January 1981, issues managers at Atlantic Richfield were warning their bosses that (1) the economy was about to take a nosedive and (2)

Reagan's proposed federal budget cuts would force economically hard-pressed states to raise taxes on corporations. ARCO maintains an issues management group of 18 full-time employees, developing action and advocacy policies on 12 different issues at any given time. As a profitable oil company operating in 28 states, ARCO felt that it would be the target of such increases and readied its lobbyists for such an event. Sure enough, almost a year later, as state tax proposals began to surface, sometimes at the rate of ten a week, ARCO lobbyists moved to block those aimed specifically at oil companies. While four states raised ARCO's corporate taxes and four others raised its severance taxes, a vast majority of the bills were defeated (P. Brown, 1984: 5).

Such individual successes, even though American business as a whole is suffering, have encouraged reevaluation of the whole field of futures studies. The monitoring and communication aspects of issues management now draw on an evolving body of experience and literature for making campaign planning more systematic (Nowlan et al., 1984). Renfro (1982) reports that at least 200 Fortune 500 corporations have established management-level groups to monitor public policy issues and to formulate corporate responses to them. One does not have to be a genius to recognize that in an information society someone must convert raw data into useful projections. Even for companies that plan for long-range issue discussion, controversies, misstatements, misrepresentations, challenges, and other problems may unexpectedly require an immediate response. Another crisis may just be around the corner, and the need for technically trained social science analysts is greater than ever.

ISSUES MONITORING

The key to planning is having research data that indicate the lay of the public policy land. Over the past decade, many corporate communication practitioners and their social scientist counterparts have developed a healthy interest in sophisticated research methods (e.g., Jones, 1975; Van Riper, 1976; Grass, 1977; Grunig, 1977a, b; Franzen, 1977; Tichenor et al., 1977; Tirone, 1977; Lerbinger, 1977; Marker, 1977; Stamm, 1977; Strenski, 1978; Zentner, 1978; Goldman and Auh, 1979; Coyle and Stephens, 1979; Bevk, 1979). Issues management involves the use of surveys and audits but goes far beyond them. Rather than treating opinion as mere response items on a survey, the preferred approach is to understand how response items cluster into arguments.

To understand an opinion, issues managers must be able to comprehend the depth and breadth of the opinion position as comprehensive thoughts or arguments (Davison, 1972; Dillman and Christenson, 1973).

Public opinion can have an impact on corporate decisions related to such matters as marketing, product development, operating standards, consumer protection, transportation and manufacturing safety standards, and environmental protection. Prior to final goal setting for an issues campaign, the company should scan its public opinion environment to establish baseline data. The 1977 IAA survey revealed that "most companies report that they have not made any effort to pre-test the effectiveness of their controversy campaigns, and that they have not attempted to measure the impact of the advertising following its appearance" (Stridsberg, 1977: 81). Cost, of course, is a factor. But without hard data one is just stumbling in the dark. Tracking an issues communication campaign has the same advantages as tracking operating costs, production figures, profits, or employee satisfaction.

Some researchers doubt that campaign impact can be accurately assessed, because so many variables are involved. Simply determining the company's or industry's image or polling for public sentiment on certain issues may not enable an issues management team to determine what a campaign has contributed. At best, survey tracking strategies can be used to determine shifts in public opinion and may ascertain which influences are having the greatest impact on opinions held by key publics (Stridsberg, 1977: 81). One major means for determining the success of a campaign is to study the track record of the issues management group, as at ARCO, to assess its legislative scorecard.

The perplexities of interpreting trends adds to the difficulties of monitoring. For instance, if the leaders in the oil business had responded to public opinion trends during the late 1970s, they would have moved to separate oil and gas reserves from the production aspects of their operation. Clearly, the sentiment in Washington, particularly as articulated by President Carter, was that oil companies should be divided into three separate units: resources, refining, and marketing. What is amazing in this issues trend example is that the exact opposite seems to have occurred. Because of various mergers, major companies have consolidated their operations. Fewer companies compete today than were competing ten years ago.

Even without sophisticated monitoring techniques, some companies and industries are able to track the subtle changes in the few issues that seem to hound them year in and year out. Many issues are like cat myths;

they seem to have nine lives, to recur and persist. Private discussions with various issues managers reveal that they are rarely surprised by the emergence of a truly new issue. What they are concerned with today is roughly the same as their worries a decade ago. Often, rather than facing dramatic shifts in public policy, their concerns revolve around technical changes such as measures of toxicity levels of pollution, or perhaps the presence of new players in the public policy marketplace.

The monitoring process can be divided into two distinct but interrelated phases: (1) Assess the company's situational environment to determine which factors influence public opinion; and (2) review campaign progress. The revised Jones/Chase-Chase/Jones interactive model (Jones and Chase, 1979; Chase, 1984) of issue identification, issue analysis, issue change strategy options, issue action programs, and result evaluation is useful in this context:

Issue identification consists of several stages: understanding the basic public policy process; monitoring anticipated social, economic, technological, and political changes; and identifying specific issue objectives/goals linked to corporate goals—all culminating in issue identification. Important are the impact and response source (business system, industry, corporation, subsidiary, or department); the geography (international, national, regional, state, or local); the span of control (noncontrollable, semicontrollable, or controllable); and the salience (degree of immediacy or prominence).

Issue analysis has as its first task to determine the origin of the issue, with particular emphasis on the political, social, and economic forces relevant to issue formation. It attempts to isolate the major influence sources that impinge on change. The issues manager is encouraged to consider the past and present issue situation—its history and current status. Because media gatekeepers and opinion leaders play instrumental roles in issues formation and dissemination, this part of the process should be sensitive to locating them. It also concentrates on elected and appointed government officials. The major concern is to locate the friendly and unfriendly constituencies for corporate issues. Qualitative and quantitative research (media content analysis, leadership surveys, legislative trend studies, and the like) are valuable. To better understand this process, Chase and Jones suggest that the issues manager discover the source and intent of each statement, its target and message, and the tactic of which it is a part.

Issue change strategy options (priority-setting considerations) involve deciding which issues the organization will commit to and in what manner. Key criteria in this stage, Jones and Chase conclude, are risks involved in undertaking the campaign, confidence in information, accuracy of forecasts, likelihood the situation will correct itself, timing, and the direction the situation is likely to take. Reactive, adaptive, and dynamic (pro-active) options exist.

An *issue action program* involves elements of communication and of the corporate behavior campaign designed to correct a given situation. It begins with the setting of goals and the discussion of strategies necessary to effect the desired change. Here the matrix comes into full effect, because a variety of disciplines are needed to determine the nature of the corporate response. This process lays the foundation for determining the targeted audiences, designing messages, and selecting channels that are helpful in reaching the audience. All of this is monitored to determine whether the campaign is meeting its goals.

According to Ewing (1980), the Allstate system developed in conjunction with Yankelovich, Skelly, and White contains stages that correspond to the natural evolution of issues. The first stage, public dissatisfaction, stems from "the belief that a right is being ignored." During this stage, a sense of uneasiness begins to grow among the public that some aspect of corporate performance is not meeting public expectations. The second stage occurs when dissatisfaction gets a name and becomes focused as a topic. The third stage erupts when the media pick up on the issue. (We might speculate that the second and third stages are really inseparable. In some instances the agitators give the topic a name, form it into a slogan, and give it some visibility. However, this topic visibility really doesn't become important until the topic has been established by the media. Furthermore, we might suggest that one monitoring strategy is to look at standard research guides, such as the *Business Periodicals Index* or the venerable *Reader's Guide to Periodic Literature,* to note when a topic becomes so well established that it is used to index articles. We can also estimate the extensiveness of discussion by noting the number of articles under a topic and the kinds of publications in which they are printed.)

The fourth stage that Ewing identifies occurs when pressure groups take note of the topic and add it to their list of grievances. In some instances pressure groups raise issues and give them visibility; in other instances these topics, as Ewing suggests, are developed by one or more persons and later adopted by larger pressure groups. Issues have reached an important state of maturity at the fifth stage when legislative representatives discuss the issues and formulate regulatory legislation.

As one of the major components in the monitoring process, Ewing advises issues managers to conduct private discussions with carefully selected leaders and experts sensitive to public opinion trends, particularly those below the surface of mass media visibility. Other needed information related to the company or industry can be acquired from industry sources, customer studies, existing syndicated research, focus groups, massive public opinion surveys, computer databases, video news services, and/or newsletters, books, and reports issued by special interest groups, foundations, and governmental agencies. Publications such as *TrendTrack, Issues Management Letter, Corporate Public Issues,* and materials provided by the Issues Management Association are worth reading (if you can afford them). In addition, issues managers should concentrate on the content analysis of leading newspapers to discover emerging issues and check their progress through the stages leading to legislative formulation. Ewing also suggests that public opinion is often reflected in popular entertainment sources such as plays, movies, novels, and television programs.

Moore (1979: 43, 45) defines an emerging issue as "a trend or condition, internal or external, that, if continued, would have a significant effect on how a company is operated over the period of its business plan." Moreover, he advises issues managers to determine the extent to which an issue is due to internal or external conditions and the likely impact it would have on the corporation. In addition, issues managers should determine where and how the issue will affect the company.

Issues managers are interested in discovering the beliefs and attitudes that key groups hold regarding crucial issues. Closely related to this concern is the need to know whether an issue is arising in internal or external environments (Brown, 1979: 9-18). Issues arise from several sources, the most important of which are special interest advocates, media commentators, governmental agencies, industry commentary, technical experts, community leaders, and other corporations. Any of these groups may begin to discuss an issue. A glimpse at Nabisco Brands demonstrates how companies deal with issues that directly affect their interests, even when conflict ensues with other companies inside and outside of their industry. Nabisco was involved in truck deregulation, railroad revitalization, Conrail, PCBs, food labeling, and sodium labeling. Robert M. Schaeberle, former chairman and CEO of Nabisco, believes that his company's involvement saved millions of dollars (Nagelschmidt, 1982: 18).

Naisbitt (1982) made a big splash in *Megatrends* when he projected which public opinion changes of the 1980s would dominate attention for the foreseeable future. To make these projections he used the news hole technique, which consists of monitoring changes in the proportion of news coverage devoted to specific issues. This content analysis of newspapers, magazines, and the electronic media works on the principle that the dominant public opinion issues and topics are those which command disproportionately large amounts of space and time. But any projection very far into the future is risky, despite the slow media agenda development revealed by news hole analysis.

Ewing (1979) discovered at least 150 forecasting techniques, although only a few of them are widely used. Several of these are worth attention, primarily as they estimate and project trends. *Trend extrapolation* assumes that media agendas change slowly, as do issue trends; therefore, current issues can be projected a few years into the future with a reasonable degree of reliability. Such projections are often adequate because most issues never reach the point of being formed into legislation, and those that do are subjected to a long and tedious discussion. In contrast to this slow, orderly development, some major events and disasters can have a dramatic and unpredictable effect on public policy formation.

Trend impact analysis takes advantage of the ability of computers to store and analyze vast amounts of data to project or extrapolate the short-term future. *Scanning* consists of brief summaries of issues constructed from specialized and general publications to sense trends and estimate the intensity of issue discussion. The *Delphi* technique, developed in the late 1950s by the Rand Corporation, has become increasingly popular. It is designed to draw upon expert opinion to gain a sense of developing issues. Once this information has been gathered, it is submitted to the people who were surveyed before to determine whether they agree with individual estimates of issue trends. Forced rankings are often used to allow survey members to prioritize issues. The technique minimizes the influence of any one expert while maximizing the knowledge of the collective group.

Cross-impact analysis assumes that a trend will be realized. The purpose of this technique is to estimate the ripple effect that would result. *Computer simulations* have been used to combine data gathering and trend projection. With increasing sophistication, computers can be programmed to help answer "what if" kinds of questions based on extrapolations of databases consisting of historical information that has been placed into a matrix of weighted variables. For instance, a computer projection can compare technological development, trends in public sentiment, economic condition projections, and issue extrapolations. "What if" questions can be answered by examining the impact of changes in variables. The strategy attempts to estimate the kinds of pressures and tradeoffs that will result. *Scenarios* clarify options and reduce the risk of decision making. Much like the betting odds at a race track, probabilities are assigned various outcomes ranging from highly optimistic to very pessimistic. Business managers, dependent on events, can use scenarios to estimate their likelihood (Linneman and Klein, 1985).

A recent development of interest is the creation in 1985 of a for-profit issues research subsidiary by the Washington, DC-based Media Institute. Known as the Communications Research Corporation (CRC), this company works with academic and commercial research firms in generating public opinion research and to complement privately sponsored content analyses and survey research. For issues managers, CRC offers a useful, comprehensive service that allows clients to see what selected media outlets actually say (content analysis) and to track how those messages are understood by and affect the attitudes of readers and viewers (survey research).

Among the keys to successful survey techniques, says Lindenmann (1977), is knowing what the study is supposed to discover, which populations are to be included, and how to be systematic in both developing and executing the instrument and reporting the data. In addition to identifying where the issues are arising and what potential they have for maturing into legislation, tracking may discover how serious various segments of the public believe an issue to be. Also, the issues manager needs to know whether the target audiences hold beliefs that are untrue. Archival research can be conducted to determine whether articles that discuss the issues are based on information that can be refuted by the corporation or industry. In preparing the corporate issues response, the issues team should begin by comparing the facts as it understands them against those believed by the public and those conveyed by opponents. Such research may include candid diagnostic studies of the company's strengths and weaknesses. After investigating the corporation's or industry's performance and comparing it to public expectations of social responsibility, corporate goals or behavior may need to be changed to conform more closely with these expectations. If the corporation is behaving as it must to achieve its corporate and social goals, a communication campaign can be designed to help targeted publics understand the company's point of view.

Companies probably cannot communicate themselves out of problems by simply proclaiming that they comply with public expectations.

The first test of performance is action, which still speaks louder than words. Consequently, corporations should make every effort to let the public know what they are doing to comply with the highest standards of corporate responsibility. In 1975, internal auditors of Levi-Strauss & Co. discovered an illegal overseas payment of $75,000. Rather than cover up the incident, Levi decided to make a full disclosure, as prescribed in its corporate policy. This action demonstrated that even though the corporate code of ethics had not prevented the indiscretion, Levi would tighten controls to prevent its repetition. The press covered this incident in a most favorable way (Steckmest, 1982: 61).

Several companies have structured communication campaigns based on their special expertise to provide valuable public information. Pfizer Pharmaceutical Company has run a series of advertisements that discuss symptoms of major diseases. While building patient goodwill and establishing product credibility, the advertising is also informative on an issue of widespread potential interest. Perhaps the most successful service-to-humanity campaign was the "Shell answer man." Shell discovered that many otherwise informed people did not understand even simple facts about automobile maintenance, repair, and safety. A series of focused pamphlets packaged useful tips, suggestions, and little-known facts. Public response helped make it one of the longest running programs in advertising history. Survey public opinion tracking shows that Shell consistently ranks as one of the most respected companies in the industry, far higher than the more aggressive Mobil. Phillips Petroleum adopted a performance focus to emphasize how its diverse range of products serves humanity in ways far beyond the typical automobile fuel and service station market. Like Shell, Phillips designed its campaign to demonstrate the company's commitment to serving the best interests of society—for profit, of course.

Monitoring is vital to corporate planning, to meeting standards of corporate responsibility, and to laying a foundation for issues communication. A case study reveals how a communication campaign by Bethlehem Steel arose from its monitoring of public opinion. In late 1975, following the direction of its Public Affairs Department management, Bethlehem isolated six issues central to its future: capital formation, environment, energy supply, foreign trade, overregulation of business, and business concentration. Bethlehem decided that one component would be an advocacy effort targeted at an audience of "opinion-leading influentials; 35 to 64 years old; professional-managerial; upscale; $20,000 annual income or above; active politically and/or in the community—those people to whom Federal and state legislators, governmental agency heads, and others look when taking the national pulse" (Latshaw, 1977: 28). Three issues survived the planning and analysis process: capital formation, environment, and energy.

To assess effectiveness, Bethlehem surveyed 4000 readers of the media used in the campaign. Part of this precampaign study was designed to determine audience response to the company position. Those in favor could be reinforced and activated to assist in the campaign. The neutrals and mildly against could be educated or informed. Through segmenting the audience by issue and comparing changes in attitude versus the cost of advertising, Bethlehem was able to quantify changes in attention and readership for its advocacy advertising created per dollar spent.

ISSUES COMMUNICATION CAMPAIGN

The communication campaign is integral to the total issues management process. Issues communication can be divided into two phases. The first is designed to prevent an issue from becoming engrained in the public mentality to the extent that it begins to demand legislative remedy. This phase is preventative, trying to help the public understand a company or industry, demonstrating corporate social responsibility, and countering false information and charges. An advantage to a successful preventative campaign is that its costs are tax deductible. The costs of a grassroots information campaign are deductible until legislation is pending; under current IRS interpretation, once the campaign undertakes grassroots lobbying asking the public to participate, the costs are no longer deductible. The second phase of the communication campaign is devoted to countering legislation as it develops and is lobbied through Congress. This is more difficult, since the opposition has been clarified and one faces a greater likelihood of losing. Many more advantages accrue from pro-active prevention of agitational controversies.

The five bits of advice that O'Toole (1975b) gives in his seminal article on advocacy advertising remain relevant today. First, he advised sponsoring companies to communicate clearly so that the identity of the company becomes part of the issue stance. Second, he insisted that dialogue with the public should begin long before the company is put under siege. Third, the campaign "*should be based on a healthy respect for the reader's intelligence.*" Fourth, the campaign position must interest readers and listeners and relate to their self-interests. Fifth, measurements should be used to test the effectiveness of the campaign (O'Toole 1975b: 16). One of the difficulties in the design of issues communication messages is avoiding a note of self-serving stridency. Moreover, issues communication is at times not inherently attention-gaining for large numbers of people until a crisis breaks out and companies no longer have the luxury of releasing information in a calm climate.

Mendelsohn (1973) has argued that information campaigns can be effective when they (1) provide information in a neutral environment, (2) show people that they know less than they thought, and (3) give information that the audience perceives to be valuable. This is not so surprising, since on an interpersonal level we tend to make friends of those people we share interests with and can talk to.

In a 1983 series of op-eds, Mobil used a version of these strategies. The basic question addressed was, "Just how profitable is oil?" At the top of each of the advertisements in the series, Mobil posed a true-false quiz. For instance, the statement, "Oil companies make a large volume of dollars," was immediately followed by the answer, "That's true." However, the response to "Oil companies are therefore very profitable" was, "That's false." The content of the advertisement was designed to prove these propositions. In a second advertisement, Mobil proposed: "In 1981, the 25 leading U.S. oil companies spent $44 billion, up from $33 billion the year before, to try to find and produce oil and natural gas around the world." In this case the anwer was, "That's true." The second statement was: "Two-thirds of those investments were made right here in the United States," followed by "Also true." The rest of the quiz ran:

> But the payout in oil and gas is so great that such huge sums can be risked safely, producing almost surefire big profits. That's false, even though a lot of people seem to believe it. The oil industry, despite all its complaining about high taxes, could afford to pay more. Also false, and there is a real danger of killing the goose in the quest for more golden eggs.

This strategy was used to introduce the other advertisements in the series. Such a strategy is attention-gaining; most people enjoy quizzes. Once readers think an answer is correct, they may be more receptive to information that confirms or disconfirms their prior beliefs.

SETTING CAMPAIGN GOALS

In preparing the communication campaign, issues communicators should objectively assess what the campaign should accomplish and design it to achieve specific goals rather than unfocused ones. The campaign objectives must arise out of and reinforce carefully defined corporate goals. A campaign that does not focus on specific objectives is doomed to failure from the outset.

Many times issues can be managed through layers of goals; in this regard, we can imagine a complex system containing many goals that coalesce around some major objective. For instance, the major goal of a campaign could be to defeat some piece of legislation or to seek amendments to make it as reasonable as possible. However, this is too global to be of much strategic advantage. As subordinate goals, the issues campaign team may strive to form coalitions, increase the understanding of targeted audiences, and mobilize grassroots resources. Goals may be established to provide specific kinds of information and to achieve desired levels of understanding on the part of targeted publics; other goals may focus on a desired attitude change. Still others relate to the level of commitment sought during mobilization. Each goal must be stated in terms of specific outcomes. For instance: (1) Bring three industry groups and two special interest groups together into a coalition, (2) create a public awareness among key segments of the population regarding the costs that will arise from unwise legislation, (3) time the implementation of the legislation so that state-of-the-art technology can be used to solve the technical problems, or (4) have targeted publics believe that voluntary corrective actions will solve the problem.

Campaigns should be sensitive to the needs and interests of the targeted audiences and make statements that are credible. Campaign planners should be objective when defining what message is going to be presented to what audience with what intended effect. The IAA reports that public relations and advertising agencies often have trouble helping corporate managers realize that in many instances they are communicating a message that they want heard rather than one that the public wants to hear. Because of the tendency to want to blame misunderstanding on ill-informed statements by special interest groups and the media, corporate communicators may have difficulty acknowledging that their company must first level with the public. As we observed in Chapter 5, the self-analysis of a social audit is an important tool, having implications not only for codes of conduct but also communication design:

> In an effort to bring discipline to the task of establishing objectives and measuring performance, some business theorists have advocated use of a "social audit," an analysis of a company's socio-economic contributions and definition, in terms of accepted norms, of what its immediate and long-term objectives should be. The procedure permits construction of an acceptable idealistic base for future corporate conduct, including communications in relations to society [Stridsberg, 1977: 75].

Such a plan makes corporate issue management more than fire fighting. It acknowledges the importance of maintaining a dialogue with the public. Such a long-term commitment may go far toward establishing a platform of information that is available during periods of crisis when corporate sponsors are under attack. It can forestall the criticism that companies only appeal to the public when they are being picked on by the media, agitators, or regulators. In conducting an audit, the International Association of Business Communicators (IABC) suggests that many companies start with the "zero-base" assumption that no communication program exists and that the public requires certain kinds of information. This approach is designed to underpin an extended communication campaign that does more than fight fires. It requires that companies determine what information the public requires and that they make a commitment to get that information to the people (Reuss and Silvis, 1981: 52-61).

Insight into the manner in which people receive and process information helps us understand how to set campaign goals and design messages. Issues managers should realize that receivers tend to accept what they want to learn about corporations and reject what they do not want to know or believe. Breaking through the barriers of doubt and refutation can be one of the most difficult tasks in the design of issues communication. Advocates of social judgment theory (Sherif and Hovland, 1961; Sherif et al., 1965; Sherif and Sherif, 1969) postulate that people encounter ideas through latitudes of acceptance, rejection, or noncommitment. These latitudes lead individuals to filter, distort, and ignore information that does not confirm their attitudes, including those toward corporations. Consequently, people who champion corporations and the role they play in our capitalistic society will accept (and may even seek) confirming information. These individuals will likely excuse most instances of corporate misbehavior because "you can't make an omelette without breaking an egg," or they will ignore certain information as false tales told by a biased media. McAdams (1981) uses a different homily: "You can't have your cake and eat it too." In contrast, those people who question the performance of companies willingly accept facts that confirm this predisposition. People who have negative attitudes toward corporations are ripe for information that can lead to regulatory constraints. Moreover, in addition to the facts that these individuals hold, they and their pro-business counterparts have a complex of values regarding the wisdom of regulating corporations.

Anchoring attitudes and values change over time, bringing about new standards of what the public will accept or reject (Rokeach, 1968, 1974; Heath, 1976). Previous to the 1960s and 1970s, consumers were usually considered to be "careless" or "foolish" if they were harmed while using a product. Now the tables have turned and public value systems hold corporations responsible. For instance, until recently parents were responsible for safeguarding their children. Then public interest groups successfully argued that the manufacturers of children's apparel should use flame-retardant fabric. When values change, the probability of regulation increases.

During campaign planning, issue information is designed to confirm the attitudes of some targeted groups and to change the attitudes of others. Reaching noncommitted segments of the population is often difficult because they may have no incentive to learn information about the issues or images involved in a particular campaign. The noncommitted may become aware of an issue and realize the need to have an informed opinion only after special interest groups and the media have made the issues salient. Moreover, issues managers should realize that attitudes do not always coincide with behavior (Gross and Niman, 1975). Although many people are critical of corporate performance, only the most ego-involved will take direct action to impose changes on companies.

Seminal work by Fishbein and his associates (Fishbein, 1967; Fishbein and Ajzen, 1975, 1980) offers a foundation for understanding human cognition and judgment which we can use to sharpen campaign design. According to this line of reasoning, individuals receive and process information into propositions that consist of two components: attitudes (the evaluative part of cognition) and beliefs (degrees of certainty). Each proposition is a belief and is measured by the extent to which it is believed to be true. To each belief is attached an attitude. Additionally, we can conceive of each statement as having a weight that is an estimate of its importance in the total cognitive structure. This approach to cognition assumes that individuals (or targeted groups) may believe many propositions about a company, product, service, industry, or issue, and that they will have many accompanying attitudes. All of these components form the total, complex opinion regarding the policies, products, or services of a corporation or industry. The advantage of the approach is its ability to help issues managers decompose complex issues or images (Denhow and Culbertson, 1985).

Using *hypothetical data* typical of the 1970s oil crisis, we can illustrate the connections among these components to show how a campaign manager can dissect opinions and identify which may be used, which must be changed, and which are irrelevant to the campaign. For the purposes of this illustration, "BS" refers to belief strength. "A" stands for attitude, which consists of two components: direction [positive (+), negative (–), or neutral (o)] and strength. The third ingredient, "I," estimates how important the proposition is in the decision. (We assume the use of Likert scales 1-7.) The context of these cognitions would be the likely impact of certain beliefs, attitudes, and important on the willingness to favor regulation.

	BS	A	I
Oil companies sell gasoline.	7	+5	2
They sell lubricants for automobiles.	7	+5	2
They spend millions exploring for crude.	5	+6	3
They receive unreasonably high profits.	7	−7	7
They pollute the environment around drilling sites.	7	−7	7
They control the market for their products.	7	−7	7
They provide chemical products which help save lives.	4	+7	2
They offer excellent investment opportunities.			
They are excellent companies to work for.	5	+5	1

All of the statements shown here combine to produce a total opinion toward oil companies. By playing with this purely hypothetical matrix, we can decompose the opinions of a population segment. The matrix helps us plot strategies for opinion change and gives us insight into which components are likely to result in regulation. Obviously, the negative components with high importance will support the effort to regulate the industry. If the campaign manager decides to provide information on product value or the company's support of the arts, it may do little to prevent regulation. The public assumes that wealthy oil companies make good products and a high profit; therefore, they should support the arts. But all of that good does not offset the behavior by the oil companies that does not match public standards of corporate social responsibility. The matrix reveals that the targeted population has strong beliefs on some positive statements, but they lack importance in the decision matrix. The strategic design could then attempt to do the following:

(1) Persuade (weaken belief) the public that oil companies do not control market prices. Since this information is in the self-interest of the companies, they have, as perceived by the audience, the incentive to lie. Because of this source credibility problem, the information could be rejected.
(2) Convince the audience that controlling prices is good, which is hardly feasible.
(3) Decrease the importance of the statement, which is hard to do for people who are waiting in line to buy gasoline that costs more than it did recently.

Other strategic choices include giving an alternative explanation for why gasoline prices have soared; in this regard, some companies played on the xenophobia of the audience by blaming the price increase on foreign (OPEC) control of the oil market. Finally, as many oil companies did, the issue could be ignored on the assumption that little positive can be done to correct false judgment, and that the issue will eventually correct itself or the public opinion environment will eventually demand new operating principles. This discussion makes apparent the complexity of opinions that allow individuals to applaud some company actions while demanding the regulation of others. Thus, for instance, individuals can believe that oil companies provide valuable products and are worthy investments and yet still prefer that they be made environmentally responsible.

Such a decision about the oil industry and its regulation is complex. Beyond the opinions surrounding the oil companies themselves, we can imagine some combination of beliefs and attitudes relating to the regulation of the industry. For instance we could imagine the following statements:

- Oil companies can provide needed products without making enormous profits and without being harmful to the environment.
- Oil companies' profits should be regulated.
- Oil companies should be heavily taxed (windfall profit tax).
- Oil companies should be stopped from polluting.
- Oil companies should be broken up to increase competition.
- The federal government should nationalize the oil industry.

Each of these statements could support regulation. Some people, according to social judgment theory, would applaud the regulation because it is consonant with a negative attitude toward oil companies. Others would reject the propositions of regulation. Still others would be noncommittal toward regulation.

By segmenting the population and selecting targeted audiences according to their opinions, issues managers can effectively design messages to have maximum impact. By approaching issues this way, campaign managers can isolate beliefs that need to be strengthened, weakened, or changed. Communicators can attempt to change attitudes attached to the beliefs or alter the weight of belief/attitude statements. Statements that do not count much for the campaign can be isolated, such as "oil companies provide lubricants." Even though the statement is widely and strongly believed, and despite the fact that it is viewed as positive, it does not counterbalance issues relating to high profits, control of market prices, or environmental impact. When the oil companies told the public that drilling/exploration costs were enormous in an attempt to justify high profits, the public tended to agree with the high cost notion but did not believe that this justified big profits. The information did not explain away what was believed to be true and what was held against the companies. Explaining to the public that environmental control is difficult and costly may not produce sympathy but rather the reaction, "So work harder!" The information integration matrix reminds issues managers that human cognition is a complex system that draws together many competing and conflicting bits of information. How it turns out determines what people are willing to accept in terms of the regulation of industry.

The public's desire for regulation can be understood by realizing that people make decisions in an effort to maximize their gains and minimize their losses. For either of these reasons, segments of the public may favor or oppose regulation. Typically, the most powerful incentive for regulation occurs when individuals are attempting to minimize their losses. Such incentives have come in the form of protection against asbestos, acid rain, visual or air pollution, noise, dangerous toys, flammable garments, or cars that are "unsafe at any speed."

Insight into the human decision process is invaluable in the design of survey instruments and the selection of communication strategies (Shelby, 1985). A viable understanding of human decision making can help issues managers divide their task into specific, measurable objectives. The execution of a campaign should be conducted from a game plan that identifies the goals to be achieved, the audiences to be reached, the strategies to be applied, the cost of the campaign (including media buys), and the tasks of specific personnel.

DESIGNATION OF TARGETED AUDIENCES

To decide which audiences to target, issues managers should determine what each group believes, how crucial that belief is to the management of issues, and what interest each group has in supporting or opposing legislation. Stressing the value of this analysis, Garbett (1981: 156) advises:

> It is essential to understand the current climate and environment within which the corporation operates. This environment can be as broad as the total population with its multitude of social factors, changing trends, and public views on issues that relate to the company. Or it can be as narrow as current trends within the specific industry in which the corporation is engaged. Whatever the scope of the examination, a solid understanding of current events as they relate to the corporation is a must.

One of the most valued audiences an issues campaign can target consists of people who have a vested interest in the success of the company and industry. The campaign must identify these "stakeholders" (Brown, 1979: 18). During the 1983 campaign against the 10 percent withholding tax on savings accounts, the sponsors of the campaign realized that anyone with a savings account was a stakeholder. Moreover, the campaign was successful in large part because it identified the outcome of the campaign with the self-interest of its targeted audiences. Many other groups of stakeholders can be targeted, such as stockholders and members of the professional financial community, especially stock analysts and brokers. Business supporters are important groups; some, such as chambers of commerce, offer potentially well positioned advocates against unnecessary regulation. Labor groups are also important audiences because they often represent a community of interest that could be detrimentally affected by dramatic changes in the operating requirements of their industries. Elected and appointed government officials must receive fact sheets and issue papers so that they can be well informed regarding the implications of pending legislation. Fear tactics, unless they are closely associated with public interests, are likely to have minimal effect. Facts are compelling for legislators and their staffs, who must be able to make reasonable and well-informed decisions if they are to resist the political pressures created by special interest groups.

Many coalitions within and outside of an industry are possible. Skillfully managed, coalitions can even be created with reasonable and moderate representatives of special interest groups who are advocating change. If corporations take a pro-active, rather than a defensive, attitude toward advocates of change, they may be able to achieve regulation that meets their interests *and* those of the agitators (or perhaps avoid it entirely). Despite their antagonism, members of special interest groups should be considered as targeted audiences. At the same time, corporate leaders must expect to compromise if they expect to develop effective working relationships with special interest advocates.

Using their increasing skills at audience segmentation, issues managers can identify and target audiences according to such factors as geographical location, age, sex, and issue position and involvement. Very little research has been made public regarding what roles specific segments of the population play in public policy formation. Voter profiles offer the most helpful guidelines for audience segmentation.

In the segmentation of audiences, most corporations overlook children because they are not yet qualified to vote and they do not constitute a cohesive power block. Nevertheless, a few companies have seen the younger segment of the population as fertile ground for explaining the nature and virtues of free enterprise. Because of the important role of primacy effects, corporations are advised to acquaint this young public with the nature of free enterprise and the details relating to the operation of corporations and their environments.

A most valuable audience comprises the employees of the corporation, the industry, and related industries who have an obvious vested interest in the outcome of policy formation and regulation (Burton, 1976). Despite the obvious importance of involving employees in corporate activities, Opinion Research Corporation (ORC) data led Morgan and Schiemann (1983) to conclude that employees believe that the quality of internal communication is deteriorating. Even at the management level, employees report that they do not get the information they need to represent the company and understand its policies and expectations. Many innovative methods have been tried, including video and meetings with executives (Farinelli, 1977). Sun Oil's SUN-PAC provides political education for its employees (Burton, 1976).

Examining employee-external environment communication, Grunig (1978) discovered that people who have constant contact with the public may have a distorted view of the public's attitudes toward a company. Moreover, he argues, unless extraordinary effort is exerted, very little accurate information flows from management to employee or from employee to management. The individuals with the most accurate information about the public's attitudes toward the company are those who are minimally involved with the public and who have to exert extra effort to find such information. These individuals are also the ones least likely to serve as liaisons with the public.

Rather than assisting employee efforts to earnestly and accurately report on the quality of their corporations, some companies have punished employees who have first attempted to report information to management and then publicly disclosed infractions of law, ethics, and/or policy. Despite the obvious advantages to be gained by building employees into the advocacy team, many companies take the stance that employees must be mute regarding corporate mistakes. Otten (1984) concludes: "Slowly but steadily, states are beginning to protect employees who blow the whistle on dangerous or improper business behavior." Even Mobil, which has been one of the most strident advocates for open corporate communication, settled out of court with an employee who had been fired as being incompetent after reporting two toxic chemical accidents at Mobil's Environmental Health and Sciences Laboratory. Such incidents demonstrate the inconsistency between corporate policy and behavior and counteract efforts to involve employees in efforts to achieve corporate social responsibility. Provisions in the Mine Safety and Health Act, the Toxic Substances Control Act, the Occupational Safety and Health Act, and the Water Pollution Control Act protect workers who report violations. Some companies, such as IBM, Bank of America, and the Prudential Insurance Company have established programs to protect employee reports of corporate mistakes.

Political education for employees is a valuable part of the corporate communication program. Edward A. Grefe (Nagelschmidt, 1982) proposes that corporations establish legislative and political support systems. Such systems would help people learn how to write letters to legislators, conduct meetings with officials, and testify in behalf of the company. Naturally, the persons who are involved in the key roles in this system must be carefully selected. Keeping everyone accurately informed and carefully coordinated thus becomes a difficult but vital issues management task. Grefe offers an example to demonstrate how the system works. Employees were involved in a grassroots effort to defeat an attempt by OSHA to require chemical companies to place labels on containers indicating the formula of the product. The company believed that this practice would cause companies to go out of business, thus eliminating jobs, and the employees fought the requirement.

Because of their gatekeeping function, media reporters and broadcast managers are often targeted audiences who make major decisions regarding what information gets to the public and how it will be phrased. Media leaders have a substantial impact on the issues agenda because they decide the content of the news and how much of the news hole each item receives. They create a version of reality by telling people what to think about (McCombs, 1977). Most issues managers recognize that media representatives pride themselves on their objectivity, even though they respond to trends in news stories. And they have their own perspectives on issues that govern what is said and how the information is presented. Not only do these persons inject their opinions into the presentation of the news, but they are also influenced by the news policy of the organization for which they work. For example, investigative reporters seek stories about corporate and industry failure to comply with standards of public acceptance.

To deal with this power and to correct the perceived bias that reporters have against business, issues communicators frequently address the press in an attempt to build a platform of understanding. One of the most important responsibilities of corporate communicators is to be sure that the press receives acccurate and reliable information to enable it to cut through the enormous flood of information available today (Finn, 1981). Issues communicators often provide information that may help media reporters understand the corporation's point of view and operations. In this way, media leaders help form what the public holds as its standards of acceptable corporate behavior. Nevertheless, the discussion between the press and business sometimes becomes a battle.

Attempts to inform media leaders and to reinforce their commitment to fair and informed reportage have been made by corporate representatives such as Tom P. McAdams (1981), chairman of the board, Independent Petroleum Association of America, and Herbert Schmertz (1983a, b) of Mobil. In a similar fashion, Robert W. Lundeen (1983), chairman of the board, Dow Chemical Company, was the keynote speaker at the annual Business Journalism Awards banquet of the Interstate National Gas Association at the University of Missouri in Columbia. He took as his theme the words of Thomas Jefferson, who had come to believe that "nothing can now be believed which is seen in a newspaper." The relevance of this observation was the gap between the "media elite" and the "business elite." Lundeen observed: "A very wide cultural gap lies between working journalists in newspapers, television and radio and most, if not all, industrial executives and professionals." The problem is that "neither side quite understands what the other is up to. Neither side quite trusts the other. And so there is hostility."

This gap translates into divergent perceptions. Dow executives see themselves as savvy, competent, and responsible, but when they read about themselves they get a picture of "arrogant polluters, insensitive to the health of their own workers, of consumers of their products and of plant neighbors." One problem is the expectation by journalists that business problems have simple solutions. Lundeen begged the press to doublecheck facts and to seek them from a variety of sources. He asked writers to try to understand that the company is not inherently evil and therefore should not immediately be approached with suspicion. He championed a dialogue but encouraged writers "to get it right and then tell it right so that 235 million Americans can judge it right." Another corporate representative, T. M. Ford (1984), CEO of Emhart, spoke as he received the 1984 Leadership Award for excellence in communication from the International Association of Business Communicators. His theme centered on the cooperation that can exist between corporations and professional communicators in their efforts to increase the quality of communication. Such messages may build a more supportive climate for corporations.

In addition to speaking before audiences of communicators, companies have targeted journalists by using trade publications. A brief glance through the March/April 1985 issue of *Columbia Journalism Review* reveals a variety of advertisements on the theme of writer/company cooperation. State Farm Insurance Companies volunteered to help writers understand the technical, specialized language of its industry. The American Trucking Associations Foundation claimed that rather than heavy trucks, the real causes of potholes are "weather, chemicals, erosion, traffic, age, and construction defects." And the Association of American Railroads argued for reduced regulation of its industry. It claimed:

> Until 1980 our nation's freight railroads were not allowed to share in the benefits of a free market. A noose of federal regulations choked the railroads for nearly 100 years. The effect of this government stranglehold was predictable: During the 1970's, railroads filed for bankruptcy at an alarming rate, affecting 22% of the nation's rail mileage.

Release from these pressures had come from the 1980 Staggers Rail Act, which now, the association worried, some wanted to "fine tune." The plea was for less regulation in order to be able to exercise the free enterprise system. (This ad was also circulated in business publications such as the *Wall Street Journal.*) Several companies, such as Dow Chemical and Phillips Petroleum, listed their information telephone numbers. Ads such as these are targeted at the media, one of the most influential issues audiences.

Throughout the planning stages, issues managers should realize that their task involves power resource management. Therefore, one of the objectives of the campaign must be the formation of coalitions. Shrewd issues managers attempt to find other corporations interested in a common issue; together they present a stronger case, particularly during the lobbying effort that may result during the development of issues. Edith Fraser (Nagelschmidt, 1982) points to two obvious advantages of forming coalitions: Numbers count and coalitions save money. Hundreds of coalitions are registered in the *Congressional Quarterly*. Fraser points to the steel industry's effective formation of a coalition of environmentalists, labor, and government in support of the Clean Air Act (in Nagelschmidt, 1982: 192-199). By trying to use coalitions, which may include critics of corporate behavior, issues managers minimize the adversarial relationship that is often inherent in combating the opposition. In 1981 the National Association of Realtors and the National Automotive Dealers Association worked together to seek lower interest rates. Such cooperation may produce superior pieces of legislation that balance many competing interests. Legislative contact is crucial, requiring efforts to provide facts and draft legislation to help in the formation of bills.

To assist issues managers, Fraser offers 20 items helpful for forming coalitions. Such efforts begin with a definition of the problems and issues and the selection of specific issue(s) to be focused on. Allies and opponents must also be identified. A game plan is then devised that decides how all of the participants will be attracted to the coalition and involved in the issues management process. The coalition effort must have budget support as well. The coalition should use poll results to keep itself informed of its progress and of public reaction to it. Experts are valuable for conducting polls and identifying issues, and for developing position statements. Fraser believes that a broadbased communication effort is best, one that communicates with as many constituencies through as many channels as possible. Many of the members of the coalition thus become channels of communication. Finally, the coalition must evaluate its results and communicate them to the member constituencies. Fraser cautions issues managers to remember that "a coalition is effective only when its issue has merit and the coalition members are organized, informed, and conscientious enough to communicate the worthiness of the effort" (Nagelschmidt, 1982: 194-197).

AUDIENCES IN TIMES OF CRISIS

Issues managers should have two major game plans, one for long-range objectives and one for crises. Many crises do not involve an issue—such as the Tylenol tampering involving Johnson & Johnson. However, if Johnson & Johnson and other companies had not proactively undertaken measures (partly out of avoiding liability and partly as marketing strategies) to provide tamper-proof packaging, legislation was likely. Because of the responsible behavior evidenced in this situation, the issue was not viewed as the result of a problem that would not be corrected by voluntary action.

Some crises do, however, provide evidence that an issue needs attention. The Three Mile Island nuclear generating plant incident increased national concern over the safety of such facilities, which brought pressure on the Nuclear Regulatory Commission. This incident produced a domino effect involving increased regulation of existing plants as well as those under construction. Some safety features were retrofitted onto existing plants to bring them up to the new levels of safe operation. Recognizing the difficulty of handling crises, Ressler (1982) advises issues managers to have a clear picture of corporate goals and access to the management personnel who must authorize the campaign. Crisis response strategies must be designed to provide accurate information as quickly as possible, and the image of the company and its industry is crucial to how a crisis can be handled. If a climate of trust has existed between the public and a company, a crisis is easier to redirect than if the public has been concerned about the company and if the crisis adds to this apprehension.

The primary objective of handling crises is to provide accurate information as quickly as possible. Employees need information, particularly if safety is a factor, and customers need to know if product safety or reliability is at issue. The crisis management team needs to send letters to shareholders if the crisis is important enough to threaten their investments. Shareholders of the corporation and of other corporations in the industry (and related industries) may have reason to become involved in a campaign. However, involving shareholders must be handled with delicacy. If a horror story is presented that hyperbolizes the implications that regulation will have on investments, rather than joining the campaign, shareholders may simply sell their shares and look for less risky investments.

Audiences are particularly attentive during times of crisis. This situation offers special opportunities to communicate and demonstrate the corporation's commitment to responsible behavior. Stephenson (1982) demonstrates how Dow Chemical turned a crisis to its advantage. Two train derailments (Mississauga, Ontario, in November 1979 and MacGregor, Manitoba, in March 1980) brought attention to Dow products which were being transported by rail. Dow took the opportunity to explain some of the properties of these products along with the safety procedures that were taken to ensure that no one was harmed. Gold (1982) proposes an issue/conflict prevention strategy that companies can use to assist people who are making major changes in their lives because of actions taken by companies. He illustrates this strategy by discussing how the Cyprus Mining Corporation lessened its impact on the lives of people in Challis, Idaho. The company created a boomtown effect when it opened a molybdenum mining project near town. Fearing that this dramatic change would produce negative local reactions, Cyprus provided direct, personal access to company officials who could keep the townspeople well informed. The corporate representatives were familiar with the community and sympathized with its concerns. The company brought in consultants to help the community accommodate its rapid growth, and the company took a leadership role in planning for the changes in the community's schools and infrastructure. Many local enterprises were encouraged to do business with Cyprus.

When coping with crisis, Ressler (1982) advises companies to make themselves available to the press immediately and to announce their findings on the situation as soon as possible. Each day's delay allows public suspicions to increase. As the investigation continues, the company should issue progress reports. After the crisis is under control, the company should announce the measures it will take to prevent similar occurrences.

MESSAGE CONTENT AND DESIGN

The content of advocacy messages can be narrowed into three overlapping categories: propositions of fact, propositions of value, and propositions of policy. The first are characterized by statements which are verifiable and objective; the second involve judgments of right and wrong. The last type should support the corporate interest to provide the best products and services in harmony with the public interest. Each of these propositions is instrumental in building understanding between the public and private enterprise.

To prevent misunderstanding, which in turn leads to unnecessary regulation, many corporations have attempted to provide a platform of fact. A review suggests the diversity of issues discussed. These samples reveal how companies and trade associations provide insight into business problems and requirements:

—the profit margin on a gallon of gasoline
—the cost of drilling for oil and gas
—costs and problems involved in generating and transmitting electricity
—costs of overregulation
—inaccuracies in the windfall profit tax controversy
—the impact of regulation on housing costs
—efforts of the railroad industry to increase productivity
—the likelihood of an electricity shortage

Such ads, whatever their purpose, provide information relevant to the operation of companies and industries.

In addition to facts, many ads discuss value issues. These ads may supply information about the ways in which a company conforms to standards of acceptable corporate behavior. Other advertisements take stands on certain values related to corporate requirements, usually emphasizing some aspect of free enterprise. Such ads may blend image and issue, as in the case of good neighbor ads used by energy companies. These seek to demonstrate that they comply with, and ostensibly champion, good corporate citizenship. By far the most prevalent values discussed are, in glittering generality, the virtues of the free enterpise system. Examples of value advertisements illustrate the kinds of positions discussed:

—virtues of incentive and free enterprise
—arguments favoring profit incentive
—virtues of companies' having access to electronic media to discuss controversial issues

—virtues of achievement and incentive
—virtues of working together to solve problems
—the value of large companies solving large problems
—the value of volunteerism in price cutting

It is impossible to apply standards of verifiability to value issues. However, as information such advertisements reveal what companies stress as being essential to productivity, profitability, and progress. Such ads compare the consequences of regulation, for instance, by pitting profits against safety or pollution. One of the major rhetorical advantages of value appeals is their ability to offer common ground with the public through the identification of common interests.

Based on the interaction of fact and value, some issue ads argue policy. The logic is this: If certain facts are true and if certain values prevail, a policy is reasonable or unreasonable. Some ads combine fact, value, and policy; others focus on only one or two of the parts. As information, policy ads give the public a view of the reasonableness of a policy and its impact. Most policy ads deal with problems of regulation. The overlap between fact and value gets us squarely at the importance of propositions of policy, as evidenced in the following examples:

—virtues of deregulation
—the value of regulation in the trucking industry
—unfairness of federal legislation affecting Bell Telephone
—the need for cutbacks in government spending
—support for air quality legislation
—criticism of regulations which give unfair competitive advantages in the loan industry
—the need for changes in domestic mineral exploration policy
—the need to unleash the oil industry

Such policy positions are subject to disagreement by opponents and supply-targeted audiences with information about the advantages and disadvantages of specific regulation.

Policy statements appear to be most persuasive when they consider the self-interest of the public as well as companies. Special interest groups build their cases by arguing that corporate behavior conflicts with the public interest. Factual and objective rebuttal, along with a discussion of the consequences of unwise regulation, can counterbalance special interest claims better than emotional appeals regarding corporate survival or character attacks on the leaders of special interest groups.

Many companies have begun to realize the advantages of reporting efforts to comply with public expectations of corporate social responsibility. To increase the impact and credibility of such reports, Cowen and Segal (1981) suggest that companies should establish a foundation for understanding why they behave as they do, and to balance their statements to show their success while acknowledging any transgressions. Over time, companies should become able to document in accounting terms the success or failure of their efforts at achieving corporate responsibility. For instance, they may report the number of barrels of oil conserved by implementing new operating techniques. Or they might report the amount of pollutants removed from the air or the positive effects of employee safety measures. The point is that corporate constituencies, like most audiences, appreciate a carefully documented case concerning the efforts corporations are making to meet public expectations (Cowen and Segal, 1981: 15-16).

Standard propaganda tricks such as transference, card stacking, and name calling may be so transparent that when the public sees through them, they do more harm than if they had not been presented at all. Moreover, strident advertisements may bait the opposition into a response that demands a counterresponse and/or public debate. All of this entanglement may have the residual effect of discrediting the combatants. "Audience receptivity [acknowledges] that the attitudes a person already possesses, combined with the information already available to him, affect how he [or she] will perceive new information" (Stridsberg, 1977: 70-75).

Bateman (1975) prefers corporate communication that features education rather than persuasion. Although this distinction is difficult to make, such an approach follows the sage advice that corporations increase likelihood of success if they provide valuable information rather than merely attempting to propagandize an issue. Additionally, Bateman suggests that message impact is increased when corporations stress economics rather than emotion. Rather than presenting themselves as bleeding martyrs of governmental regulations, corporations are likely to have more success when the targeted public receives information regarding the economic consequences of pending legislation. Issues communicators should build their campaigns on the least hostile ground and repeat a central theme (Bateman, 1975: 8-9).

Stridsberg (1977) discovered that controversy advertising utilizes a variety of themes and messages: (1) Some advertisements are used to correct misinformation and misunderstanding. (2) One-time reply advertisements reflect the belief "that a single statement should be sufficient to bring opponents to reason, or to rally sufficient support to overcome them. In the cases where this supposition is naive, based on conviction in a righteous cause, the advertiser may pay only cursory attention to the communications qualities of the advertisement. Such advertising tends not to succeed, nor to be remembered." (3) Some ads warn targeted publics of dire outcomes that will result if they do not support the company's cause. (4) Upon this foundation, advertisers may mobilize constituent support. (5) Industry associations may create and disseminate advertisements so that no single company's name is associated with the issue. (6) Sometimes a prominent figure is used as a spokesperson for the corporate position. (7) Advertisements may be designed for a "direct counterattack." (8) Others may offer a rational explanation that compares and contrasts both sides but draws a conclusion in favor of the corporation and industry stance. (9) Some advertisements request supporters to do something in behalf of the cause. (10) In keeping with the commitment to establish a platform of fact, this kind of campaign make a long-term commitment to providing information. "Such 'platform of fact' campaigns are generally characterized by long-term planning, continuity, access to all kinds of media, and a high degree of professionalism in their preparation. Subjects focus on how a company's products and activities link it to socioeconomic questions currently in the news, and how the company has an effect on the life of the individual." (11) When products are controversial, issue advertising and product advertising may merge. The content may indicate how the products are helpful, and safe. (12) Conversely, "an advertiser will attempt to tie a product into a fashionable controversy, in the hope of increasing its sales. When it is deliberate, this may be viewed as a cynical strategy, since it attempts to exploit public concern for selfish, short-term purposes." Whether they are cynical or naive, such advertisements usually lack credibility and undermine that of advertising displaying genuine social and economic concern (Stridsberg, 1977: 61-68).

Controversy advertising copy should be tested before it is placed into channels of dissemination. Because issue copy is different from that in corporate, product, or service advertisements, it may require special considerations. One of the reasons for the matrix organization of issues management is the need to bring together a wide variety of disciplines (and outside topic specialists) which can be utilized in the research and development of arguments and the design of copy. Once this is done, ads should be tested on focus groups to determine whether they are clear and address reasonably and believably the issue they are designed to affect.

Campaign preparation should ensure that the campaign is not talking to itself.

One of the most important considerations in the design of ad copy is whether it addresses the issues in a way that seems relevant to the audience. One of the worst mistakes an issues campaign can make is to tell the public what it already believes or acknowledges, while not addressing directly the key issues it wants answered. Such campaigns waste money because they do not accomplish valuable goals. Moreover, they work against the company's credibility because the poor design of the campaign reinforces the public sentiment that the company does not care to provide sufficient and worthwhile information. Many oil companies, during the time when they were reporting huge profits, attempted to divert public anger by arguing that oil exploration, refinement, and transportation costs a lot of money; therefore, large profits are needed. The public was unimpressed. It was willing to acknowledge these extraordinary costs, but it did not see how the enormous profits could exist if the costs were great and if the public was not charged more than the fair market value for the products.

One of the side effects of modern advocacy advertising is the increased involvement by major executives, especially CEOs, in the public discussion of major issues. Emphasizing this trend, Thompson (1981) speculated that CEOs have made enough public statements "on the unnecessary violence done to the industry in the name of public policy" to thicken substantially the *Congressional Record*. He uses data from Howard Chase to suggest that CEOs spend half of their time on "external affairs." Many corporations, such as Sperry, have launched campaigns to upgrade the ability of executives and managers to communicate publicly. In some instances this task is even written into job descriptions (Thompson, 1981: 79). A few advertisements have been presented through the words of employees. In its coal strip-mining reclamation advertisement, Gulf Oil Corporation spoke through Ben Sorrell, a Gulf Land Reclamation Supervisor who is a Navajo. The implication was that he and Gulf would be especially careful in reclaiming land where the Navajo had grazed sheep for "centuries."

CHANNEL SELECTION

Channel selection depends primarily on three factors: the audiences targeted, private media editorial standards, and the extent to which regulation permits access. Typically, the following channels are utilized:

paid advertising, sponsored articles, books, editorials, legislative position papers, CEOs' comments, sponsored public affairs programming, press releases, personal contact by key staff and management personnel, annual reports, newsletters, employee communication, and speeches. According to Cowen and Segal (1981), approximately 85 percent of all major corporations (1978 survey) use their annual reports to explain their efforts to meet their social responsibility. The most sophisticated campaigns are based on the premise that every available channel of communication must be used. Of these channels, paid advertising may be one of the least effective, if the most visible.

Using the ostensible credibility of the media, some companies have hired broadcast journalists or actors to portray a network reporter to present vital information and discuss favorable business activity. For example, the Fertilizer Institute hired Martin Agronsky to "anchor" the film, *One to Grow On*, which was designed to inform the public about the value of chemical fertilizers and to distinguish them from other kinds of chemicals targeted for regulation. Mobil used this format to present interviews of its executives discussing key energy issues, such as the one entitled *Energy at the Crossroads* which was shown on 62 stations. One danger in using this format is the potential for a hostile boomerang effect which could result when the public learns that the ostensibly neutral public affairs format is sponsored by an energy company (MacDougall, 1981).

One of the key objectives of issues communication is to have favorable information reported in typical news stories. Often, newspapers and magazines seem more willing to present bad news regarding corporations; this is probably so because good news (thereby being no "news") is expected. A recent pro-active story in the financial section of the Houston *Post* is a case in point. Utility companies have been under considerable scrutiny for the past two decades because of their desire to use coal and nuclear fuel. One of the major problems in using coal, as the American Electric Power Company argued in the 1970s, is the cost of cleaning the discharge from smokestacks. On November 25, 1984, the Houston *Post* carried a story in its financial section which extolled the efforts of New York State Electric and Gas Company's ability to build a plant that used electrostatic precipitators to clean the air. Not only was the facility notably clean, but it was built at $70 million under budget. The story proclaimed that the air cleaning equipment removed 99.86 percent of the fly ash from the flue gas, and between 90 and 95 percent of the sulfur dioxide. In addition to discussing the success story of this plant, the article explained that gas-burning plants were more popular today because of the enormous amount of regulatory requirements imposed by the Nuclear Regulatory Commission. In 1983 the commission implemented over 900 new requirements. Thus, aside from carrying information about the coal-burning facility, the article provided information on the utility industry's efforts supplied by the American Electric Reliability Council and the Edison Electric Institute. Such a news story ostensibly cost the industry no money, yet it presented details on the success of one utility and commented on the problems of government regulation.

Unlike product and service advertising, advocacy advertising relies more heavily on words than pictures. By their nature, issues topics usually require lengthy discussion not easily reduced to standard product, service, or image ad copy length. The IAA found that print media constitute a particularly well-suited environment for messages needing clarification, explanation, or argumentation, with newspaper editorial pages and financial sections also being hospitable locations for such discussions (Stridsberg, 1977: 58). For this reason, as well as the influence of the FCC's fairness doctrine, print media are used more extensively than broadcast media. Issues advertisers prefer daily newspapers (short response time to critics), specific magazines (good demographic appeal), and radio (quick/inexpensive production). Newspapers and radio also allow virtually instant modification of messages.

Some advertising practitioners believe that television should not be available for advocacy advertising. President Edward Ney of Young & Rubicam International has concluded that the broadcast media are so inherently persuasive and so subject to propaganda that they should be barred from use in public controversy, even though the problems involved in trying to visualize issues means that TV ads risk becoming "talking heads." Ney believes that issue managers would abuse the power of the electronic media. He particularly fears the use of the 30-second spot commercial, which is insufficient for a comprehensive discussion but which can be used to lead viewers to believe that they have received valuable information (Stridsberg, 1977: 60).

CAMPAIGN ASSESSMENT

The standard methodologies for campaign assessment feature pre- and post-campaign issue position comparisons. Tracking studies establish baseline information which is used to assess changes in attitudes and beliefs regarding the relevant issues. One of the most important problems in issues campaign assessment is isolating the influence of the campaign from all other variables that could produce positive or negative changes in opinion. One measure that is less subject to confounding variables is the information level. If the public knows more on the issue (platform of fact) after the campaign or at milestones during the campaign, the issues manager can more safely conclude that the campaign was a success. By taking the facts, values, and policies approach, a campaign manager can estimate the shifts in levels of fact (information), understand and appreciate what values are relevant to the issue, and understand the policy and its implications for the company, industry, and public.

The measurement of public affairs success or failure is extremely difficult. The first step in measurement is to state the desired objectives as specifically as possible—to know what is to be measured. If the campaign objectives are stated in behavioral or opinion outcomes, they constitute the foundation for assessment.

Discussing strategies for measuring effects, Grass (1977) builds a solid case for using specific rather than global questions for measuring the effects of advertising on the public perception of a company's image. Likewise, the survey should not try to encompass all of the opinions embedded in a large public policy debate. The campaign should be designed to affect attitude changes only in some of the key issues of the public policy contest. Advertising budgets and executive time do not allow the company to take a stand on every issue in the public discussion. The issues must be carefully selected to be only those most crucial; likewise, the monitoring effort to determine the success of the campaign should be narrow. The company should not be interested in how the whole public policy contest is going; rather, it should focus on essential issues.

Drawing on their involvement with tracking opinions relevant to container legislation activities, Goldman and Auh (1979) propose four population segments that are important to monitor: legislative trends; leadership surveys to determine the stands of "key bureaucrats, legislators, and influential civic and business leaders"; surveys of public opinion; and media content analysis to determine what messages are being transmitted. "The analysis of newspaper clippings on the issue was conducted to bridge the gap between the thought leaders and the general public" (Goldman and Auh, 1979: 21). The research design corresponded to the traditional communication model components: They wanted to know who was saying what to whom through what channels and with what effect. Part of the research design focused on discovering the targeted audiences by both sides of the controversy. By doing such analysis, the research disclosed which issues (recycling, litter, energy, cost/prices, and jobs) dominated the discussion. Also discovered was the fact that 61 percent of the statements contained no theme. Many of the messages were general claims that the "other" side had the facts wrong in the controversy. This kind of tracking revealed the kinds of themes proposed by specific groups; for instance, labor messages tended to concentrate on jobs, and advocates of the bill championed an end to litter. By tracking opinions and monitoring competing groups, tracking analysis can give valuable feedback.

The campaign cycle continues through several stages: *reevaluate goals, reassess strategies, redesign the campaign, select channels, execute new strategies*, and *reevaluate the corporate commitment*. This model assumes that corporate communication constantly seeks to adapt corporate behavior to standards of public expectation. Throughout the various stages and cycles of issues management, one realization stands out. Because of the overlap among corporate image, standards of corporate social responsibility, and regulation, corporations are wise to provide preventive maintenance to their reputations. If such efforts are successful, the likelihood is decreased that a legislative campaign on public policy issues will have to be waged.

7

ISSUES MANAGEMENT AND SPECIAL INTEREST GROUPS

Because systems of government work imperfectly, solutions to problems often occur only when facing a crisis or political mass mobilization by power-based organizations. Political advocacy is closely linked to social agitation and propaganda, both of which have a long historical tradition in America (Nelson, 1981). Although discordant, such public policy contests are fundamental to our power system, with special interest groups playing a particularly influential role in the issues management environment. More than 200 years after the Declaration of Independence, our nation still holds the efforts of the patriotic Founding Fathers in reverence. Even while helping frame the U.S. Constitution and its accompanying Bill of Rights, James Madison worried that factions would be the death of the new republic. But George Washington, Samuel Adams, Thomas Jefferson, and Patrick Henry, to mention only a few, had already established the precedent embodied in the First Amendment for citizens to band together to change their circumstances.

Any view of issues management which ignores the power of public interest agitation is naive. Not only are issues management and advocacy advertising used by corporations but by religious organizations, associations, unions, clubs, political parties, action committees, other committed interests, and even individuals. Public interest coalitions commonly press for government intervention on issues that they have helped to publicize in the mass media. In matters of corporate regulation, government responds reactively, instead of pro-actively, to public appeals for change. Because government is vital to efforts to change society, special interest groups often try to introduce their issues into political campaigns. To increase the likelihood of success, interest groups use PACs and political endorsements to encourage or coerce candidates to take stands on key issues.

Accustomed to doing business in a relatively tranquil manner, many corporate leaders view special interest groups as threatening. Consequently, a negative, combative attitude toward such groups has led some business people to desire to defeat, even to destroy, the "enemy." Shants (1978) describes the win-lose attitude of some members of the nuclear generation industry who wanted to fight anti-nuclear "activists not with facts but with closed factory gates, empty schools, cold and dark homes and sad children." This philosophy hardly endears public relations experts to their management or to the agitators who already do not trust them. The statement implies that the company is correct, the movement is wrong, and only through punishment can the public understand. This combative stance is ironic because many public interest groups would like nothing more than to punish corporations. This adversarial or win-lose stance occurs when both sides presume to have the truth and can use force to silence the opposition. Corporations are advised to seek to harmonize their efforts with special interest issues positions before polarization occurs. A combative attitude increases the likelihood of the hostile polarization that typically matures into confrontation. Such public visibility can do little to improve the public attitude of corporations. When corporations confront a group which seems to be acting in the interest of "the people," they appear to flaunt their contempt for the public interest. On the other hand, some firms, such as Nestlé, have used agitational groups intelligently to help establish criteria for socially responsible performance.

Special interest agitators try to use regulation to limit the options that businesses have. In contrast, issues management arises from a corporation's desire to increase its options. If companies can skillfully monitor their environment, they should be able to spot the efforts of agitators while issues are emerging and before they become focused into pending legislation. Early warning systems can alert corporations to emerging issues and to highly motivated individuals who are attempting to focus public attention on those issues. Many issues arise as the product of the efforts of a few individuals who are troubled by some aspect of society and/or corporate behavior. By articulating the issue and demonstrating the extent to which it affects the interests of others, social movement agitators can increase the size of their following, make the issue more visible, and foster interest by legislative bodies. Standard lore in issues management underscores the reality that once an issue has entered the legislative process, it is no longer emerging; it has emerged. Even then, however, once issues arrive in legislative halls, they develop slowly. For instance, development of the Employment Retirement Income Security Act of 1974 started 15 years earlier in congressional hearings (Nagelschmidt, 1982: 137).

The politics of polarity are often played to the advantage of special interest groups (Navarro, 1984). This outcome is more likely when the agitators have successfully associated their cause with some corporate behavior that is contrary to the public interest. Profit, shareholder responsibility, job security—such themes hardly defend corporations against public wrath when toxic waste, indiscriminate deforestation, air pollution, or other problems are set in balance. Once the press gets involved, if the agitators couch their appeals in broad humanistic and self-interest values, such as public safety or toxic waste, corporations are likely to damage their cause by making a frontal attack. A win-win strategy of conflict resolution increases the likelihood that corporations can take a position that can be demonstrated to support the public interest.

Whereas a win-loss outcome may be the lifeblood of a movement, it is the death knell of a corporation. Movements seek to defeat. They want a company or industry to capitulate. Anti-nuclear generation advocates seek to stop the construction of generating facilities and/or prevent the loading of nuclear fuel. They want corporations to admit to having dumped toxic wastes, and they want companies to clean up the environment. They want to prevent smoke and water pollution. In short, they want victory—wins for them, losses for companies. Companies must take a stance of seeking to win by convincing the public, if not the agitators, that it has also won. Companies, unless they are attacked by terrorists, are at a substantial disadvantage because of their size, especially if the public believes the accusations made by special interest agitators.

PUBLIC INTEREST AND POWER POLITICS

Two early writers, Gabriel Tarde in *The Public and The Crowd* (1922) and Gustave LeBon in *The Crowd: A Study of the Popular Mind* (1925), viewed special interest groups as being disruptive to an otherwise systematic and well-managed society. This elitist notion arose from the belief that the best class deserved to rule without challenge. Such writers typically viewed agitators as "rabble rousers." Those who dissented were either of the elite class, who used permissible means, or from a lower class unworthy to share power and participate in government.

Objective observers of social agitation recognize the pejorative rhetoric inherent in the use of the word "rabble" to describe the supporters of environmental issues or the religious champions of decency on television. Social movement membership, especially in recent years, often draws on every economic and educational stratum of society. The membership as well as the leaders represent many professions and other occupations. Housewives protesting unsanitary food processing conditions can hardly be characterized as rabble, and any issues manager who thinks of the opposition as such may be at a disadvantage. Such a narrow and stereotypic response may swing the power balance to those members of the special interest group who understand how to use themselves as a power voting bloc pressuring Congress to act in the "public interest." When people become so dissatisfied with certain conditions that they are willing to join together to change those conditions, the foundations have been laid for a social movement group.

Of several theoretical approaches to the nature of social movements, the most accurate view is that special interest groups are enjoined in power struggles. Those groups which are successful are most skilled at obtaining and wielding power resources (Gamson, 1968, 1975; Oberschall, 1973; Simons, 1972). Following this line of reasoning, agitation is best viewed as a complex of strategies designed to acquire and manage such resources.

One misconception regarding social movement conflict is that it arises from misunderstanding. Somewhat in this vein, Tichenor et al. (1977: 107) argue: "Community conflicts to an increasing degree involve a contest over information and its interpretation." Such a viewpoint is accurate to the extent that it is founded on the conclusion that information is power. The interpretation of fact and the contest over information may be part of movement conflict, but ultimately the contest centers on the acquisition and use of power.

An equally erroneous view treats social movements as arising from a disagreement; this viewpoint suggests that the remedy is to achieve harmony through agreement. The problem with this conception is its failure to realize that the combatants may be unwilling to compromise, even when they see their opponent's power. For instance, we can hardly imagine companies changing policy every time some group disagrees with their policies.

Despite this emphasis on power, persuasion is vital to social movements; Simons (1974: 177) concludes that persuasion "is not so much an alternative to the power of constraints and inducements as it is an instrument of that power, an accompaniment to that power, or a consequence of that power." Power and persuasion interrelate. Power helps individuals, groups, and corporations be persuasive, certainly in terms of affecting public policy. Likewise, persuasion supports power. Properly used, persuasion can keep people committed to the belief that the groups that have power deserve to keep it and that their policies are correct. Issues only begin to have audience impact when members of the public realize how their lives are affected (or could be affected) by some aspect of corporate behavior. Movements give visibility to ideas, so that others may learn that their sentiments are shared.

POWER RESOURCE MANAGEMENT

Roughly defined, power is the ability to make and implement policy and to take actions which in turn affect the actions and well-being of others. Power resource management arises from the ability to control and manipulate economic, political, and social sanctions and rewards through such means as boycotts, strikes, embargos, layoffs, lockouts, legislative regulation, executive orders, police action, and judicial review. The essential characteristic of power resource management is the ability of a group, company, or governmental agency to give or withhold rewards. At the extreme, coercion implies the actual granting or withholding of punishment or rewards. In contrast, coercive persuasion draws its potency from the fear on the part of a group, company, or agency that punishment will be given or rewards withheld (Simons, 1972: 228).

During the early stages of the movement, the agents of change lack power and must acquire it. Mere outbursts of rage are unlikely to result in emergent issues. Movement power consists of the number of people who support the movement, alliances and other third-party assistance, media attention, and favorable responses by key people in power institutions such as the judiciary, members of Congress, administrative officers, leading educators, and religious leaders. Persuasion is necessary to help obtain, maintain, and marshal resources of power and to develop a public opinion favorable to their use.

Organizations that have power must work to maintain it. "Established groups," Gamson (1975: 140) observes, "must maintain the loyalty and commitment of those from whom they draw their resources; challenging groups must create this loyalty." This loyalty can be maintained by the use of rewards, threats, and persuasive appeals. Saul Alinsky's tactics in the struggle with Eastman Kodak Corporation of Rochester, New York, illustrates the dynamics of power. Black citizens of Rochester held disproportionately fewer and lower-paying jobs at Kodak than did white members of the community. The leaders of the black community had attempted to use moral suasion to convince Kodak to change its hiring and promotion policies and practices, but this strategy failed. To create a viable struggle, the black group had to obtain power resources.

The leadership decided not to use boycotts and strikes because the local black population was too small; organizing a national boycott would have been too difficult and probably would not have had lasting impact. With only a few competitors in the photograph industry, people could hardly suppress their desire to capture the memories of their family, even in behalf of an important principle. The first step in the movement was to unify and rally the black community in support of the issue. Next, moral appeals were used to persuade churches and other organizations to commit their Kodak stock proxies which the black group could use. With these proxies, the black group became a visible and legitimate force at the stockholders' meeting; the proxies served as power resources to force Kodak to alter its hiring and promotion practices. The proxies and the coalition with third-party institutions were also power resources. Their use as coercive tools was supported by appeals to the moral principles generated by the nationwide civil rights movement. The proxies provided power, but persuasion was vital to their acquisition and use (Alinsky, 1968, 1971, 1972).

Persuasion in social movement operates out of a combination of two essential principles. The first is the ability of words to demonstrate to people how their self-interests are affected by corporate "misbehavior." Through language, critics can provide facts about corporate behavior and argue that certain values should be applied to impose new regulatory policies which can require corporations to behave in the public interest. The second use of persuasion is to create new terms, a new vocabulary, with which to discuss the behavior of corporations. Recent contributions to our public policy vocabulary include toxic waste, smog, endangered species, fluorocarbons and the hot house effect, discrimination, and equal opportunity.

Persuasion, including the rhetoric of identification and redefinition, involves the use of words and other symbols to create and change opinion and to motivate people to act as a group. Followers of a social movement come to have a new perspective through the redefinition created by the movement's ideologists. The followers become identified with one another through new labels, such as "environmentalists," or through the sharing of a common interest, such as the prevention of indecent television programming. Such rhetorical themes appeal to followers to join the fight for some point or action. Words create division by contesting political, social, and economic issues and images. Through persuasion, agitators appeal for support and motivate resistance against the "enemy." The language of agitation develops a climate of public opinion which justifies the tactics of resource management.

Ellul (1971) observes: "Although revolt invariably centers on what is concrete, immediate, and palpable, once revolution is rooted in the hearts of men it cannot fail to support elements of myth and ideology." One of the biggest mistakes issues managers can make is to confuse an "act of revolt" with a revolution. Some believed the 1960s was a period of revolt, an outburst of anger that would quickly dissipate, somewhat like a temper tantrum. Those who believe this way tend to think, "It will soon go away." What companies must watch for is a shift of opinion and the creation of new beliefs that support new norms of behavior. If the change is strong enough, it can lead to the implementation of those norms through governmental regulation. Corporate critics believe they have been wronged, and issues managers should not lose sight of the possibility that a revolution is occurring, a revolution that goes beyond an act of revolt. As Ellul (1971: 47) concludes, "Revolution is bound to embody a journey to the absolute in the hearts of those who take part in it."

Movements are strongest, McLaughlin (1969: 349) concludes, when their "ideology is in accord with the *Zeitgeist* of the era." Social movement agitators, like corporate communicators, must court favorable public opinion. For example, antiwar advocates encountered much hatred in the 1960s because they exhibited disdain for traditional symbols such as the American flag. Oberschall (1978) argues that the successful 1960s agitation groups created favorable opinion or joined their movement with established opinion; the groups that failed did so because they did not manage public opinion. Ideas are vital, not incidental, to the growth and development of a movement. They define the climate of the movement and produce divisions between factions. But more important, when strongly believed they help unify movement members.

Movements survive by associating the interests of their followers with dominant political and moral symbols (Edelman, 1964, 1977: 41). Because freedom is so central to the public mentality, it can be used in many ways. Social movement agitators can use it to argue for antitrust legislation: The people should be free from the tyranny of monopolies. Labor rights have been championed in the name of freedom. Free enterprise is the corporate version of freedom. Another value, a world of beauty, has been used to try to stop pollution. Equality, fairness, safety, and many other values underpin social movement persuasion, and they all have their counterparts in corporate responses. "Political forms . . . symbolize what large masses of men need to believe about the state to reassure themselves" (Edelman, 1964: 2). Groups can exploit the principles reflected in these symbols and use them as identification and for moral suasion. Under attack, major institutions struggle to stop the erosion of their authority. Basic documents give authority to control agents. "The constitution thereby becomes the concise and hallowed expression of man's complex and ambivalent attitude toward others: his wish to aggrandize his goods and powers at the expense of others: his fears that he may suffer from powerful positions of others and from their predations" (Edelman, 1964: 19).

Movements are so individual that characterizing them is often difficult. Gamson (1968, 1975) has achieved one of the most comprehensive definitions of groups and has identified many of the variables that make them successful. At the same time he finds very few patterns universal to all successful groups. Some agitational groups are successful with minimum effort; some change the conditions or policies which they find troublesome merely by pointing out certain conditions. In some instances, very little has to be done to convince the public that a certain corporate action is wrong. The scene in which conflict transpires and the size of the group are major variables. The probability of charge is also influenced by the competing individuals' ability to exert power, to use threats and inducements, and to create a climate of opinion favorable to their efforts (Gamson, 1968: 53-57, 60-69, 72).

Some movements are very large, involving thousands, even millions, of followers. They may last for a brief moment or for many years, decades, or even centuries. They often start by focusing on one idea or object, but if they are successful they tend to grow in confidence and undertake more issues. The leaders of the most successful movements are extremely competent in performing three major functions. They articulate a set of values and express the self-interest of followers to attract them and keep them loyal. These leaders are able to structure the movement and create a division of labor and an exchange of information. Thus they attract attention to the group.

Many groups begin by petitioning the people in authority. If these grievances are satisfied, the movement loses its impetus. In this regard, companies can do well by listening to customer complaints to monitor what issues may be emerging. But if the interests of the petitioners are denied, they may fight for acceptance, visibility, and power. Depending on how ego-involved the members of the group are and how resistant corporations and governments are, the movement can escalate to violence. Fortunately, few movements get that far, and those that do so before they have sufficient popular support are bound to fail. The public must be willing to accept violence before it can be used effectively. Corporations that are met with acts of violence can win public sympathy by demonstrating their goodwill efforts to compromise and be responsible citizens.

In any test of power, combatants seek to exploit each other's vulnerability. Corporations are vulnerable if they cannot withstand public scrutiny. For instance, during the muckraker era, once the public learned that packing companies were not using sanitary procedures, companies were doomed to suffer the sting of regulation. Corporations are also vulnerable to product or service boycotts; they hate to lose part of their market. They worry about having their facilities closed down by an injunction, and they fear court battles, which they may lose and during which they can appear to be Goliaths fighting Davids. Likewise, they may be vulnerable to competing views of corporate social responsibility, and to the willingness of employees or consumers to take risks in order to achieve the goals of the movement. Vulnerability is related to the quality of ideas which provide the rationale for the movement. The movement tests the content of new ideas and their use to reshape institutions and norms.

Movements help shift public opinion, which may constitute a new orientation as well as new norms and values. For example, child labor was once accepted practice. Through powerful arguments, however, a power constituency began to believe that children were better off in school than in coal mines or sweat shops. In *Muller* v. *Oregon* (1908), Louis Brandeis argued that women should not be required to work long, hard hours because of their weaker constitution. This view, which seemed enlightened nearly 80 years ago, has since been opposed by women who argue that many jobs should be open to them because they have the strength to perform the same tasks as males. Neither position is correct or false; each reflects a different set of beliefs and values created by a particular context in the convolutions of public opinion.

Beyond ideas, social movements may test the willingness of combatants to risk lives, property, position, and/or economic stability (Heath, 1979). Corporations have an advantage in those communities where people may, at least for a time, be unwilling to risk losing income. But if the risk of other losses, such as those resulting from the danger of radiation or toxic waste, begins to outweigh the economic loss, agitators may confront the company with a new set of dynamics.

STAGES OF MOVEMENT DEVELOPMENT

Many writers have proposed models to depict movement life cycles. Thus Griffin (1952) identifies inception, rhetorical crisis, and consummation, and Oberschall (1973) argues that movements progress from commitment formation through mobilization and finally to confrontation. In a later study, Stewart et al. (1984) propose a five-stage model: genesis, social unrest, enthusiastic mobilization, maintenance, and termination. Any list may be misleading because social movements vary so much. However, without some sense of movement development, monitoring is quite problematic.

As the following model indicates, movements can be monitored by examining how they progress through five separable but interdependent stages: *strain, mobilization, confrontation, negotiation*, and *resolution*. Of course, not all groups progress through all stages. Some will make the mistake of trying to get to one of the later stages before the prerequisite foundation has been established; consequently, the later stages may collapse because they lack the necessary support. Likewise, movements may fail if they are unable to progress beyond the first stages. However, because of favorable circumstances some movements may be successful without going through all stages.

The value of this model is its ability to provide insight into the ways and places corporations can intervene to prevent the movement from achieving a point contrary to their business interests. Much regulatory legislation is created and imposed during confrontation, negotiation, and resolution. If the movement never progresses that far, however, we may assume that the corporate monitoring system worked so that corporate planning could adapt to the emerging issues, or that the issues communication strategies blunted the appeals of the movement. Or we can conclude either that the movement leaders were incapable of promoting the movement or that it was not founded on a deeply and broadly felt issue. If corporations understand movements, they can work pro-actively to solve problems of corporate performance before they mature into regulatory legislation.

Strain

On a given day, hundreds of people feel some discomfort about their lives. Isolated instances may occur where families suffer the tragedy of children losing their lives or being seriously harmed because of flammable clothing. People may be having difficulties concerning car warranties. Strange rashes may appear on people living near chemical complexes. Also, scholars may be examining the effects of fluorocarbons on the atmosphere or of chemicals on declining predatory bird populations. These feelings can be called "strain," a comparison of *what is* versus *what should be*, or a perceived impairment (Smelser 1963: 47).

A movement gets its impetus from a desire to change some condition which causes discomfort or prevents people from obtaining or enjoying advantages they believe they deserve. "A social movement represents an effort by a large number of people to solve collectively a problem that they feel they have in common" (Toch, 1965: 5). Thus the first requirement of persuasion used by movement leaders is to convince potential supporters that strain exists and that it is of sufficient magnitude to warrant collective action to change it. The feeding ground of movements is "the ranks of persons who have encountered problems" (Toch, 1965: 9). Following the classic problem-solution persuasion model, most people seek to eliminate strain by moving toward equilibrium or comfort.

Strain does not only occur during economic hard times. In fact, it is even more likely to erupt during or shortly after periods of well-being. One of the classic examples of this phenomenon is the outburst that occurred during the mid-1960s following two decades of phenomenal corporate growth and prosperity (Brown, 1979). The IAA observes:

> The historical view of controversy advertising suggests that it is a product of periods of economic expansion. The spread of affluence in such periods encourages new publics to expect or demand a voice in social and economic decision-making. Discussion has moved over the years into the public media, where controversy receives wide coverage, with new adversary points of view commanding the most attention [Stridsberg, 1977: 96].

Strain is most persuasive when established social, economic, or political norms are violated. Sometimes the foundations of strain are present, and at other times agitation groups must present facts calling for change. Agitators may have to change norms and establish the value of using new norms to evaluate corporate behavior. One of the interesting by-products of the agitation of the 1960s was the development of new operating norms of corporate business behavior. If, for instance, companies could make huge profits from chemicals, they were not to be trusted. The bottom-line requirement in this regard is persuading targeted publics that their self-interest has been damaged, that norms have been violated, or that new values need to be applied to evaluate corporate behavior. Until the appropriate challenge is met, agitators have no hope of building a social movement.

Smelser (1963) views movements as ranging from a relatively undefined interest, such as fads, to norm-oriented or value-oriented changes. Fads are passing crazes or panics which have little permanent impact on the social, political, or economic character of a society. In contrast, major movements attempt to change either norms or values. Some movements are built on a collective desire to restructure norms so that they correspond to dominant values. For instance, the civil rights movement has struggled to appropriate and implement the norms implied by freedom, equality, and the pursuit of happiness. Agitators may assert that norms are inconsistent with major values or are applied so that some people suffer. In contrast, value-oriented movements work to reform social, economic, or political values prior to changing norms. Communist revolutions are thus classic instances of a totally new value system. But less drastic changes have resulted from battles between the public interest and corporations. The value of unrestrained corporate free enterprise was repudiated by the Populists and Progressives, who feared it would lead to corporate monarchy. Product safety and environmental protection are two values that have dramatically altered corporate operating environments. As values are redefined, business issues monitoring must accurately estimate which changes are mere fads and which are more permanent.

Corporations are wise to be alert to opinion shifts marked by a change in *intensity* regarding how deeply certain population segments feel about some issue. The intensity of feeling can be empirically measured by the strength of beliefs or attitudes. The *extensiveness of support* is another measure. Indeed, strain can be measured by the number of people attracted to a movement or aware of an issue. Because agitators are required to obtain large numbers of supporters to increase the movement's power base, the extensiveness of support is a crucial measure. Complementing this measure is the ability of the movement to attract *third-party or allied* support. Such support may come in the form of coalitions with existing groups who have become concerned about a problem. If a movement can obtain the support of a governor, mayor, president, religious leader, or celebrity, its power may increase substantially.

Monitoring can ascertain the extent to which a movement has *legitimacy*. Unless movements can become legitimate representatives of some issue, they are unlikely to be able to bring about legislative change or to impose other pressures and sanctions on an industry. Whether the media treat the voices of change as legitimate or aberrant can be crucial. Another measure of increasing strain is the extent to which people *identify* with the leaders of the movement and the cause that they champion. By charting shifts in opinion, corporations can track the flow of opinions relevant to the development of a movement's power base. By observing the standard press and by listening to the movement's statements, an estimation can be made of the extent to which coalitions and associations with power figures are being achieved.

Strain is frequently expressed in rhetorical statements which blend emotional terms and careful reasoning. The former are required to gain attention for the problem. The latter are needed to give the issue permanence. Out of the substance founded on the conditions of strain, the movement builds "a fire under its members by stressing the intolerability of their fate. . . . The result is *to reinforce the member's conviction that he must take action*" (Toch, 1965: 83). A "sufficient condition for the outbreak of collective behavior is communication" when united with "a shared culture and a common orientation among the discontented group." But this communication must focus "attention on the same incidents, and the shared culture ensures that a similar interpretation of those events will be made" (Oberschall, 1973: 310-311).

In the development of strain, atrocities can have an explosive impact. The civil rights movement of the 1960s was given impetus when the nation learned about the horrors of racism which led some people to bomb a church, killing several children in a Sunday School class. Labor atrocities, employment inequities, rivers catching fire, chemically produced birth defects, dioxin pollution, and cancer resulting from asbestos production—these are only a few dramatic instances which have changed the dynamics of corporate life. Corporations typically call instances such as these crises, but in terms of the credence they lend to social movement rhetoric, they are "atrocities."

One of the most difficult problems facing corporate communicators *and* agitators is to reach the public with simplified versions of often complicated issues. During the pollution battles, even the regulators could not arrive at a consensus of the components of pollution, a safe level of various pollutants, or the best technology for its correction. Because of this difficulty, movements attempt to simplify and freeze attention on a few defensible statements which are believed by followers to be true and which can be easily communicated and remembered. For this reason, the atrocity has impact; it is hard to explain away, and the burden of proof has shifted to the corporations. Corporations under such situations are often hard pressed to communicate with the public to explain the complexity involved. Indeed, attempts to indicate that technology is unavailable or that the process of correcting a problem is not as simple as the movement suggests can be interpreted as sandbagging, which invariably hurts the corporate cause if the problem is generally believed to harm the self-interest of a segment of the population.

Social movement rhetoric attempts to increase the chances of mobilization by trumpeting atrocities and demonstrating how the public's self-interest is jeopardized by corporate actions. Social movement rhetoric is often most effective when it is expressed in hyperbole. After a while the dramatic effect of hyperbole wears off, but the residual shift in redefinition and new perspectives lingers in the public mentality. When this occurs, the movement has made a major step toward the establishment of strain.

Agitators utilize redefinition throughout their efforts. They try to place a new interpretation on a situation, on some aspect of the products or services, or on a corporation so that companies become vulnerable to change. Under normal circumstances, Dow Chemical, during the Vietnam years, would have been seen in a positive light as the manufacturer of napalm. With napalm, U.S. troops could be more effective against the enemy. However, after the negative characterization of napalm by antiwar activists, napalm became known by many as an indiscriminate and horrifying weapon that destroyed innocent victims as well as the enemy.

Some ideological movements never advance beyond wrangles over facts, values, and ideology. Individuals may be so compulsive in their commitment to ideas that they organize more as a cult of true believers than as a formidable instrument for social change. As a cult, they may create unity but are not likely to achieve confrontation. A movement becomes strong only when ideas are coupled with action. Consequently, a movement takes a vital step toward the establishment of strain once it creates a perspective that, like a new pair of glasses, allows a segment of the public to see its world in a different way. This new perspective does not constitute the movement, but it is a vital step toward developing the power resources without which the movement stands no chance of forcing changes in regulatory policy.

To develop and maintain follower commitment, agitators try to create the impression that they present a righteous purpose. Movements are presented as solutions to problems created by business. In a sense, movements are like morality plays; they symbolize good, while the adversary epitomizes evil. To some degree, movements become an extension of each follower's identity, since they symbolize each follower's hopes and aspirations for a better life.

Mobilization

Mobilization is the stage in the life of a movement when it must begin to marshal its power resources. In the case of Nestlé, public opinion quickly turned against the company, and a boycott was started to pressure management into abandoning its marketing techniques. One of the most formidable supporters of the boycott was the United Methodist Church Task Force. The purpose of the boycott was to persuade Nestle to support a United Nations World Health Organization code of ethics. When Nestlé began to manage the issues involved, it obtained the assistance of the Methodist Task Force to help draft a code and work it through the United Nations. As noted in Chapter 5, once progress by Nestle was demonstrated, the Methodists and other churches voted to abandon the boycott (Pagan, 1983).

Social movement persuasion uses strain to produce intense commitment in followers who become willing to sacrifice time, money, and, in some instances, personal security. Persuasion's primary roles are to establish an ideology to justify the movement's activities. Persuasion supplies ideals, emphasizes self-interest, and establishes identification sufficient to sustain the movement. In the battle of wills, however, corporations usually have the advantage of being able to outlast a movement. In some instances corporations can simply ignore the movement, which eventually runs out of ideological fuel and self-interest and fades into little more than a fad, at best, and perhaps nothing more than a "waste of time."

Strain is a movement's energy source. If the strain is sufficiently strong, people will be motivated to join the movement or at least support it with their opinion. However, social movements do not exist on fire and brimstone alone. If they are to become potent forces of change, they must develop structure and stability to conduct routine tasks of organization and maintenance between the more visible acts of confrontation. Movements require a division of labor, motivated supporters, monetary resources that can support the movement's activities, two of which are mass communication and lobbying.

Beyond the rhetorical parts of commitment building, the movement must accomplish some victories which evidence its ability to solve its followers' problems. The sagest movement leaders pick easy battles that they know they can win to establish symbolic power. They call upon followers to participate in ways which do not go outside their experience or willingness to act, and they minimize the perceived level of risk to motivate followers that the rewards of participation are justified. Less astute movement leaders often bite off such a large chunk of the power task that they are unable to devour it. Such a failure weakens their credibility and causes people to lose interest and withdraw support. They must be able to isolate and focus on the enemy and challenge it in legislative combat.

Movement leaders quickly realize that "to be effective, they must show evidence of widespread support—hence, they frequently resort to mass rallies, demonstrations, petitions, and other forms of visible aggregation of the discontented groups and their sympathizers" (Oberschall, 1973: 308). For instance, if the group asserts that it can force a reduction of violence and sex in television programming by boycotting sponsor products, it must be able to deliver. Idle threats are the death knell of social movements. Eventually, no one takes them seriously. Corporations and governmental agencies are barraged with so many complaints and appeals to change that they are willing to resist or ignore all but those which seem capable of effecting a change in business as usual. Corporations can defend themselves against these tactics with appropriate countermeasures.

During mobilization, movements must continue to attract attention, and yet achieving favorable attention is sometimes difficult. Nevertheless, unfavorable media treatment is better than no attention. The ultimate goal is to be prominently and favorably featured on front pages and editorial sections. Even at the strain stage, movements must use the standard media, as well as their own, to disseminate messages. However, one major requirement is to appear favorably in the standard media and to at least *seem* to have broad and enthusiastic support.

This last requirement is important for issues monitoring as well. Prior to becoming visible in the media, a movement should have a fairly broad and deeply committed following. Thus, if issues monitors are alert, movements can be discovered before they become visible to large groups of interested people. Moreover, standard channnels, such as major daily newspapers, may not begin to carry information about a movement until it has established its own channels of information and has a substantial infrastructure in place.

Many social movements develop their own mobilization communication system, which typically includes some variety of newsletters, magazines, newspapers, films, and speakers' bureaus. Typical of the kinds of sophisticated and slick magazines which are developed are *Audubon* and *National Wildlife*. Both are products of wildlife groups that engage in environmental lobbying. They circulate stories and articles that reinforce their followers' love of nature and wildlife. Both discuss and monitor ecology issues. For example, the February-March 1985 issue of *National Wildlife* answered the question, "Is the nation losing its impetus to conserve energy?" The article champions those corporations which have developed new products for conserving energy. The magazine argues that environmentalism is good business. In an environmental watch, the magazine concludes that "progress continues but toxic clouds are on the horizon." The article took issue with corporate complaints about pollution controls. It observes: "The notion that cleanup pays was further reinforced by a report prepared last year for the EPA by a private research firm. Among its findings: while corporations have blamed pollution requirements for decisions to close 155 plants at a loss of 33,000 jobs since 1971, the nation's air and water cleanup laws will have stimulated some 524,000 new jobs by 1987" (p. 35). In addition to articles, such magazines use exquisite color photography to make their points about the beauty of nature and the disaster of abuse.

When mobilizing, the movement experiences its first test of power. It must resist the dangers of fracturing. Movements tend to fragment as they develop. Leaders vie for followings and may challenge one another. In fact, they may actually destroy one another in what they think to be the best interest of the movement. A second requirement is to develop slogans and symbols that foster identification and simplify the movement ideology. The symbols of identification used by the combatants must be strong. "To be a part of an organization viewed as potent is evidently to derive some feeling of effectiveness" (Edelman, 1964: 109).

During mobilization, a movement is strengthened by its ability to achieve coalitions that add to its legitimacy. If judges, legislators, administrators, and regulators are unwilling to support a movement, it is unlikely to mobilize any power resources (Chubb, 1983). In this regard, a powerful agitation strategy is to threaten the legitimate leaders of society with the prospect that they must support the movement or lose their own authority and position. Movements seek celebrities who identify with the cause and who lend their name to making it visible and legitimate. Petition drives give a social movement a sense of legitimacy;

they suggest that the movement's cause has popular support. Special interest groups often buy full-page ads to proclaim their endorsements.

Corporations may resist the special interest mobilization by many means. Among the most obvious are discovering and disrupting the source of funds. Major figures in society can thus be discouraged from associating with and endorsing the group. Corporations may also increase the risk of supporting the group. They may do so directly, through threats of layoffs or shortages, or by showing the costs that will result if the group's efforts are successful. Corporations may argue that support of the groups is not needed because they cannot solve the problems, or that the agitators' activity is unlikely to be productive. Corporations may co-opt the movement by bringing some key leaders into the corporation in an advisory capacity. All of these strategies are designed to prevent special interest groups from gaining enough power to significantly influence the corporation in a negative way.

Confrontation

Public affairs consultant Patrick Jackson underlines one of the realities of working with special interest groups when he observes: "Issues can't be 'managed'; confrontation can" (quoted in Nagelschmidt, 1982: 212). Jackson believes that too many participants are involved in the formation of public opinion for a company or industry to reach all of them and correct and refute the points of disagreement. For this reason, Jackson advises issues managers to follow several principles while dealing with controversy. The first piece of advice is to try to avoid confrontation when the issues are so complex that they cannot be explained easily and quickly. He cautions issues managers that conflict can help the special interest group maintain its momentum and increase its fund-raising success. Issues managers must be able to recognize when the opposition is so strong that it cannot be defeated. Issues groups can be ignored only when they are too weak to cause damage. But issues managers should not fear conflict. Indeed, Jackson argues, it can be used to get the corporation's message across to the public. Conflict is a good time to put the company's issues into the public agenda and to use that vehicle to lead the public to pay attention to the company. Conflict can be managed by diverting attention away from some undesirable point of view, and companies can blame problems on scapegoats. They can prove that the special interest groups are ill informed or are following shallow reasoning (see Nagelschmidt, 1982: 213-314). In essence, Jackson advises issues managers to understand the power variables at play and know when to exert their influence. He also cautions companies to know when a low profile is best.

The social movement is ready to confront its enemy it believes it has obtained and marshaled the requisite power resources. After focusing on the advantages and disadvantages of believing two competing points of view, confrontation occurs when the special interest group polarizes society by trying to force a choice between its position and that of its corporate adversaries. "Radical confrontation reflects a dramatic sense of division" (Scott and Smith, 1969: 2). This conclusion points out the stark reality that by the time confrontation occurs, the situation has gone so far that the corporation must work very hard to mend fences and build bridges. One of the greatest powers of any corporation is being able to ignore or deny a group's demands. Confrontation is that moment when the group attempts to force a corporation or governmental agency to recognize the group and implement its demands. Confrontation tests whether or not the group can be ignored.

If at all possible, corporations should manage their issues involvement so that they never reach confrontation. Jackson (quoted in Nagelschmidt, 1982) argues that as one of the earliest stages in preparation for conflict, corporations must try to identify their own vulnerabilities. They must change their behavior as much as possible to minimize their vulnerability. Once the conflict begins, Jackson proposes several tactics for corporations: (1) Stick to the issue at hand. (2) Be able to admit you're wrong, or could be. (3) Don't be afraid to alter your position. (4) Find good things to say about others and their viewpoints. (5) Present your views forthrightly and do not apologize for your self-interest. In addition to these strategies, Jackson cautions companies to use their power judiciously. They should not call in the authorities unless public sentiment is solidly on their side. Flagrant use of money can be counterproductive. The veterans of such battles from whom Jackson draws advice caution companies to avoid counterattacking the credibility or personality of the agitators; rather, they should focus on providing valuable information to help interested parties understand the corporate side of the issues. Companies may be hurt more than helped if they escalate the controversy. They should use media to inform those segments of the public which are only minimally involved in the issues. Throughout Jackson's advice runs one dominant theme: Maintain a win-win attitude (Nagelschmidt, 1982: 216-220).

During confrontation, each side uses persuasion to continue its fight for legitimacy and recognition. Agitators struggle to be recognized as the bargaining agents for change by associating their power and issue position with the public interest. While corporations attempt to keep public opinion on their side by trying to portray the confrontation as likely to result in negative consequences or to be motivated for base reasons, agitators try to keep their followers committed to maintain favorable public opinion by characterizing corporations in negative terms. Agitators must demonstrate to their followers the virtues and necessity of confrontation. Consequently, they argue that change can come only through movement efforts. At such times they often try for a positive image by associating their cause with commonly held principles. In response, corporations may associate their cause with competing principles. In the battle over the development of nuclear generation, for instance, antinuclear advocates have portrayed utilities as being unwilling to change from dangerous nuclear energy to more inexpensive and safer energy sources. Management is often portrayed as reluctant to admit defeat, and ratepayers have been told they will have to pay a great deal more for electricity because of the faulty judgment of the corporate leaders. Agitators sometimes bring in the risk factor and characterize nuclear technology as unsafe and inadequate. If the agitators attempt sit-ins and picket lines to prevent the construction of such sites or the loading of fuel, they do so because only they, as they say, are standing between the public interest and corporate misjudgment and avarice. In this manner, confrontation can come from a division of opinion and interfere with corporate "business as usual."

Agitational groups attempt to become part of the established governmental system by creating agencies that oversee their special interests. One such agency, the Center for Auto Safety, survives even in the unfriendly climate of the Reagan administration. One report suggests that as many as 100 public interest groups operating in the federal government continue to be influential because of the tenacity of their leaders. The Natural Resources Defense Council, which has been active in controlling hazardous waste, has seen its budget increase from $400,000 in 1970 to $5 million annually. Even though they are only quasi-regulatory, they often stay in business because many of these watchdog groups provide government officials with valuable information and help to draft legislation (Schorr and Conte, 1984).

Special interest groups use many methods to gain legislative attention for their policy recommendations. One of the major objectives of agitational groups is to bring their point of view to a vote, especially if the situation can result in legislative action. They may use referenda and initiatives seeking to require legislatures to deal with issues they might otherwise avoid because of corporate lobbying efforts. These strategies are a mixed blessing for agitational groups, since battles over propositions often place agitation groups at a disadvantage. Once an issue is placed on a ballot, the electronic media can no longer deny corporations access to issue advertising. According to the FCC, ballot issues constitute a controversy; therefore, stations must accept advertisements that address the merits of the propositions.

Special interest groups gain power if they wage a successful proposition battle, but corporations have proven formidable. On a recent proposition in California, despite favorable public opinion corporate interests defeated an attempt to ban handguns. In most cases, corporations can outspend special interest groups. In a November 1982 proposition battle in California, corporate interests spent approximately $1.50 *per vote* to defeat a container law that would have required recycling beverage bottles and cans. Nearly 60 percent of the companies' approximately $3.5 million budget, managed through Californians for Sensible Laws, was spent on radio and television advertising (Waz, 1983).

For years, shareholder meetings were agitators' prime vehicles to criticize the actions of targeted companies. For a few shares of stock, a person or a group could address issues regarding some corporate policy. Despite new rules by the Securities and Exchange Commission, such groups are still able to protest corporate actions by owning as little as $1000 of company stock. Under the old rules, a resolution had to receive 3 percent of the shareholders' votes to be resubmitted; that level has since been increased to 5 percent. In addition, companies are protected against any one group being able to submit multiple resolutions. They can also forbid more than one resolution per issue to come before the shareholders (Ingersoll, 1985). Nevertheless, shareholder protest can attract media attention, since such meetings are otherwise typically uninteresting. Reporters are looking for drama, such as that created when a group of Catholic teachers, Sisters of the Sorrowful Mother, purchased a few shares of stock and used the shareholder meeting to protest the construction of a nuclear generating plant by Houston Industries, a major utility company.

Such religious groups, because they often hold sizable amounts of stock, use this strategy to bring attention to key issues. Religious groups are not to be taken lightly as special interest protesters. One of the strongest religious groups is the Interfaith Center on Corporate Responsibility (ICCR), which represents approximately 100 religious orders with a combined stock investment of $10 billion. Taking defense as a major issue, five church groups have demanded that Burlington

Northern reveal its contracts for the transportation of nuclear warheads and nuclear fuels for atomic submarines. Two orders are challenging Eastman Kodak's participation in the "star wars" defense planning. Chevron and Texaco have been challenged to withdraw from South Africa. Such action against Wells Fargo led it to withdraw loans from South Africa to prevent a resolution from going to the shareholders. Other issues of importance include unfair labor practices in Latin America and South Korea (Coca-Cola and Control Data), discrimination against Catholics in Northern Ireland (TRW, General Motors, United Technologies), international lending practices (Bank of America, Chemical Bank, Bankers Trust), infant formula marketing (American Home Products), the development of economic minorities (Sears, Roebuck and K-Mart), and acid rain (American Electric Power) (Moskowitz, 1985).

In response to such activities, and even to forestall them, corporate issues managers may join hands with investor/shareholder relations. The shareholders of a company typically are interested in its continued financial success. For this reason, they can be led to believe (one hopes for the right reasons) that a protest group is incorrect and that what it advocates is contrary to company and shareholder interests. This targeted audience can be used in many other aspects of the campaign, but the greatest fear on the part of management is that issues management will become mixed with the performance of executives in such a way that the management team is subject to being challenged by shareholders.

To decrease the likelihood of confrontation or to weaken its impact, companies can create a coalition with special interest groups. Pires (1983) has described her efforts as Planning and Constituency Relations Manager with Texaco. The impetus for this cooperative effort was a move by several civil rights groups in 1982 to consider credit policies in the petroleum industry. The NAACP, along with several other constituency groups, had a membership of 16 million people, a sizable power bloc. Pires explains that the desire by Texaco to work in a constructive manner grew out of a 1979 audit of Texaco's image conducted by Fraser Associates, which disclosed that Texaco had an opportunity to work with such constituencies. Pires's appointment charge was "to systematically open lines of communication with influential third-party groups; in short, to develop the interaction necessary for proactive public relations/public affairs." This function was situated "in the Public Relations and Advertising Department, rather than Government

Relations, since its focus was to be the broad one of developing sound two-way communication with major national constituency groups, as opposed to only searching out legislative allies."

Along with this reorganization and appointment, Texaco made a commitment to *listen* to the leading spokespersons of the constituency. Texaco "decided that it wouldn't promise anything it couldn't deliver" and was "resolved not to develop 'checkbook relationships.' " Again using outside counsel, Texaco discovered several constituencies that could assist the firm. Pires and her department head, Paul B. Hicks, Jr., vice president of public relations and advertising, placed the groups into a priority. Visits were made to the leaders and members of these groups to establish rapport. From these visits, Pires and others learned that members of these groups could understand how their stake in certain issues coincided with that of Texaco. The Texaco people came to understand that despite their differences the groups were willing to listen to Texaco's side of the issue and that the people in the groups were respectable. The members of the groups were quite serious in their efforts to achieve what was in the best interest of their groups. These relationships laid the foundation for an ongoing communication relationship in which Texaco provided information on issues of interest to the various constituencies. By trying to understand these constituencies, and through providing communication on vital topics, relationships were strengthened; the lines of communication and cooperation were indeed proactively opened.

During confrontation, issues are framed into propositions and set before the court of public opinion. The parties in conflict seek to define the issues to their advantage. How they are worded can be essential to the willingness of the public to participate in the combat. Both sides take part in this contest of issue development, since any contest of issues challenges each side to produce information and facts in support of its position and against the other. Part of the contest centers on the interpretation of these facts, and on their implications in light of various value perspectives. Moreover, the confrontation may center on competing values or the interpretation of what the values and norms of society require in the way of corporate behavior. Finally, the confrontation is likely to center on the wisdom of the policy changes advocated by the agitators. The latter will argue that a specific set of regulatory policies should be implemented in the public interest. Corporations, in turn, are prone to rejoin that those policies are ill advised and will result in negative outcomes instead of the desirable consequences sought by the agitators. Corporations may, under these circumstances, contest the technical, financial, or managerial expertise of the agitators which allegedly warrants their advice on the particular regulation.

Schwartz (Nagelshmidt, 1982: 123-134) reports survey data which indicate that businesses are improving in their ability to communicate with legislators and other Washington, D.C. thought leaders to explain their side of controversies. One of the major advances in this kind of communication is the ability to take a perspective that fairly represents and balances business and public interests. The survey generated the following elements that characterize effective communicators: well informed, knowledgeable, accurate, accessible, candid, open, and avoiding high-pressure/hard-sell tactics.

Confrontation is the stage in which the power resources of the combatants are tested. Persuasion supports the requirements of confrontation by maintaining and marshaling resources, by intensifying commitment, and by drawing and contesting issues.

Negotiation

Conflict is often conceived of as a clash over valued resources or positions; the clash is heightened in proportion to the value each combatant places on the outcome—the winning of resources or positions. Social movement controversy demands resolution. If strain is the foundation of the movement, then the impetus for change must be taken away or the agitational group must be defeated before peace can occur.

The fourth stage in movements is negotiation. At times corporations are smart to accede to the demands of agitators without waging open battle. The circumstances, particularly if strongly contrary to public opinion, can be more dire if corporations fight. Corporations can be made to look like the villain in a political melodrama. The crowd is sure to hiss and boo. Thus negotiation is often the better part of valor.

During the negotiation stage, each side seeks to gain as many advantages or minimize as many losses as its power allows. Much negotiation tends to be unspectacular. However, sometimes radical agitators (and corporate leaders) have difficulty settling a dispute. If tradeoffs favor corporations, most radical agitators have a hard time agreeing to them. In some instances, agitators get burned when they think they have struck a deal with a corporation or have tried to strike a bargain only to learn that they have been betrayed. Sometimes merely debating the issues in public satisfies some needs felt by agitators.

Negotiation can also take place in legislative halls and the offices of administrators and regulators. For that matter, some negotiation transpires in courts and judges' chambers. In some instances corporations can use these means for their own advantage. Often they have talented lobbyists who can help draft legislation and move it along (or slow it down) in Congress. In these settings corporations may be expected to provide information, especially on technical, financial, and managerial issues, in areas where the legislative group and the agitators lack expertise. This is one of the major roles in the legislative fact sheets which corporations develop to help legislators understand an issue and its implications. The Koupals, who led the People's Lobby (PL) in California,

> contended that all the facilities of the state of California were pitted against them. Whenever they made a statement on pesticides or some other aspect of agriculture, the Agriculture Department would come up with a big promotional program indicating either that the state was already working on it, had thought of it in the first place, or the PL's program was unworkable and PL's statements had no scientific proof [Sethi, 1977: 206].

Public opinion continues to be important during negotiation. The advantage that each side in the controversy is capable of exacting depends, to an extent, on what the public can be led to believe is fair. A countermeasure of grassroots lobbying may have begun during the conflict stage. If the pressures of this effort can be maintained, and if the swings in public opinion seem to favor the corporation, a special interest group may have a harder time imposing rigorous standards. If the agitators have been successful in bringing public opinion to bear on legislators and executives, the corporation may be advised to attempt to blunt it and thereby lessen the stringency of the regulatory measures. Power resources are crucial during negotiation because the competing sides are likely to gain only the amount of advantage warranted by the power they have to wield.

Even in the announcement of the outcome of negotiation, corporations or special interest groups can characterize the situation to their advantage (or disadvantage, if they intend to continue the fight). They may, for example, describe the constructive role they played in the development of effective legislation. Beyond this, corporations can offer an olive branch of peace, if not to the agitators then to those who are less closely associated with the movement. Announcements of changes being made in the public interest can go a long way toward building a positive, supportive operating environment for the future. Such a stance may also blunt the agitators' chances of persuading followers and potential followers that the strain still exists. One of the key requirements at the end of the negotiation period is the attempt to persuade the public that new conditions prevail which will eliminate the problems that produced the controversy.

Resolution

Skillfully managed, such appeals can bring about the resolution of controversy. The major requirement of a resolution is to determine how society can be adjusted to accommodate the results of negotiation. Claims regarding the positive impact of the change will be to the corporate advantage.

One of the largest problems in the resolution of conflict is participating in the selection of the people who will administer regulatory programs. Isaac and Isaac (1984) have studied the ways in which agitators become a part of the established governmental system. According to these authors, agitators often take their political agenda with them and attempt to implement it through their appointment. For instance, under the Carter administration, the Legal Services Corporation set about to transform the legal system. It went so far as to become involved in state ballot initiative measures. The Reagan administration has attempted to keep this organization functioning within its mandated guidelines. Also, the Reagan administration curbed the flow of funds through the Environmental Protection Agency to various environmental groups. Nevertheless, the Environmetal Action Foundation received $179,644 in June 1981. The group has been one of the strongest critics of corporate actions regarding the environment. Its agitational tactics have included sending dead fish to shareholders of corporations alleged to be polluters and filling gasoline tanks with sugar.

Many issues battles consist of a dialogue among technical specialists, particularly natural or behavioral scientists and engineers. Some researchers are not willing to take stands on issues, but others translate their science into issues politics, or vice versa. For instance, on matters of toxic waste, nuclear generation, pollution, or chemical toxicology, the special interest groups have their scientists, as do the companies. In some instances the government will have its cadre of specialists who give opinions. Many times these specialists wage a battle among themselves, which would occur even if it did not find its way into legislative and regulatory matters. Even when public opinion is for or against some issues position, the weight of scientific evidence and the efforts of politicians will be key factors in how the regulatory battle will be played out. Politicians, whether or not they represent any specific constituency on an issue, have their own agendas. Some will favor the special interest group side of the issue on a technical question, while other politicians will take the corporate side. Like poker, how the regulatory battle plays itself out depends on the relative power and skill of the players.

If the circumstances during confrontation and negotiation have been such that resolution seems to be disadvantageous to corporations, they must decide whether they are willing to attempt to persuade members of the public that problems exist which harm their interest. Such a statement would indicate that the roles of the combatants have changed. Now the companies are in a position to develop arguments to prove that strain exists which the public should seek to correct, in alliance with corporations.

POLITICAL ACTION COMMITTEES

One of the most important innovative power resources in public interest group combat has been the advent of PACs. Corporations, unions, trade associations, and special interest groups have started many PACs as a means for channeling money to candidates and participating in the power game through established politics. PACs got a boost in 1974 when the Federal Election Campaign Act was changed to restrict large individual or corporate donations and encourage broad-spectrum election participation. Two theories exist. One holds that to be effective (meaning most powerful), PACs must work for candidates who would otherwise not win. Supporting a sure winner is not as decisive as backing a candidate who becomes indebted because of the participation. The alternative position involves contributing to incumbents and other likely winners to at least gain access after the election.

Many business PACs have the natural inclination to give money to Republicans instead of Democrats. However, because of their positions on many House and Senate committees, Democrats have also received large shares of PAC money. They also understand that their committee standings can be used to "encourage" PAC contributions. Democrats appear to be more reliant on PAC money than their Republican counterparts. Democrats running for House seats got 41 percent of their money from PACs, whereas Republicans reported only 28.8 percent from PACs. In the Senate the pattern was the same, although the margin was less, with Democrats claiming 21 percent and Republicans 18 percent (Jackson, 1984a, b).

One of the major contributions PACs make is to share information valuable to understanding an issue and its public policy consequences. Besides raising funds, PACs often develop and circulate issues books that employees can use for their own public policy education and to contact legislators. Special interest PACs are also sponsored by a variety of business interests, realtors, physicians, defense contractors, and others. The realtor PAC and the PAC of the American Medical Association are two of the richest. Their combined funds have risen from less than $100,000 in 1978 to $700,000 in 1984 (Jackson, 1984b). In contrast, various other interest groups support PACs, particularly those devoted to the environment, quality of life, civil rights, arms control, and nuclear freeze issues.

Mapes (1984) provides evidence that PAC funds given to one side of a controversy encourage a counterattack of spending. She notes that the large amounts of money spent by those who support weapons systems are being countered by contributions to members of Congress who will support arms control and a nuclear freeze. She concludes: "Contrary to the hue and cry raised about the corruption of the political process by PAC money, the record shows that some members of Congress can accept money from PACs, even a great deal or money, and still cast votes that defeat utterly the interests of their benefactors." She observes how defense spenders have pushed tons of money into the campaign of Joseph Addabbo (D-NY). As chairman of the House Appropriations Subcommittee on Defense, he also receives large sums from arms control PACs. He has a nearly perfect voting record on arms control but is still in a position to be fair and understanding to the interests of armament. Military contractors particularly interested in the MX missile and President Reagan's space defense system contributed more than $900,000 to Senate candidates in 1984. The targeted candidates were either members of the Senate Armed Services Committee or the Defense Subcommittee of the Senate Appropriations Committee (*New York Times,* 1985).

Some PACs are more interested in promoting an ideology (and the candidates who adhere to it) than in targeting specific issues. The most visible of the conservative PACs is the National Conservative Political Action Committee; other well-known conservative PACs are the National Congressional Club, the Fund for a Conservative Majority,

Citizens for the Republic, and the Committee for the Survival of a Free Congress. PACs have also become popular with liberal political ideologues. These include the National Committee for an Effective Congress, the Fund for a Democratic Majority, the Committee for the Future of America, Independent Action, Democrats for the '80s, and the Progressive Political Action Committee. Donors to the right-wing PACs are typically business people or those with argricultural interests. The left-wing contributor profile is a young professional educated in the humanities and social sciences (Green and Guth, 1984). As long as they are not outlawed, general PACs will continue to play a vital role in politics. They offer issues managers a creative opportunity to help shape the political agenda and to keep updated on issues that are likely to mature into legislation.

WIN-WIN: DISARMING THE OPPOSITION

Persuasion can be used to create favorable or unfavorable attitudes toward the outcome of a conflict. If it is successfully managed, both sides will feel they have prospered from the confrontation. If the agitators feel that their side has not achieved all the desired changes, they will likely be back to do battle again. If corporations come out of the conflict at a disadvantage, they must consider how they can best stage a campaign to correct the difficulties. In the best case scenario, if a corporation has successfully managed its efforts in a win-win mode, it may have disarmed agitators, granted the corrections that seemed most necessary, and built a foundation for cooperation with the public interest.

Corporations have instrumental roles to play in the tug-of-war with special interest groups. From this description we can conclude that prevention is preferable to combat, and that a win-win attitude is more constructive than win-loss. Sophisticated issues monitoring and strategic planning can be supported by insight into the dynamics of social movements.

8

ISSUES MANAGEMENT IN THE NEW CORPORATE INFORMATION ENVIRONMENT

Not only do the media constitute the means for reaching targeted audiences, but they also shape the issues agenda. Business executives, like most people subjected to scrutiny, are sometimes uncomfortable with what they see of themselves in newsprint or on the screen. More so than any other medium, the unblinking eye of television serves as an electronic pop culture window into company practices, presenting a picture of U. S. business seen by nearly everyone in the country. For good or bad, TV typically opts for the easy stereotypes of executive ruthlessness, foolishness, or incompetence which various publics often uncritically accept as true. Not surprisingly, corporations reached new image lows in news and entertainment programming during the 1970s and early 1980s (Aronoff, 1979; Divelbiss and Cullen, 1981; Nelson-Horchler, 1982; Chickering, 1982; Lichter et al., 1982, 1983). These developments reflect broad societal trends in which traditional assumptions as to the proper role of government, the press, business, and other institutions underwent reevaluation—a process that continues today (*Society*, 1979; Nimmo and Combs, 1981; McKenzie, 1983).

MEDIA AND THE IMAGE OF BUSINESS

The communication environment is frustrating for business communicators because what they try to say is reshaped by the media.

Corporations would like to be unfettered in the ways they communicate publicly. As Paskowski and Donath (1981: 48) observe, however, "The free enterprise system's right to free speech by its corporate entities runs head on at times against the American sense of fair play when large profits, funneled through big media, overwhelm the voices of underfunded grass roots viewpoints." On the other hand, media gatekeepers, "journalists bent either on rectifying unfair play or typing a story, at times get caught leaving important pro-corporate information on the cutting room floor. And business people think media unfairness is far more pervasive than they can prove. Corporate communications remains a controversy because everyone in society has a story to tell, justified or not."

One mistake in analyzing news coverage is to expect balanced treatment. By its very nature, news is a selective presentation of reality. Much news is not even really new, but rather cyclical updates of mostly predictable events (weather, sports, air crashes, and the like). Another component involves non-investigative handout journalism of events in local, national, and foreign power centers tied to government. Less attention is paid to private sources, but nonprofit groups somewhat antagonistic to corporate values (such as think tanks, universities, and public interest lobbies) often successfully create news through the release of surveys and other studies. Until recently, few resources and little airtime were devoted to a host of institutions unfamiliar to most journalists (including religion, education, science, medicine, agriculture, and labor) except as they related to some political action or were caught up in governmental investigations. To make regular fill material attractive, the headline or lead story imperative is to feature the unusual, the visual, the dramatic, the bizarre, and the unexpected—not the normal.

Good business, unfortunately, is thus rarely perceived as newsworthy. Dominick (1981) contends that bad news about business heavily outweighs neutral and positive news. The Institute for Applied Economics, a nonprofit organization sponsored by 39 major American corporations, confirmed this in a report analyzing all evening TV newscasts of ABC, CBS, and NBC for the last six months of 1983. The survey concluded that while the amount of economic news had increased over previous years, "television's coverage of the economy continued to highlight bad news, not healthy economic trends. . . . Good economic news was simply not reported—or, more often, not reported in depth" ("Study," *Broadcasting*, 1984). Similarly, investigative reportage usually concentrates on the conflict between public and corporate interests and features the worst side of business life. Occasional nefarious acts, such as toxic waste dumping, cost overruns, ethical misbehavior, misleading advertising, and irresponsible development receive disproportionately large amounts of media attention for obvious and justifiable journalistic reasons precisely because ethical malfeasance in corporate America is far rarer than the day-to-day production of high-quality products and services. Coverage of the Union Carbide explosion in Bhopal, for example, was more newsworthy than reporting that thousands of products were handled safely by the chemical industry on the day of the disaster.

No company or industry can expect the media to serve as unthinking conduits to forcefeed the public on pro-business propaganda. On the other hand, companies should not have to contend with reporters who make predetermined conclusions without conducting thorough research. Reporters are particularly open to fault for neglecting business sources and abrogating their investigative responsibilities in pursuit of emerging stories. Many journalists already know what their report will be before arriving for interviews, seeking useful "sound bite" or "actuality" video and audio quotes rather than new information to complete the story package. Commenting on the credibility gap between reporters and companies, Finn (1981: 6) observes: "Reporters suspect that businessmen often lie and more often fail to tell the whole truth. Businessmen are convinced that the press is out to get them whatever the facts may be, and they are wary of saying anything lest they be quoted out of context."

One of the major differences between the print and electronic media has been the plentitude of the former and the scarcity of the latter. Because of the variety of publications, people can pick those magazines, books, and newspapers, or parts of newspapers, which confirm their world view. This publication specialization means that corporate communicators can more strategically position advertising and public relations messages to particular kinds of audiences. But short of using the persuasiveness of their message or the clout of their advertising dollar, business has little direct control over what appears. Few have been willing to take the frontal attack of openly refusing to cooperate with a publication or broadcaster with which they may disagree editorially, as Mobil did with the *Wall Street Journal*. If that controversy seems surprising, Lagerfeld (1981) suggests that the free enterprise system does not necessarily receive fair or balanced treatment even in the popular business press. Although his analysis of *Business Week* is skewed toward a strongly conservative viewpoint on corporate practices and economics, he charges that the magazine performs "a tremendous disservice" to readers by editorial policies "undermining and attacking the very ideas and values that give their work meaning and moral status" (Lagerfeld, 1981: 75).

Even in science reporting, bias and distortion unintended by journalists affects conceptions of social reality. All too typically, reporters react to disasters and other events for which they could have more adequately prepared themselves and their readers/viewers/listeners. For example, based on precoverage of the nuclear industry and later developments from the Three Mile Island incident, Friedman (1981) concludes that the media and power utility communicators were both in error for failing to adequately forewarn the public of possible dangers.

Too often when issues involve technical details, journalists simply lack the competence to judge the facts reported. Space and time limitations also restrict what can be said. One of the costs of communicating on terms dictated by broadcast journalists is the need to compress information, however complicated, into 20-second segments, because TV and radio "think" in that timeframe. Consequently, a story requiring a couple of pages of print or an hour of television may not receive full treatment.

Mazur (1981: 106) demonstrates how "reaction against a scientific technology appears to coincide with a rise in quantity of media coverage." Taking a hard look at nuclear issues, Cohen (1983: 70-71) reports that "pack journalism" also leads some reporters to simply become blinded to alternatives. He charges that public perceptions of reactor safety have been shaped by those who do not understand nuclear energy but recognize the popularity of a negative stance. Cohen is disconcerted by press usage of the safety issue to rail against nuclear generation when many other more immediate safety concerns receive lesser treatment. To support his argument, he reviewed the number of entries in the computerized New York *Times* to check the frequency of reporting on certain safety topics. Some 50,000 people die in car crashes yearly; Cohen found 120 stories on automobile safety. Industrial accidents, with 13,000 fatalities each year, received only 50 entries. Reports on asphyxiation dangers got just 20 mentions, even though they account for 4500 deaths. Other issues were largely ignored. In contrast, although not a single person has died directly from radiation exposure due to nuclear generation, over 200 entries discussed its safety, technology, progress, and regulation.

Similarly, in motion pictures and series television, many negative views of business are presented. Nuclear disaster, whether viewed from military or peacetime use, is a recurring theme in films such as *On the Beach, Dr. Strangelove, The China Syndrome, Silkwood, Special Bulletin,* and *The Day After.* The relationship between corporations and television programming is particularly paradoxical. Despite its reliance on corporate advertising, network television tends to show the darkest side of corporate life in entertainment programming as well as investigative journalism. A glance at broadcasting today reveals that the J. R. Ewing-type of scoundrel holds much more prime time interest than the generally unspecified business roles exemplified by earlier TV shows such as *Father Knows Best* or *Leave it to Beaver.* Through content analysis, the Media Institute discovered:

—Two out of three businessmen on television are portrayed as foolish, greedy or criminal.
—Almost half of all work activities performed by businessmen involve illegal acts.
—The majority of characters who run big business are portrayed as criminals.
—Television almost never portrays business as a socially useful or economically productive activity [Theberge, 1981: ix].

The institute concluded that the typical "crooks, conmen, and clowns" portrayal of business leaders constitutes a social reality instrumental in the formation and reinforcement of public opinion.

With great delicacy we note a parallel here with stereotypes of Blacks, Hispanics, women, and other social segments. For instance, the NAACP has argued that radio and television shows such as *Amos 'n' Andy* slowed the implementation of civil rights progress by reinforcing buffoonish role models. In a similar vein, Hispanic leaders have charged that the "Frito Bandito" character used in Frito-Lay product advertisements damaged the image of their people. Feminists have challenged narrow portrayal of women as weak, dependent housewives worried only about "ring around the collar." Nor are southern sheriffs as vicious or incompetent as typically pictured.

If such characterizations confound the understanding of these groups, so do inaccurate portrayals of business leaders. The danger of regulation by false stereotype is real. Users of television classified in the heaviest network-viewing quintiles have their access to information artificially restricted when the major networks take stands on corporate behavior and then refuse to sell corporations issue advertising spots—even coupled with offers such as those from Mobil, Kaiser, and others to pay for equal reply time by anti-business advocates chosen by the networks. This places an added burden on business communicators to market information via alternative channels and to present it without legerdemain. Otherwise, journalists and knowledgeable citizens come away believing they have been misled, as when Republic Airlines presented a slanted view of its profits (Young, 1981). Surely, some percentage of people who run corporations are driven only by greed. But the vast majority are responsible individuals who value their reputations, respect their communities, and care about the positions their companies occupy in society.

MEDIA IMAGE AND MEDIA EFFECTS: CREATING A TWO-TIERED SOCIETY

"Today," as Noelle-Neumann (1983: 157) notes, "most researchers assume that the mass media have a decisive effect on people's conceptions of reality." However, media effects research is problematic because television programming probably reflects opinion as much as it creates it. If a sizable segment of the public were not convinced that corporations are corrupt and acting against public interests, negative broadcast portrayals of business on entertainment and information programming could not maintain their ratings. We can postulate that because television news and entertainment programming presents narrow and negative portraits of corporations and the people who run them, heavy prime time viewers will develop different perceptions about corporations than will light viewers. Since the media follow public opinions as well as reinforce them, the extrapolation of this analysis is that if groups of people receive different information from different media, they will develop different conceptions of reality to form a broadly two-tiered society.

We believe that these two major audience tiers include one large group—the majority—composed of "know nothings" as well as those who watch a significant amount of prime time "crooks, conmen and clowns" television. A smaller second group—lighter viewers and those with interests skewed toward investment opportunities—probably has a more favorable perception of corporate behavior. Contrary to a smattering of earlier research which found that light viewers are not more attracted to intellectually low-rated shows than heavy viewers (Katz, 1981), the emergence of business-oriented programming is in fact drawing new viewership. This minority population is composed of individuals inclined to seek out narrow-cast information by accessing alternative video sources to those controlled by the three major commercial networks. Moreover, second-tier group members are also more prone to read upscale magazines and newspapers carrying issue advertisements that explain corporate points of view.

Many studies have supported different versions of this conclusion, even though research to date has not provided definitive answers regarding the nature of these groups nor fully explored their viewing patterns. Nevertheless, after reviewing the literature and acknowledging the methodological problems of effects studies, Hawkins and Pingree (1981) agree that televiewing and demographics interact so that social realities are created, amplified, and reinforced. Another perspective of this problem is provided by Burke (1969), who contends that one of the most powerful social forces involves living a shared view of reality, or what he calls "identification." Of significance here is the fact that, according to a 1982 Roper Organization national survey, over 60 percent of respondents named television as their regular business news and information source ("TV Outpolls," Adweek, 1982). A moment's reflection on this finding reveals that these self-reported data may underestimate the effect that television viewing has on public perceptions of business behavior, people, and ethics.

Evidence to confirm the emergence of two tiers is further found in a demographic segmentation study by the Magazine Publishers Association (1985). Despite having an apparent vested interest in the survey results, the association examined the buying and media use of the "super innovator," a 25- to 54-year-old college graduate with a minimum household income of $35,000. Super innovators are policy-active; 72 percent are in the heavy magazine/light (more selective) television viewing category. These facts suggest that a vital, politically involved segment of society obtains its impressions of business from reading more than televiewing.

What can be speculated is how group attitudes are shaped and reinforced by the media they use, a question open to subsequent analysis by a sophisticated demographic system integrating the Simmons Market Research Bureau's "Media Imperatives," Donnelley Marketing Information Services' ClusterPlus, the Stanford Research Institute's Values and Lifestyles (VALS) categories, and/or similar programs. Funkhouser (1973) has argued that the amount of media time and space influences public awareness of an issue. Many subsequent studies have found that heavy viewers of television believe that the amount of crime is greater than it actually is (Gebner et al., 1980). Reinforcing the danger of media-based reality, a group of researchers discovered that network claims of momentum shifts in candidate popularity during the 1976 presidential election were often based, not on poll data, but on the subjective opinions of the reporters. Such shifts, as reported, lead viewers to believe a totally contrived social "truth" (Meyers et al., 1978). On political communication, Graber (1982: 557) views the media as "active creators of political reality, rather than mere mirrors of the passing scene and transmitters of the views of others." Consequently, perhaps because of the attempted balance of television, heavy viewers call themselves political moderates and avoid liberal or conservative labels (Gerbner et al., 1984).

Similar findings indicate that advertisements can lead children to make inaccurate inferences about the operation of products and to prefer advertised to nonadvertised products (Adler, 1977; Comstock et al., 1978; Roberts et al., 1980; Robertson and Rossiter, 1977). Meyer and Hexamer (1981) claim that consumer socialization, and not cognitive development, accounts for the differences in information processing regarding advertising content.

ISSUES MANAGEMENT AND MEDIA ALTERNATIVES

Having a broadly two-tiered society sharply contrasts with Marshall McLuhan's (1969: 17) prediction that advancing communication technology will produce an electronic age sealing "the entire human family into a single global tribe." Television is the crucial channel, McLuhan argues, because it allows millions of people to have common viewing experiences.

The observations of McLuhan and the other researchers cited above are cause to worry about the magnified consequences of fragmented and misinformed public opinion. In seeking a level of consensus, corporations are looking at widening their media reach (Miller, 1981; Business Week, 1980; Much, 1980; Maher, 1982; Friendly, 1977; Simmons, 1978; Rowan, 1984). Despite antagonism to politically motivated commercial speech and the lack of guaranteed access, a weakened economy has led many local broadcasters and cablecasters to reconsider accepting advocacy communication. A number of individual licensees and cable franchise holders now televise some relatively innocuous corporate messages. Precedent exists among the some 1200 commercial, public, and cable TV stations/systems regularly requesting promotional "public service" public relations films from producers and distributors of sponsored motion picture products (Klein, 1983; DeWitt, 1983; Perkins, 1982). Compared to 1975, when only 50 percent of its member stations said they would accept more controversial issue advertisements, Television Bureau of Advertising (TVB) data indicate that by 1981 the figure escalated to 93 percent of those reporting. These figures are somewhat misleading, however, in that licensees still control which issues, sponsors, advertisements, and daypart airtimes will be allowed.

As noted in Chapter 4, information-based issue broadcast ads might be more widespread if it weren't for the fairness doctrine. Network managements present a "Catch 22" dilemma for corporate communicators and the public, since ABC, CBS, and NBC (even with audience erosion) jointly still control over 70 percent of all viewers. This gives senior executives inordinate power in determining the news agenda and directing public opinion. Network broadcasters have long argued, without substantive proof, that news and public affairs programs created by their own staffs—rather than first-come/first-served common carrier acceptance of advocacy advertising—are the best way to explore issues and keep the public informed (Pool, 1983; Woolward, 1982).

Though frustrated in their efforts to use the major television networks to balance negative business reportage, issues managers will not find their time productively filled by carping about the problems of media bias. Corporations are cautiously realizing that past press release denials, the stonewalling of reporters, and other "low profile" practices are no longer acceptable in many instances and, worse, can prove quite damaging in the critical arena of public opinion (Steckmest, 1982; Genthe, 1982). As Ronald Rhody (1983), vice president of public relations for the Bank of America, candidly observes:

> Most of the misimpressions, or errors, or unfairness that so many are concerned about is business's own fault. We, in our institutions (just like the media and government), have been guilty of ignorance, arrogance, bad judgment and negligence. Silence, evasiveness, the lack of candor, the unwillingness to respond, have been like lead weights pulling business down lower and lower in public esteem. The fact that the public may be misinformed on key economic or business issues, may be misled about our respective operations and intentions, is largely our own doing. We have permitted this because, out of fear of either criticism or controversy, we have failed to take the initiative.

Drawing insight from earlier experiences while with Kaiser Aluminum & Chemical Corporation, Rhody (1983: 46-47) challenges business leaders to "stop grousing about the media and really learn how to work with it. . . . The 'it's none of their business' school of public information and press relations has no place in the '80s. Business is so much a part of the society and the economies in which it operates—has such an impact on jobs and taxes, and therefore on government services and community life and health—that what a company is doing, and why and how, is very much 'their business' . . . that is, the public's business."

Such sage advice—or pro-active prescription—is evidenced by Kevin Phillips (1981), president of the American Political Research Corporation, who optimistically points out:

> The battleground of business-media relations is changing. Television network news is still simplistic, inflammatory and more than occasionally biased, yet it is a problem corporations have begun to take seriously. The larger context of press coverage of business-economic issues is one of improvement, however, and in the growing area of corporate-related First Amendment interpretation, press groups are now frequently emerging as *allies* of the business community.

A 1981 study by the American Management Association further reveals that while broad areas of misunderstanding continue to exist between business executives and the media, at the same time there are also some surprising new areas of agreement. Companies are simultaneously exploring a variety of alternative cost-effective strategies and channels for issues communication (Gandy, 1982; Moriarty, 1983). Their experiments include the following:

(1) meeting directly with broadcast executives to explore possible improvements in business-media relations;
(2) counter-advertising/informational advertising in journalism trade magazines and newspapers;
(3) counter-advertising/informational advertising in leading general and opinion publications;
(4) establishing trade association information offices for liaison with television/film producers;
(5) underwriting academic news and policy studies by pro-business and independent nonprofit institutes;
(6) distributing videotaped rebuttals via a variety of outlets; and
(7) filing a lawsuit (Miller, 1981).

Major growth areas involve internal communication (corporate television, videodisc, and videoconferencing) and external communication (cable programming, direct mail, and data retrieval) (Media Institute, 1983; Budd, 1983a, b; Sambul, 1982a). All offer desirable audience pinpointing and hold tremendous promise for influencing our information landscape.

Despite the apparent difficulties and overestimates of the new technologies, writers such as Patrick R. Williams (1982) encourage corporate communicators to become proficient in using them. The need to explore many new communication alternatives is also expressed by Bleecker and Lento (1982: 11), who issue a challenge to public relations practitioners: "As people who manage and disseminate information, we should be in the vanguard of the information revolution. To play out our role in the transformation of our jobs, we must keep up with the technology."

Well-established videotex/teletext/on-line data search and retrieval services, such as The Source, Knowledge Index, Dialog, CompuServe, NewsNet, and Nexis/Lexis, conveniently offer users key word/topic access to hundreds of publications and other documentation. Most organizational issues managers find these services helpful as a tracking and monitoring tool. But since the field is open to innovation, creative opportunities also exist to cooperate with these and other text services in establishing credible new encyclopedic and specialized alternative information banks. As in other communication efforts, the end user audience should be specified and the content tailored to its interests. As a supplement to traditional media efforts, on-line communication offers participating companies and industries the potential to bypass reporters and speak directly via articles, fact sheets, position papers, and other useful data. This is an ideal propaganda vehicle, to be sure, but one that serves the public interest by expanding access. Rather than relying simply on the editorial discretion of newspapers, for instance, readers can go into large data systems and find authoritative, unedited information (which would otherwise be unavailable) about corporate operations and industrial practices. Multiple addressing via electronic mail services such as Western Union EasyLink offer additional message-tailoring options.

Further underscoring this change is the fact that corporate-related news itself is of increasing importance to journalistic organizations. Additional staff reporters now regularly cover the economy and "more air time than ever before is devoted to financial events" by the major networks and a growing roster of business news programs on public radio and television, independent stations, and cable channels (Grasser, 1982). An estimated 100-plus hours of business and financial programming goes out each week through Financial News Network (FNN), Cable News Network (CNN), Satellite Program Network (SPN), Modern Satellite Network (MSN), Public Broadcasting Service (PBS), and syndication. Made possible in part by a greater effort on the part of corporations to publicize their commitment to social responsibility, these broadcasters offer an alternative to the three-network sameness. It is also worth noting that hundreds of cable system operators also require on-air video "product" as more and more channels come on line.

Corporations are particularly well placed to service this new market with professionally produced materials. Internal corporate/institutional (or business) videos already account for a $4 billion industry. Over 7000 private and nonprofit organizations regularly produce 20,000 hours of video programming for viewing by employees, shareholders, customers, and other targeted audiences. The 1981 market research study by D/J Brush Associates for the International Television Association estimated that this constituted "substantially more programming" than was produced by all four major national broadcast networks combined during the preceding year (Brush and Brush, 1985). Most of this programming discusses technical and financial topics, showing developments as well as telling about them. Some companies run these programs in-house on a weekly or monthly basis. Others believe that the impact of information is increased by communicating only when some issue or topic is salient in employees' minds.

Despite the potential to repackage in-house material for other audiences, the external airing of business productions is still largely an undeveloped area. Currently, only a handful of corporate television studios specifically produce programs for the general public now shown either in local offices, at trade shows, or during nationwide seminars via satellite. A smaller number of corporate TV reports are screened on individual cable systems and regional networks, including material generated by Kaiser, Emhart Corporation, Mobil, W. R. Grace & Co., and Standard Oil of California (Chevron), among others. Further opportunities are being explored to expand business involvement through video news releases, video brochures, video annual reports, "informationals," "advertorials," and "newsitorials" running up to ten minutes or longer (Buske, 1983a, b; Sambul, 1982b; Rubin, 1985).

The technology exists for providing videotaped commentary and visualization to help interested publics understand company operations or to give the company's version of a crisis situation. Interactive videoconference setups enable specialized users immediate, "face-to-face" access to communication experts and corporate executives. One of the major success stories in this use of videoconferencing was effected by Johnson & Johnson in its response to the September 1982 Tylenol crisis. When several people died in Chicago after taking cyanide-laced Tylenol capsules, myriad dimensions of issues management were employed to protect the company's product image. Moreover, this crisis gave J&J an excellent opportunity to demonstrate its commitment to achieving the highest corporate social standards. The fact that the public outcry was shortlived demonstrates that the company's reputation for responsibility was high to begin with. Its image rose even higher afterward.

Of course, J&J had an advantage over other corporations in hot water; as far as the evidence indicates, the company was not responsible for the tragedy. Senior managers gave the crisis their full attention, meeting twice a day for its duration. One of their primary commitments was to show that the company cared by stressing its concern for people and emphasizing the statement on corporate responsibility that J&J had adopted 40 years before. As the backbone of the crisis management effort, the executive decision from the start was to open the company's operations to public scrutiny. The company allowed Mike Wallace and a *60 Minutes* crew to video a strategy session, and Chairman James E. Burke volunteered to appear on major national television programs. Going beyond the obvious reliance on communication to solve a crisis, J&J immediately recalled millions of bottles of its product. But perhaps the highlight of the crisis management effort was a 30-city teleconference used to introduce new triple-sealed Tylenol capsule safety packaging. The satellite teleconference cost approximately $400,000 and attracted representatives from over 6000 news organizations (Leon, 1983).

This innovative video press conference gave the company impressive visibility in major markets as it solidified reporter perceptions that J&J executives were telling the truth. Still, there is always room for performance improvement. Although he awards high marks to the marketing team at J&J, Snyder (1983) only gives a "good" rating to the public relations effort. He finds two major faults: First, J&J lacked a crisis management plan. What was done, although brilliant, had to be developed after details of the incident began to unfold. Second, there were no specific prior guidelines on how general corporate philosophy could be applied in a given crisis. Despite these valid criticisms, the fact remains that J&J masterfully utilized a major new communication technology. Rather than relying on unimaginative media efforts, the company decided to make itself vulnerable; it went live to the press. And it was successful.

Sometimes, however, you can win the battle but lose the war. The striking Air Line Pilots Association (ALPA) in 1983 used a national videoconference to charge that Continental Airlines planes were being flown by inexperienced and psychologically stressed crews shortly after the carrier voided labor contracts, eliminated routes, and declared

Chapter 11 bankruptcy. ALPA president Henry Duffy's claim that Continental committed 152 safety violations was featured on *60 Minutes*. Believing that Continental would respond to these charges, ALPA executed a video press conference beamed by Telstar 301 (at a cost of $4000) to media representatives, including 200 commercial television stations in the 32 cities served by Continental. Newsrooms were notified by telex that the broadcast would be available for airing. The short-term result: Approximately 11 million homes with 28 million viewers saw the releases (Hattal and Hattal, 1984). In its more important long-range objective to put public and court pressure on Continental to restore earlier contracts, however, ALPA failed.

Videodisc/computer interconnects are an intriguing related on-demand text and picture option. Despite the commercial failure of home videodisc players, on-site laser videodisc facilities will likely be data-base-integrated to provide employees convenient call-up access to operational procedures and policies. The videodisc is an immediate and tireless source allowing for either pictorial, spoken voice, or written information about a company and its industry. Another advantage of this medium is its transmission, if desired, via satellite directly into homes, businesses, and newsrooms.

Beginning in September 1983 an all-commercial cable network—The Cableshop—launched programming services in Atlanta, Boston, Chicago, Detroit, Erie, Los Angeles, and northern New Jersey. Initially some 250,000 subscribers had access to the channel, which is promoting itself as a cable TV information service. Subscribers see 3- 7-minute messages about national products and services, as well as retail shopping opportunities in the community. Viewers can tune in and watch informationals that are running on a "loop" or access a specific advertisement or business report by phoning the Cableshop and dialing a computer. Code numbers for individual ads appear in participating systems' cable guides.

Private Satellite Network (PSN) is another bold attempt to use new technological options creatively. PSN is launching an institutional business-to-business direct broadcast satellite (DBS) service. Initially, PSN is being offered to large corporations as a form of in-house communications, but as its market penetration expands it will also provide a service for advertisers to use television to reach key industrial targets (Mandese, 1983).

Although Cableshop and PSN test marketing have offered more traditional product- and service-type messages, other avenues are being explored in terms of news. Public relations news organizations staffed by professional broadcast journalists are also springing into existence to take advantage of new low-cost satellite and other technologies. Most newsrooms are computerized today, and stories placed on the PR Newswire are instantaneously distributed to major newspapers and other clients throughout the country for convenient desktop call-up by reporters. For under $3000 the North American Precis Syndicate, Inc. (NAPS) will guarantee a corporate client that its TV release—a script and four chromakey slides illustrating the story—will be placed on over 40 stations with Households Using Television (HUT) levels exceeding 10 million. The cost includes usage cards returned by the stations, computer printouts with audience demographic data, and coverage maps. Another example is Washington Broadcast News, which reaches 3400 radio news departments via satellite facilities of Mutual, UPI, and the Associated Press networks with daily feeds of news releases and actualities for their clients. PubSat (the Public Affairs Satellite System), an audio and video public relations news service operational since 1981, is an increasingly popular option. It delivers electronic news releases to over 1450 radio and 300-plus commercial television stations reaching 80 percent of the nation's potential audience, with more coming on line as earth stations are added. An additional 4000 cable systems may be accessed.

Recognizing that electronic journalists utilize predictable format conventions preaccepted by audiences, corporations and trade associations have been attracted by the relatively low cost of delivery for radio and TV spots virtually indistinguishable from station-produced reports. A variation of this strategy features a well-known personality who presents information in an ostensibly neutral news fashion. In one TV spot, produced by the Chemical Manufacturers Association (CMA) and distributed by PubSat, former CBS commentator Rod MacLeish affects a standup microphone reporter pose to describe how the chemical industry is solving pressing waste and environmental safety problems. Another example sponsored by the association featured Meryl Comer as correspondent. This shows the precautions taken by the chemical industry during the transportation of its products. The story made two important points: (1) Federal figures indicate a continued drop in the frequency of chemical transportation accidents; and (2) Chemtrec, a CMA-funded agency, is on the job assisting fire protection and police agencies when they encounter a chemical accident. Similarly, Mobil has reached a syndicated national audience through sponsorship of the *Independent News,* with its Mobil Information Center commercials stylistically crafted to harmonize with the "news sandwich" surrounding them.

The U.S. Chamber of Commerce, through its American Business Network (BizNet), operates one of the more ambitious programming operations. BizNet is a business-oriented, closed-circuit private television service transmitted via satellite from the chamber's $4 million studios in Washington, D.C. to its members (local chambers, companies, associations, and law firms) and non-members (colleges, hotels, and cable companies). BizNet is also an interactive on-line network with receiver sites throughout the country for private use. BizNet, for example, has been used to bring PAC managers together by video to coordinate lobbying efforts.

Members of the U.S. Chamber and home satellite dish users receive up to seven hours of weekday programming via Satcom F4 84W. Programs include in-depth reports on legislative, political, and regulatory events in Washington as well as the 50 state capitals. BizNet also features business and political experts, forecasts and trend analyses, educational workshops, and seminars. Through BizNet's state-of-the-art two-way audio capability, subscribers are able to interact with program participants in Washington for an annual subscription fee.

Nonmembers of the chamber are also targeted to receive *BizNet News Today*, a daily one-hour talk show patterned after *Good Morning America*, with hosts Meryl Comer and Carl Grant. *BizNet News Today* offers policy analysis reports on issues affecting the business and financial sectors. It airs in the morning on BizNet's own satellite system, plus a mix of conventional broadcast and cable outlets. Many cable television systems are airing *BizNet News Today* as the cornerstone for an entire business service, welcoming the business community as a potential new market for cable penetration. Segments from selected shows are also offered on video cassettes to businesses for internal corporate TV screenings to employees.

The chamber additionally produces *Ask Washington*, an hour-long call-in talk program aired daily with leading Capitol Hill figures, and *It's Your Business*. In this half-hour syndicated program available on over 155 stations and cable systems, Chamber President Richard Lesher and three different guests use a moderated discussion/debate format to discuss topical issues. According to BizNet marketing representative Kathryn VanLier Michael (1983), "this revolutionary business advocacy network is improving communications throughout the business community and the grassroots to affect the public policy process."

Besides BizNet, several other cable TV programs feature general business news and discussion. The 60-minute format of *Business Times* (until recently aired on ESPN) consisted of interviews, features, and hard news. These are packaged into a morning "business briefing" of 60-90 stories targeted at upscale executive males ($70,000+ household income). *Business Times* boasted an exclusive hookup with the *Financial Times* of London and its worldwide network of correspondents. Ratings estimates moved as high as 1.2 but tended to hover at .7 and .8 for the show. This inability to break out into viewing numbers attractive to advertisers hurt its future. A noncommercial *Business Times* audio version airing on National Public Radio is proving more successful.

PBS has two of the most popular series. The *Nightly Business Report* (Public Broadcasting System, in conjunction with WPBT-TV in Miami) emphasizes stock market developments, economic commentary, and CEO interviews; the program reaches an estimated audience of 4 million on 234 stations covering virtually the entire nation. *Wall $treet Week,* which appears to have the largest audience of all U.S. business programs, is hosted by Louis Rukeyser, who reviews the market developments for the week, chats with three analysts, and concludes with an interview of a special guest. This 30-minute show airs on Friday nights. *Wall $treet Week* reaches an estimated 10 million viewers—a figure nearly one-third the size of the nation's 32 million total shareholders. PBS sources report that 47 percent of *W$W*'s audience is made up of women. Less well known airings on PBS are featured in *Enterprise,* which pictures the human side of business in a series of 13 topical 30-minute shows per year.

The most emulated format centers on news of value for active investors. *Financial News Network* offers 13 hours of financial and business news, including the BizNet feed, 6:00 a.m.-7:00 p.m. ET, Monday through Friday, via the Satcom F3 131W satellite and cable systems. A six-hour *Marketwatch* from 10:00 a.m. to 4:00 p.m. features in-depth coverage of bonds, stocks, real estate, options, commodities, ventures, and other technical analyses invaluable to the serious investor. Early morning and late afternoon one-hour blocks contain programs such as *Business Today, Money Talk,* and a daily wrap-up called *Wall Street Final.*

The Tulsa-based Satellite Program Network (SPN) innovated a variety of programs to test audience appeal, including *Investor's Action Line*, a 30-minute discussion show; *Money, Money, Money*, with specific advice on investment themes; *Money Talks*, targeted to viewers with a household income of $35,000+; and *Get Rich With Real Estate.*

American Express earlier worked with SPN to experiment with a pilot half-hour series called *How's Business* airing in 1982 on 1400 cable systems in more than 120 cities (Video Systems, 1983).

Cable News Network (CNN) offers a strong roster of programs. *Business Morning* is a 30-minute segment of *Daybreak*. Later, *Market Update* airs brief reports on key market developments, appearing every hour on the half hour Monday through Friday. *Moneyline,* with Lou Dobbs as executive producer and anchor, has been the highest rated CNN program since breaking ground in 1980 as the first nightly business newscast (7:00 p.m. ET, repeated at 11:00 p.m. with occasional updates). This fast-paced 30-minute program, with a heavy emphasis on market and economic information, drew an estimated audience of 221,000 households in the first half of 1983. *Inside Business* (CNN) interviews major corporate leaders, who are quizzed by host Myron Kandel; it airs Sunday evenings for 30 minutes. *Moneyweek* is a 30-minute weekend summary of the week's action on Wall Street and in Washington, supplementing CNN's personal finance show, *Your Money*.

The Modern Satellite Network (MSN), an outgrowth of the world's leading audio-visual public relations information distributor (Modern Talking Pictures Service), is also actively providing outlets for corporate, foreign government, and other sponsored film producers into cable systems reaching nearly 9 million homes. MSN programs such as *Business View, Consumer Inquiry, Modern Life, Viewpoint,* and *Let's Travel* all have been packaged in response to Nielson survey data commissioned by MSN which show that 44 percent of cable subscribers want more travel information, 50 percent seek more documentaries, and 63 percent desire additional consumer information. The causes and effects underlying these findings are open to several interpretations. The desire for consumer information can indicate public interest in combating what it believes (and perhaps rightly so) to be poorly built products. It may exhibit a negative, anti-business attitude. However, it may reveal the desire of certain people to become as fully informed as possible in dealing with corporate America. *Business View*, for example, provides paid half-hour reports from business, industry, and government presented to demonstrate how clients' efforts are working to benefit consumers. *Viewpoint* is a proprietary interview-format program that presents opinions and ideas from leading associations, corporations, and not-for-profit organizations. Each interview explores a timely topic in depth, with an attempt to provide audiences with a better understanding of relevant issues. MSN program purchasers can also opt for an "800" telephone number for viewers to call toll free for more information, giving them near-instantaneous feedback on the effectiveness of their messages.

Other syndication program options are being explored. *Moneyworks*, an interview program produced by Hardie Mintzer, airs weekly in a number of markets. *Business Week Final* (syndicated by *Business Week* magazine in cooperation with Newslink, Inc.) is a nightly five-minute television news insert offered on a market-exclusive basis to local stations. Similarly, *The Wall Street Journal Report* (Independent News/WPIX-TV, New York, in conjunction with Dow Jones & Company) offers an entertaining 30-minute weekly videomagazine selection of feature stories drawn from daily editions of the paper. It airs to an average audience of 1.3 million viewers per week (with a potential national reach of 83 percent) on 96 local stations. In a related service, daily *Wall Street Journal* broadcast scripts are offered to subscribing stations for a five-minute newscast insert slot using local anchors. *Taking Advantage* again features a similar format to *The Wall Street Journal Report* but aimed at a broader investor/consumer audience. Its airdates began in October 1983 on 145 local stations reaching 90 percent of American households. Several other business shows are in their trial stages, and undoubtedly there will be change and attrition just as in other television formats.

What impact does this proliferation of business television programming have on the corporate information environment? Most shows, as we have seen, consist of economic news, business commentary, and investment advice. It is true that many are nothing more than public relations marketing vehicles designed to attract investors, not directly addressing issues related to one side or the other of regulation controversies. However, some programs—*Pinnacle* on CNN to name one—feature person-to-person-style interviews of leading business figures and give insight into the human aspect of corporations. Viewers get a rare opportunity to listen to CEOs discuss management perspectives on issues facing their firms. These programs currently appeal to a narrow but influential market, probably not very different in composition from the upscale readership of business magazines and financial newspapers. This is a potentially receptive constituency for a company or industry. Particularly as individuals gain greater sophistication in finance and economics, cable becomes a psychographically desirable supplement to print issue advertising campaigns.

One problem in attempting to analyze the significance of these developments involves the current inadequacy of conventional Nielsen/Arbitron ratings methodologies to determine cable audience demographics. Beyond sketchy demographic profiles, the size of the audience reached by this programming has not been fully calculated, nor is much else definitively known about the viewers of such programs. For example, we do not know answers to such questions as what percentage are high users of television, how distinctive their newspaper and magazine reading habits are, or whether their attitudes toward business in fact differ from other viewers of television. Continuing reliance by cable program packagers on potential audience figures, instead of actual Persons Using Television (PUT) statistics, further undermines credible media usage analysis but is understandable given their marketing needs. Except for specially commissioned reports, to be rated a cable network first must demonstrate that it has a 15 percent national audience penetration, with both diaries (inaccuracies in recording actual usage) and meters (only experimental introduction of people meters, and on conventional systems of limited sample size for important subgroups such as business executives making $50,000+ per year) seemingly incapable of yielding precise, reliable data for the fragmented and specialized viewership tuned to new technology channels. How viewing estimates will take into account consumer-oriented DBS narrowcast programming, if that appears in the late 1980s as predicted, is also a concern.

Obviously the challenge before corporations is not only the status quo in terms of news reportage and standards, but also the ethical and philosophical problems created by efforts to inform various publics. Some of the programming is obviously biased and one-sided in its point of view. As audiences grow, broadcasters and cable operators are likely to be confronted with increased efforts to apply the fairness doctrine. The redirection of media used by corporations and parts of the viewing audience also evidences the critical need to understand the convergence of information technologies now taking place. Federal deregulation and the rapid expansion of such opportunities necessitates identifying cable business programming as an emerging electronic publishing format with audience demographics and information society legal issues similar in many ways to the traditional print media (Hartman, 1983; Jacobson, 1983; Kelley, 1983; Pool, 1983; Nelson and Heath, 1984).

Pioneering communicators have nevertheless welcomed alternative opportunities to disseminate their pro-business views. Indeed, the purpose of most of the business advocacy and informational programming efforts is to spearhead major changes in our society. Viewers may not know they are seeing a video handout rather than an objective report. Corporate public relations, done with flair, may end up looking like another news spot or documentary, prostituting the news environment to one of capitalist propaganda (Green, 1982).

Balancing this situation is that business, of course, is not alone in looking toward new technological options (Lacayo, 1984; Kelley and Donway, 1983). Members of Congress, for example, have ready access to the professionally equipped Congressional television studios, complete with a backdrop of the Capitol, for video news releases directed at TV/cable constituents in their home districts. Many political, public interest, religious, labor, and educational groups seeking greater exposure for their views are also exploring similar opportunities opened up by 30-channel cable, low power TV, direct broadcast satellites, and electronic bulletin boards. Funding comes from donations, foundations, advertisers, and union dues.

The AFL-CIO in the 1980s established a new media affiliate, the Labor Institute of Public Affairs, with a $3 million annual budget to create informational television programming. The union has also helped form an ambitious "CableLINE" service testmarketed in Pittsburgh, Atlanta, and Seattle during late 1983. Included were pro-labor feature films such as *Harlan County, U.S.A.* and a half-hour *Labor Visions* weekly news magazine that presented worker views on issues such as the Greyhound Bus Company strike. The AFL-CIO additionally spent $600,000 producing the 12-part issue-oriented *America Works* for the screen in nearly 40 selected local television markets. The initial episode describes the economics of plant closings and the resulting impact on workers. The United Auto Workers spent $2 million to air commercials aimed at bolstering support for domestic content legislation and offsetting "improper" Reagan administration interference in GM/Ford labor contracts. The Communications Workers of America have also aggressively communicated their union's position on issues such as high technology by airing the television and radio public affairs series *Rewiring Your World* (*Videography*, 1983; Sheler, 1983; Buske, 1984; Brown, 1984).

IS THERE A FUTURE TO ISSUES MANAGEMENT?

Much continuing research is needed before we fully understand all the implications of contemporary network and cable programming policies. Rudimentary evidence suggests that prime time network televiewing further alienates a sizable segment of the public from business and establishes a social reality unfounded in fact. To the extent that prime time viewers are a different segment of the population from those who regularly see business-oriented programming, a two-tiered nation is being created. Responding to what they perceive as a generally hostile media environment, and because the mass dissemination of issues advertising has liabilities, corporations are pro-actively seeking new channels to inform key message audiences.

The more important concern, at least in the sense of societal fragmentation, is whether we can effectively balance public and private interests to achieve reasonable business and communication regulatory policies meeting future needs. A workable consensus on the role of corporate responsibility has so far eluded us. In the end, our society may be inexorably drifting toward polarized "global villages" where consubstantiation on many serious issues is impossible. Assuming the need for a common platform of fact and a common-sense evaluation of the contributions made by business, some constructive alternative is necessary.

Social involvement and responsibility is at the heart of issues management. As Abraham Lincoln wisely observed long ago, "You cannot fool all of the people all of the time." Even in a high-tech conglomerate society, no one company or industry can entirely squelch independent inquiry or buy out the media, even if it wanted to. Nor do most business leaders seek such power. Instead, the need is for more openness. If error is to occur in regulating business speech, we suggest that it be made in attempting to give corporations every opportunity for public communication.

What philosopher Ayn Rand called "the virtue of selfishness"—in this case, business attempts to extend influence by expanded exploration of new technologies—is ironically contributing to a broader understanding of regulatory policy options. The public interest is well served by continuing private participation in this process, since the result is a more informed and balanced discussion of critical financial, economic, and political issues. Such open debate is far more likely to provide valuable insight than any repressive system artificially limiting communication by one or more parties. At the very least, these alternative channels offer many intriguing possibilities for alternative messages by information practitioners. But more importantly, in defending corporate speech and libertarian values perhaps rests the lasting worth of the First Amendment to those of us really concerned, like the Founding Fathers, about truth emerging from the welter of competing voices.

CONCLUSION
The Future of Issues Management

A FOUNDATION OF UNDERSTANDING AND THE MANAGEMENT OF POWER RESOURCES

Over the past two decades, the history of issues management has been stormy. Public relations/affairs practitioners and scholars question whether issues management is unique or nothing more than the natural evolution of the maturing practice of corporate communication. Certainly the explosive, assertive style used by Mobil scared many companies from using advocacy communication. Regulatory policies at the FTC, FCC, and IRS have been exploited by pressure groups as a form of weaponry to curtail the public discussion of issues. Some corporate critics propose strengthening rather than relaxing these restrictions. Others (e.g., Buchholz, 1985) have challenged companies to communicate in a more responsible and meaningful manner, while writers such as Post et al. (1983) argue that the value of issues management is the narrowing of the gap between corporate performance and public expectations by harmonizing corporate practices with public interests.

As we have attempted to show, the major debate today should not be whether corporations should improve their ethics or commitment to social responsibility. That battle has already been won. The business leadership that has emerged during the past decade is devoted to the public interest and does not need to be preached to (Useem, 1985). Rather, the focus of concern should shift toward how most effectively to encourage dialogue between business and other critical sectors. This relationship seems to center on three key questions. Do various publics understand companies? Do companies understand these publics? And, on the aggregate, are these publics satisfied that corporations are meeting the prevailing standards of corporate social responsibility? In the uncertain years ahead, issues management (if not artificially restricted) should play an increasingly important role in resolving these questions by shaping the information agenda.

In many ways, issues management seems to be on the verge of becoming institutionalized. For one thing, it has been the object of House of Representatives and Senate investigations (U.S. Congress 1978a,b). Another major step toward institutionalization was taken with the creation of the Issues Management Association (IMA). Most of the leadership instrumental in its birth in the mid-1970s came from corporate ranks or those closely associated with consulting practices. Many of the early articles, often written by corporate communication practitioners, extolled the virtues of issues management while paying little attention to whether it was a unique or valuable corporate function with an identity separate from other established planning and communication functions. Academic scholars have now joined the effort to examine issues management. A glance at the 1985 IMA program reveals that issues managers for the Clorox Company, the Public Service Company of New Mexico, and Atlantic Richfield were on programs with faculty members from San Jose State University and the University of California at Berkeley. Despite this mingling, the association still leans heavily toward leadership from the corporate ranks.

Issues management is now finding its way into university curricula and highly respected studies such as *The Public Affairs Handbook* (Nagelschmidt, 1982); HRN's guidebook, *Leveraging the Impact of Public Affairs* (Nowlan et. al, 1984); and the ninth edition of Moore and Kalupa, *Public Relations: Principles, Cases, and Problems* (1985). Moore and Kalupa (1985: 63-64) observe: "Issue management, while still relatively new, is an increasingly significant method of meeting the pressure resulting from rapid social-economic changes and proliferating political activism." They continue:

> For a corporation faced with current or emerging public issues which may affect its business, issue management can be likened to war or diplomacy strategy. The focus is not on the weapons but on decisions as to whether the issue requires combat, on what grounds a battle will be fought, and when it will be engaged. Effective issue management also can often prevent an issue from arising at all, or redirect its course.

Xerox is right. One of the major problems facing companies is not the acquisition of information, but rather its use. The world of issues management resides at the conflux between agreement and controversy over the control of power resources. Four factors seem central to the future of issues management. None of these relate to questions about whether it is unique or old hat public relations/affairs, nor do they concern where it is housed in the corporate structure. Rather, the future of issues management depends on the hostility of the regulatory climate, the executive philosophy and social vision of specific corporations, the value of public policy monitoring and advice to corporate planning, and the economic and social benefits of establishing a continuing public dialogue.

REGULATORY CLIMATE

As long as corporate managements associate public affairs and issues management with short-term fire fighting, its popularity will fluctuate with the temper of the regulatory climate. Advocacy advertising increases when special interest agitation challenges business practices. Despite the Reagan administration's tilt toward corporate interests, the problem with becoming complacent is the likelihood that another period such as the 1960s will catch companies off guard. A favorable regulatory environment can lull corporate leaders into abandoning the "distant early warning system" of monitoring and refining standards of corporate social responsibility when pro-activity is most possible. Support for issues management, including budgeting, should not be put off until crisis management time. Then it is too late to utilize the full value of what issues management can provide in terms of environmental monitoring and pre-crisis planning and communication.

Over time, special interest groups can become an institutionalized part of the establishment. Many environmental groups, for instance, have become entrenched players on certain issues. They use grassroots politics to bring their memberships into the fray. They have research and political staffs which direct their lobbying efforts. They even draft legislation. Some groups are so integral to the system that their activities are funded in part or whole by the government.

The conflict between special interest groups and business advocates may occur more often in legislative hearings than in the public media. How the regulatory battle ends will depend on the relative power of the players. The balance of power, to a large extent, depends on how effectively corporations respond to the public interest and how well they communicate that response.

CORPORATE MANAGERIAL PHILOSOPHY

The future of issues management depends on the corporate vision that develops over the coming years. Arrington and Sawaya (1984) hit the nail on the head as they observe: "An issues management function will prove effective in direct proportion to senior management's understanding of its utility and commitment to its success." A major trend in managerial philosophy in the past two decades has been to incorporate the data and advice from many people into the process of strategic planning. Senior executives can become isolated from the external realities of how their company meets public standards of accountability. To this end, Arrington and Sawaya argue: "Senior management should subscribe explicitly to the charter of an issues management function and substantiate the charter by full involvement in the issues management process. Issues management will not relieve corporate decision makers of their responsibility to participate in the public policy process; it can insure their participation is coherent." In addition to a charter, issues management must be more than futures research and a means for institutionalizing corporate social responsibility. The scope, in their judgment, must be this: "Operations always bound issue agendas, and issue agendas are, therefore, always company specific. . . . The fundamental responsibility of an issues management 'team,' as part of the strategic process of a company, is to help exercise foresight about and collectively develop options for corporate accommodation to the discontinuities present in society."

Arguing that issues management does not need a large hierarchical staff because it is a core function, Arrington and Sawyer (1984) conclude that in the final analysis the heart of issues management is this:

> Issues analysis must balance the legitimate interests of a company with a consistently disinterested view of issues under considerations. This is not merely a matter of the politically possible; it is also a matter of the changing contract society makes with business. If issues management is regarded only as a tool to shape public policy to serve near-term business objectives, it will inevitably prove unsatisfactory as a legitimate function, both inside and outside the company. At its best, issues management is neither sophistic nor ideological—it is pragmatic. The habit of mind it requires and fosters may be fundamental to all decision making that has consequences for society [Arrington and Sawaya, 1984: 156-160].

The advice of these experienced practitioners can be wisely heeded by those executives who have not yet acknowledged how central issues management should be to their managerial philosophies.

VALUE TO ORGANIZATIONS

If they bridge the credibility gap between corporate planners and themselves, issues managers can play more critical roles in corporate planning. Nevertheless, many practitioners complain that their executive managements do not take full advantage of public policy information during strategic planning. Only if corporate leadership realizes the potential benefits of issues management will it use the skills and knowledge available to pro-actively forestall issues from becoming serious and contentious. One of the most serious challenges of the future centers on the ability of issues managers to demonstrate how their knowledge of issues emergence, special interest group agitation, and pro-active communication can help harmonize the company with its external environment. Job descriptions and titles that contain "issues" periodically appear in company manuals and employment advertisements.

One of the questions for the future is whether issues management will be a relatively visible function in many companies, or whether it will be absorbed by corporate planning. Each company is unique in its structure and personality. Because issues management can be embedded throughout a company, rather than concentrated in one department, it can be vital to the way operating decisions are made using information. In fact, one of the characteristics of issues management is its ability to be a vital part of ongoing planning, operation, and communication activities. Closely associated is the problem of managing the enormous amounts of information that companies acquire. To improve controls on the information management process requires many innovations. The most important among these is increased sophistication in (1) calculating the impacts of public policy changes on operations and (2) estimating the effects of company activities on public sentiment.

Companies also need to concentrate on internal as well as external constituencies and monitor issues in both arenas. A major value of issues management specialists is their ability to train people throughout the company to use public policy information to conduct operations planning and to communicate with constituencies as often and as fully as possible. Employees have a vested interest in the survival of the company, but they can also be forced to become contentious if their welfare is being harmed by a company that seems disinterested in employee interests.

Because the mass dissemination of issues advertising has so many liabilities, companies will develop many forms of communication which may preclude the need for extensive issues advertising. It is easier to gain audience attention and communicate a little information about corporate behavior over time rather than trying to communicate during a public policy crisis.

CREATING A PLATFORM OF UNDERSTANDING

The history of issues management grew out of a clash between corporate interests and public standards. Effective issues management coincides with broad corporate recognition that public policy considerations are inseparable from ethics. Public relations efforts to shape a corporate image and achieve publicity fall short of the more demanding requirement to help the public understand the facts and values involved in public policy considerations. Rather than thinking only of a platform of fact, issues specialists can go a bit further and strive to develop a platform of understanding and agreement between the public and corporate management.

One-directional, corporation-to-audience communication approaches will not work for long. Moreover, corporate communicators and planners will quickly learn the pitfalls of the use of surveying techniques to learn what the public thinks about the company and its industry, or they will discover what issues are on the minds of the public and special interest groups. If the assumption is that various publics are incorrect, misinformed, or malicious, corporate communication will fail. Public opinion changes in response to changes in the world and because of the ways in which influence leaders characterize these new conditions. As conditions change, the public receives some new information (platform of fact), realizes what values should be used in assessing corporate performance, and becomes willing, even supportive, of certain regulatory measures. Consequently, an awareness of the currents of fact, value, and policy can be central to the listening functions of corporations. The foundation of trust is laid when corporations seek to understand the public and when they want to be understood in return.

Because it is at the nexus of corporate planning, public expectations of corporate behavior, and every effort of companies to participate as citizens, issues management has a substantial burden. It has many critics and debunkers. Undoubtedly, some underestimate what it can do to bring harmony between companies and the public. Likewise, some believe that this task is one-sided, requiring the defeat of public interest groups and the dissemination of simplistic information that champions free enterprise. Most practitioners fall somewhere in this continuum. Moreover, some campaigns are fraught with self-serving apologia. An even larger problem is the age-old nightmare of public relations: Corporate actions and statements sometimes contradict one another. While companies are preaching their virtues, their actions may not prove that they are virtuous. These conditions make necessary a stronger effort to discuss issues and provide information, not on the broad, free enterprise issues, but the more specific issues about which corporations have real expertise. Some of the most important issues, for instance, regarding the performance of the oil companies were those which helped the public realize the tremendous costs of discovering, refining, and marketing petroleum products. Even if the public was unimpressed, at least it was informed; it met this information with a businesslike attitude that it expected the companies to perform, and they did. Such awareness seems essential for the narrowing of the gap between expectations and performance, which is one of the best yardsticks of corporate success, whether in the provision of goods and services or of issues management strategies.

By applying the standard ingredients of the communication model (source/sender, receiver, message, channels, and feedback), we can diagnose the interaction transpiring during the development and contest of public policy issues. The struggle involves a variety of players, ranging from corporations (good or bad), agitation groups, the media, and governmental officials. What each says and how it fits into the entire communication context can help us understand what is going on. Message strategies concentrate on standard types of evidence and propositions of fact, value, and policy. Channels are essential to issues managers because they are the means by which to reach targeted audiences. Despite their ostensible objectivity, the media are prime players in these controversies. In some instances they may be little more than channels through which the various combatants attempt to communicate. At other times they are directly involved in waging the controversy. The underlying realization, however, is that issues conflict is not only a matter of understanding; it entails power resource management as well.

Issues management offers business the means to intervene between key groups to prevent the public from being convinced by business critics that regulation is necessary; in conjunction with the pro-business faction, corporations try to get the public to support less rather than more regulation. The world of issues management resides at the confluence between a platform of understanding and a war over the management of power resources. Its future rests with the dynamic need of the public to have a reasonable relationship with companies and the concomitant contest to subject corporations to the will of special interests.

REFERENCES

ADKINS, L. (1978) "How good are advocacy ads?" Dun's Review 111 (June): 76-77.

ADLER, R. (1977) Research on the Effects of Television Advertising on Children. Washington, DC: National Science Foundation.

ADONI, H. and A. A. COHEN (1978) "Television economic news and the social construction of economic reality." Journal of Communication 28 (Autumn): 61-70.

ALEXANDER, H. E. (1983) The Case for PACs. Washington, DC: Public Affairs Council.

ALINSKY, S. (1972) "Interview." Playboy 19 (March): 59-78, 150, 169-173, 176-177.

———(1971) Rules for Radicals—A Practical Primer for Realistic Radicals. New York: Random House.

———(1968) Organizing for Power—Through Conflict to Negotiation (John Kemeny and Barrie Howells, Dirs.). National Film Board of Canada.

ALTER, J. (1984) "Mobil boycotts the Journal." Newsweek 104 (December 17): 101.

American Advertising Federation (1981) "Comments of the American Advertising Federation with respect to proposed regulations on the treatment, for tax purposes, of expenditures for attempts to influence legislation." Statement filed with Commissioner of Internal Revenue, January 26.

American Association of Advertising Agencies (1980) Statement by the Board of Directors, June.

American Management Association (1981) "The business-media relationship: countering misconceptions and distrusts." New York: Author.

ANSHEN, M. [ed.] (1974) Managing the Socially Responsible Corporation. New York: Macmillan.

ARMOUR, J. O. (1906) "The packers and the people." Saturday Evening Post 178 (March 10): 6.

"Arms concerns called heavy donors to PAC." (1985) New York Times (January 20): 19, section 1.

ARONOFF, C. E. [ed.] (1979) Business and the Media. Santa Monica, CA: Goodyear.

ARRINGTON, C., Jr. and R. N. SAWAYA (1984) "Managing public affairs: issues management in an uncertain environment." California Management Review 26: 148-160.

BAILEY, R. N. (1983) "Issues management: a survey of contemporary practice." M. A. Thesis, University of Florida, Gainesville.

BAKER, J. C. (1985) "The international infant formula controversy: a dilemma in corporate social responsibility." Journal of Business Ethics 4: 181-190.

BARNET, S. M., Jr. (1975) "A global look at advocacy." Public Relations Journal 31 (November): 17-21.

———(1976) "How to organize for controversy advertising." Public Relations Journal 32 (November): 23-25.

BARNOUW, E. (1978) The Sponsor: Notes on a Modern Potentate. New York: Oxford University Press.

BAROVICK, R. L. (1979) "Status report: code of conduct for MNCs." Public Relations Journal 35 (October): 30.

———(1982) "Activism on a global scale." Public Relations Journal 38 (June): 29-31.

BASKIN, C. (1985) "On-line services." Popular Computing 4 (March): 74.

BATEMAN, D. N. (1975) "Corporate communications of advocacy: practical perspectives and procedures." Journal of Business Communication 13 (Fall): 3-11.

BATES, D. (1982) "Signal trends in not-for-profit public relations." Public Relations Journal 38 (November): 22-23.

BECK, B., N. F. GREENBERG, M. HAGER, J. HARRISON, and A. UNDERWOOD (1984) "Could it happen in America?" Newsweek 104 (December 17): 38-44.

BEEKEN, S. H. (1981) "A tax practitioner's primer on grassroots lobbying." Taxes—The Tax Magazine 59: 93-96.

BELL, C. (1983) "Advertisers seek link between sales, corporate ads." Houston Chronicle (December 18), p. 16, section 4.

BERELSON, B. and M. JANOWITZ [eds.] (1966) Reader in Public Opinion and Communication (2nd ed.). New York: Free Press.

BERGER, P. L. and T. LUCKMANN (1966) The Social Construction of Reality: A Treatise on the Sociology of Knowledge. Garden City, NY: Doubleday.

BERGNER, D. (1982) "The role of strategic planning in international public affairs." Public Relations Journal 38 (June): 32-33, 39.

BEVK, K. L. (1979) "Literature search and analysis: key to vital information." Public Relations Journal 35 (February): 12-13.

BLEECKER, S. E. and T. V. LENTO (1982) "Public relations in a wired society." Public Relations Quarterly 27 (Spring): 6-12.

BLOCK, E. M. (1977) "How public opinion is formed." Public Relations Review 3 (Fall): 5-11.

BLUMLER, J. G. and E. KATZ [eds.] (1974) The Uses of Mass Communication: Current Perspectives on Gratifications Research. Beverly Hills, CA: Sage.

BOE, A. R. (1972) "The good hands of Allstate: a spectator exclusive interview with Archie R. Boe, Allstate's chairman of the board." Spectator (October).

BOFFEY, P. M. (1984) "Bhopal: the case for poison factories." Denver Post (December 23), 1D, 12D.

BOGART, L. (1984) "The public's use and perception of newspapers." Public Opinion Quarterly 48: 709-719.

BOOTH, M. (1978) "Single-issue advocacy: a new trend in nonprofit PR." Public Relations Journal 34 (December): 13-14.

BORDUA, D. J. (1983) "Adversary polling and the construction of social meaning." Law & Policy Quarterly 5: 345-366.

BOSTICK, G. H. (1981) "Prop. regs. on grassroots lobbying: analysis of the area and special problems involved." Journal of Taxation 54: 332-338.

BREMNER, R. H. (1956) From the Depths: The Discovery of Poverty in the United States. New York: New York University Press.

BRODWIN, D. R. and L. J. BOURGEOIS III (1984) "Five steps to strategic actions." California Management Review 26: 176-190.

BROOM, G. M. (1977) "Coorientational measurement of public issues." Public Relations Review 3 (Winter): 110-119.

BROWN, J. K. (1979) This Business of Issues: Coping with the Company's Environments. New York: Conference Board.

BROWN, M. V. (1976) "Corporate reporting in a changing environment." Public Relations Journal 32 (April): 14-16.

BROWN, P. (1984) "The prophets of profits." Grey Matter: Thoughts and Ideas on Advertising and Marketing 55: 1-8.

BROWN, W. (1984) "UAW advertising campaign stresses jobs." Washington Post (August 28): A6.

BRUSH, J. M. and D. P. BRUSH (1977) "Corporate video: burgeoning role for PR." Public Relations Journal 33 (October): 14-15.

———(1981) Private Television Communications: Into the Eighties. Berkeley Heights, NJ: International Television Association.

———(1985) Private Television Communications: The New Directions. Cold Spring, NY: Highland Institute.

BUCHHOLZ, R. (1982) "Education for public issues management: key insights from a survey of top practitioners." Public Affairs Review 3: 65-76.

———(1985) Essentials of Public Policy for Management. Englewood Cliffs, NJ: Prentice-Hall.

BUDD, J. F., Jr. (1983a) Corporate Video in Focus: A Management Guide to Private TV. Englewood Cliffs, NJ: Prentice-Hall.

———(1983b) "Video, a corporate communication tool." Vital Speeches 49: 592-594.

BUDNOVE, E. C. (1973) "The internal revenue code's provisions against legislative activity on the part of tax-exempt organizations: a legitimate safeguard or a violation of the first amendment?" New York University Review of Law and Social Change 3: 159-178.

BURGER, C. (1976) "Trends affecting future skills." Public Relations Quarterly 21 (Summer): 18-19.

BURKE, K. (1969) A Rhetoric of Motives. Berkeley: University of California Press.

BURROUGH, B. (1983) "Company's handling of radioactive items stirs a bitter fight with Texas regulators." Wall Street Journal (August 1): 17, 25.

BURTON, K. R., Jr. (1976) "Getting the corporation involved in politics—legally." Public Relations Journal 32: 14-15.

Business Week (1979) "The corporate image: PR to the rescue." (January 22): 47-61.

Business Week (1980) "The business campaign against 'trial by television.'" (June 2): 77-79.

Business Marketing (1985) "Leading 100 business/industrial advertisers spend $420 million." Vol. 70 (May): 60-163.

———(1983b) "Regional networks: fact or fiction?" Video User 6 (October): 17.

———(1984) "Labor now plugging into cable." Video User 7 (January 1): 16.

BUSKE, S. M. (1983a) "Crossing the nonbroadcast line: corporate cable programs." Video User 6 (July/August): 12.

"Carbide was warned disaster possible." (1985) Houston Post (January 25): 5A.

"Carbide's U. S. plant fined for violations." (1984) Houston Post (December 17): 3A.

CARLSON, R. O. [ed.] (1975) Communications and Public Opinion: A Public Opinion Quarterly Reader. New York: Praeger.

CARSON, R. (1962) Silent Spring. Boston: Houghton-Mifflin.

CARSON, T. L., R. E. WOKUTCH, and J. E. COX, Jr. (1985) "An ethical analysis of deception in advertising." Journal of Business Ethics 4: 93-104.

CATO, F. W. (1982) "Procter & Gamble and the Devil." Public Relations Quarterly 27 (Fall): 16-21.

CATHEY, P. (1982) "Industry has a new advance guard—issue managers." Iron Age 225 (April 23): 64-70.

CHASE, W. H. (1976) "Organizing for our new responsibility." Public Relations Journal 32 (May): 14-15.

———(1977) "Public issue management: the new science." Public Relations Journal 33 (October): 25-26.

———(1982) "Issue management conference—a special report." Corporate Public Issues and Their Management 7 (December 1): 1-2.

———(1984) Issue Management: Origins of the Future. Stamford, CT: Issue Action.

Chemical Risks: Fears, Facts, and the Media (1985). Washington, DC: The Media Institute.

CHICKERING, A. L. (1982) "Warming up the corporate image." Public Opinion 5 (October/November): 13-15.

CHRISMAN, J. J. and A. B. CARROLL (1984) "SMR forum: corporate responsibility—reconciling economic and social goals." Sloan Management Review 25 (Winter): 59-65.

CHUBB, J. E. (1983) Interest Groups and the Bureaucracy: The Politics of Energy. Stanford, CA: Stanford University Press.

CLAVIER, D. E. and F. B. KALUPA (1981) "Are corporate rebuttals working? A study of '60 Minutes/Our Reply.'" Business and the Media 3 (Fall): 1, 6-7.

———(1983) "Corporate rebuttals to 'Trial by Television.'" Public Relations Review 9 (Spring): 24-36.

CLEVELAND, R. W. (1981) "Grassroots lobbying and the public's right to hear: first Amendment implications of I.R.C. Section 162 (e) (2) (B)." Cardoza Law Review 2: 597-638.

CNN vs. The Networks: Is More News Better News? (1983) Washington, DC: The Media Institute.

COCH, L. and J.R.P. FRENCH, Jr. (1948) "Overcoming resistance to change." Human Relations 1: 512-532.

COCHRAN, P. L. and R. A. WOOD (1984) "Corporate social responsibility and financial performance." Academy of Management Journal 27: 42-56.

COE, B. J. (1983) "The effectiveness challenge in issue advertising campaigns." Journal of Advertising 12, 4: 27-35.

COHEN, B. (1983) "Nuclear journalism: lies, damned lies, and news reports." Policy Review 26 (Fall): 70-74.

COHEN, D. (1982) "Unfairness in advertising revisited." Journal of Marketing 46 (Winter): 73-80.

COHEN, S. E. (1976) "Social responsibility can win friends in government and in the marketplace." Advertising Age 47 (May 31): 6, 59.

"Competition is concern in TV deregulation proposal." (1983) Broadcast Management/Engineering (August): 12-14.

COMSTOCK, G., S. CHAFEE, N. KATZMAN, N. McCOMBS, and D. ROBERTS (1978) Television and Human Behavior. New York: Columbia University Press.

CONNOR, M. J. (1975) "Mobil's advocacy ads lead a growing trend, draw praise, criticism." Wall Street Journal (May 14), pp. 1, 20.

"Conversation with Larry Kirkman." (1983) Videography 8 (June): 46-54.

COPULOS, M. (1985) "It's effective—but is it safe?" Reason 16 (March): 24-32.

"Corporate ads influence stock prices." (1982) Adweek (March 22): 9.

"The corporate imperative: Management of profit *and* policy." (1982) Corporate Public Issues and Their Management 7 (March 1): 1-4.

"A corporate video alternative." (1983) Video Systems 9 (August): 48-49.

COWEN, S. S. and M. G. SEGAL (1981) "In the public eye: Reporting social performance." Financial Executive 47 (January): 11-16.

COYLE, R. J. and L. F. STEPHENS (1979) "Why practitioners should master sampling and survey research." Public Relations Journal 35 (February): 14-16.

CRABLE, R. E. and S. L. VIBBERT (1985) "Managing issues and influencing public policy." Public Relations Review 11 (Spring): 3-16.

———(1983) "Mobil's epideictic advocacy: 'observations' of Prometheus-Bound." Communication Monographs 50: 380-394.

CRESPI, I. (1977) "Attitude measurement, theory, and prediction." Public Opinion Quarterly 41: 285-294.

CUTLIP, S. M. and A. H. CENTER (1982) Effective Public Relations (rev. 5th ed.). Englewood Cliffs, NJ: Prentice-Hall.

DARDENNE, P. (1982) "Corporate advertising." Public Relations Journal 38 (November): 34-38, 47.

DAVISON, W. P. (1972) "Public opinion research as communication." Public Opinion Quarterly 36: 311-322.

DENBOW, C. J. and H. M. CULBERTSON (1985) "Linkage beliefs and diagnosing an image." Public Relations Review 11 (Spring): 29-37.

DeWITT, J. B. (1983) "Films can project your association's message." Association Management 35 (March): 85-91.

DIAMOND, E., N. SANDLER, and M. MUELLER (1983) Telecommunications in Crisis: The First Amendment, Technology, and Deregulation. Washington, DC: The Cato Institute.

DIAMOND, S. (1984) "A global question of ethics." Denver Post (December 23): 1D, 12D.

DiBACCO, T. V. (1982) "Business ethics: A view from the cloister." Wall Street Journal (June 10): 30.

DICKIE, R. B. (1984) "Influence of public affairs offices on corporate planning and of corporations on government policy." Strategic Management Journal 5 (January-March): 15-34.

DILLMAN, D. A. and J. A. CHRISTENSON (1974) "Toward the assessment of public values." Public Opinion Quarterly 38: 206-221.

DINSMORE, W. H. (1978) "Can ideas be sold like soap?" Public Relations Quarterly 23 (Spring): 16-18.

DIVELBISS, R. I. and M. R. CULLEN, Jr. (1981) "Business, the media, and the American public." Michigan State University Business Topics 29 (Spring): 21-28.

DOMINICK, J. R. (1981) "Business coverage in network newscasts." Journalism Quarterly 58: 179-185, 191.

DOUGHERTY, P. H. (1983) "Advertising: Grey's corporate survey." New York Times, (November 30): 40.

DOVER, C. J. (1965) Management Communication on Controversial Issues. Washington, DC: BNA Inc.

DuBOS, T. J. (1982) Letter to Jack Hart, School of Communication, University of Houston, October 8.

DYKES, C. (1983) "The stranglehold of 'big business.' " The Freeman 33: 323-327.

EDELMAN, J. M. (1964) The Symbolic Uses of Politics. Urbana: University of Illinois Press.

———(1977) Political Language: Words that Succeed and Policies that Fail. New York: Academic Press.

EDELSON, A. H. (1981) "Advocating their position." Advertising Age 52 (July 6): S16.

EHLING, W. P. and M. B. HESSE (1983) "Use of 'issue management' in public relations." Public Relations Review 9 (Summer): 18-35.

EHRBAR, A. F. (1978) "The backlash against business advocacy." Fortune 98 (August 28): 62-68.

ELLUL, J. (1971) Autopsy of Revolution. Patricia Wolf (trans.). New York: Alfred A. Knopf.

EPSTEIN, E. M. (1969) The Corporation in American Politics. Englewood Cliffs, NJ: Prentice-Hall.

EWING, R. P. (1979) "The uses of futurist techniques in issues management." Public Relations Quarterly 24 (Winter): 15-18.

———(1980) "Evaluating issues management." Public Relations Journal 36 (June): 14-16.

———(1982) "Advocacy advertising: the voice of business in public policy debate." Public Affairs Review 3: 23-39.

FARINELLI, J. L. (1977) "Fine tuning employee communications." Public Relations Journal 33 (January): 22-23.

FIDLER, L. A. and J. D. JOHNSON (1984) "Communication and innovation implementation." Academy of Management Review 9: 704-711.

FIELDS, J. M. and H. SCHUMAN (1976-1977) "Public beliefs about the beliefs of the public." Public Opinion Quarterly 40: 427-448.

FINN, D. (1981) "The public relations role in coping with the information crisis." Public Relations Quarterly 26 (Fall): 5-7.

FISHBEIN, M. (1967) Readings in Attitude Theory and Measurement. New York: John Wiley.

———and I. AJZEN (1975) Beliefs, Attitudes, Intentions and Behavior: An Introduction to Theory and Research. Reading, MA: Addison-Wesley.

———(1980) Understanding Attitudes and Predicting Social Behavior. Englewood Cliffs, NJ: Prentice-Hall.

FITZSIMMONS, S. J. and T. E. FERB (1977) "Developing a community attitude assessment scale." Public Opinion Quarterly 41: 356-378.

FLETCHER, S. (1982) "TV's coverage of oil crisis branded 'superficial.'" Houston Post (March 7), p. 10D.

FOOTE, S. B. (1984) "Corporate responsibility in a changing legal environment." California Management Review 26: 217-228.

FORD, T. M. (1984) "Talk is too cheap." Presented at the annual meeting of the International Association of Business Communicators, Montreal, Canada, June 13.

FOX, J. F. (1982a) "Communicating on public issues: a changing role for the CEO." Public Relations Quarterly 27 (Summer): 19-26.

———(1982b) "The politicizing of the chief executive." Public Relations Journal 38 (August): 20-24.

FRANKLIN, M. A. (1981) The First Amendment and the Fourth Estate (2nd ed.). Mineola, NY: Foundation Press.

FRANZEN, R. S. (1977) "An NBS internal communications study: a comment." Public Relations Review 3 (Winter): 83-88.

Freedom of Expression Foundation (1984) "Comments of the Freedom of Expression Foundation before the Federal Communications Commission in the matter of inquiry into Section 73.1910 of the Commission's rules and regulations concerning the general fairness doctrine obligations of broadcast licensees." Gen. Docket No. 84-282 (September).

FREUDENBERG, N. (1984) Not in Our Backyards! Community Action for Health and the Environment. New York: Monthly Review Press.

FRIEDMAN, R. (1985) "Beer and wine industry girds for battle as campaign to ban ads gathers steam." Wall Street Journal (January 30), p. 16.

FRIEDMAN, S. M. (1981) "Blueprint for breakdown: Three Mile Island and the media before the accident." Journal of Communication 31 (Spring): 116-128.

FRIENDLY, F. W. (1977) The Good Guys, The Bad Guys and The First Amendment: Free Speech vs. Fairness in Broadcasting. New York: Vintage.

FUNKHOUSER, G. R. (1973) "The issues of the sixties: an exploratory study in the dynamics of public opinion." Public Opinion Quarterly 37: 62-75.

GALAMBOS, L. (1975) The Public Image of Big Business in America, 1880-1940: A Quantitative Study of Social Change. Baltimore, MD: Johns Hopkins University Press.

Gallup Report (1983) "Honesty and ethical standards." Report No. 214 (July).

GAMSON, W. A. (1968) Power and Discontent. Homewood, IL: Dorsey Press.

———(1975) The Strategy of Social Protest. Homewood, IL: Dorsey Press.

GANDY, O. H., Jr. (1982) Beyond Agenda-Setting: Information Subsidies and Public Policy. Norwood, NJ: Ablex.

GARBETT, T. F. (1981) Corporate Advertising: The What, The Why, and the How. New York: McGraw-Hill.

GAVAGHAN, P. F. (1983) "Alcohol industry campaigns against alcohol abuse." Public Relations Quarterly 28 (Summer): 11-16.

GAY, V. (1982) "Mobil—they speak their mind." Marketing & Media Decisions 17 (Spring): 87-97.

GENTHE, W. K. (1982) "Building bridges to public trust." Public Relations Journal 38 (August): 28-30.

GERBNER, G., L. GROSS, M. MORGAN, and N. SIGNORIELLI (1980) "The 'mainstreaming' of America: Violence Profile No. 11." Journal of Communication 30 (Summer): 10-29.

———(1984) "Political correlates of television viewing." Public Opinion Quarterly 48: 283-300.

GIGOT, P. (1982) "Some corporations trying to turn shareholders into a political force." Wall Street Journal (January 19), p. 27.

GLASSER, I. (1983) "Introduction," pp. 1-2 in L. Siegel, Free Speech, 1984: The Rise of Government Controls on Information, Debate and Communication. New York: American Civil Liberties Union.

GODOWN, R. D. (1981) "Should the I.R.S. call the tune?" New York Times (January 22), p. A27.

GOLD, R. L. (1982) "Accommodation preempts confrontation." Public Relations Quarterly 27 (Fall): 23-28.

GOLDMAN, E. and T. S. AUH (1979) "Public policy issue analysis: a four-posted research design." Public Relations Quarterly 24 (Winter): 20-25.

GOODMAN, S. E. (1983) "Why few corporations monitor social issues." Public Relations Journal 39 (April): 20.

GOTTSCHALK, E. C., Jr. (1982) "Firms hiring new type of manager to study issues, emerging troubles." Wall Street Journal (June 10), pp. 21, 28.

GRABER, D. A. (1982) "The impact of media research on public opinion studies," pp. 555-564 in D. C. Whitney and E. Wartella (eds.) Mass Communication Review Yearbook, Vol. 3. Beverly Hills, CA: Sage.

GRASS, R. C. (1977) "Measuring the effects of corporate advertising." Public Relations Review (Winter): 39-50.

GRASSER, J.L.C. (1982) "Business news is big business." Business and the Media 4 (Spring): 1.

GREEN, A. (1982) "Canned news: serve sparingly." Videography 7 (November): 78-80.

GREEN, J. C. and J. L. GUTH (1984) "The party irregulars." Psychology Today 18 (October): 46-52.

GRIER, P. (1984) "Poisons in our midst are well-kept secret." Rocky Mountain News (December 26), p. 81.

GRIFFIN, L. M. (1952) "The rhetoric of historical movements." Quarterly Journal of Speech 38: 184-188.

GROSS, S. J. and C. M. NIMAN (1975) "Attitude-behavior consistency: a review." Public Opinion Quarterly 39: 358-368.

GRUBER, W. H. and R. L. HOEWING (1980) "The new management in corporate public affairs." Public Affairs Review 1: 13-23.

GRUNIG, J. E. (1977a) "Evaluating employee communications in a research operation." Public Relations Review 3 (Winter): 61-82.

———(1977b) "Measurement in public relations—an overview." Public Relations Review 3 (Winter): 5-10.

———(1978) "Accuracy of communication from an external public to employees in a formal organization." Human Communication Research 5: 40-53.

GWIN, L. M., Jr. (1984) "Mechanisms for public participation at the Tennessee Valley Authority." Public Relations Quarterly 29 (Spring): 27-30.

GWYN, R. J. (1970) "Opinion advertising and the free market of ideas." Public Opinion Quarterly 34: 246-255.

HAMMOND, G. (1976) "Public opinion: do we understand its function?" Public Relations Journal 32 (July): 9-11, 22.

HANEY, C. (1980) "Public rights and corporate social responsibility: a profitable marriage." Retail Control 48 (March): 16-27.

HARDING, M. (1967) "Corporate vs. product advertising." Industrial Marketing 52 (September): 59-61.

HARRISON, B. (1982) "Environmental activism's resurgence." Public Relations Journal 38 (June): 34-36.

HARTMAN, C. (1983) "TV gets down to business." Inc. (October): 52-53, 56.

HASKELL, F. K. (1984) "Correcting the corporate myth." Denver Post (December 23), p. 4D.

HATHAWAY, J. W. (1984) "Has social responsibility cleaned up the corporate image?" Business and Society Review 51 (Fall): 56-59.

HATTAL, A. M. and D. P. HATTAL (1984) "Videoconferencing." Public Relations Journal 40 (September): 21-24.

HAWKINS, R. P. and S. PINGREE (1981) "Using television to construct social reality." Journal of Broadcasting 25: 347-364.

HAX, A. C. and N. S. MAJLUF (1984) "The corporate strategic planning process." Interfaces 14 (January-February): 47-60.

HEATH, R. L. (1976) "Variability in value system priorities as decision-making adaptation to situational differences." Communication Monographs 43: 325-333.

———(1979) "Risk as a dimension of social movement vulnerability," pp. 491-505 in D. Nimmo (ed.) Communication Yearbook 3. New Brunswick, NJ: Transaction Books.

———(1980) "Corporate advocacy: an application of speech communication perspectives and skills—and more." Communication Education 29: 370-377.

———and R. A. NELSON (1983a) "Image/issue advertising tax rules: understanding the corporate rights." Public Affairs Review 4: 94-101, 104-105.

———(1983b) "An exchange on corporate advertising: typologies and taxonomies." Journal of Communication 33 (Autumn): 114-118.

———(1985) "Image and issue advertising: a corporate and public policy perspective." Journal of Marketing 49 (Spring): 58-68.

HELM, L. M., R. E. HIEBERT, M. R. NAVER and K. RABIN [eds.] (1981) Informing the People: A Public Affairs Handbook. New York: Longman.

HESSEN, R. (1979) In Defense of the Corporation. Stanford, CA: Hoover Institution Press.

HILL, D. (1982) "Congruent communications." Public Relations Journal 38: 12-15.

"How PR executives shape corporate advertising." (1976) Public Relations Journal 32 (November): 32-33.

HUSH, M. (1983) "Corporate advertising: stacking the odds." Grey Matter: Thoughts and Ideas on Advertising and Marketing 54: 1-12.

INGERSOLL, B. (1985) "Annual meetings are much calmer affairs under changed SEC shareholder rules." Wall Street Journal (April 24), p. 35.

ISAAC, R. J. and E. ISAAC (1984) "Subsidizing political hidden agendas." Wall Street Journal (September 6), p. 28.

"Issues management: preparing for social change." (1981) Chemical Week 129 (October 28): 46-51.

IVERSON, A. C. (1982) "Advertising in a hostile environment." Presented at the annual meeting of the Popular Culture Association, Louisville, Kentucky, April.

JACKSON, B. (1984a) "Democrats lead in PAC donations." Wall Street Journal (October 29), p. 56.

———(1984b) "Realtor, doctor PACs show clout." Wall Street Journal (November 6), p. 56.

JACOBSON, H. (1983) "Cable shows give viewers the business—money matters." On Cable (October): 19-21.

JONES, B. L. and W. H. CHASE (1979) "Managing public issues." Public Relations Review 5 (Summer): 3-23.

JONES, J. F. (1975) "Audit: a new tool for public relations." Public Relations Journal 31 (July): 6-8.

KAHN, H. and A. J. WEINER (1967) The Year 2000: A Framework for Speculation on the Next Thirty-three Years. New York: Macmillan.

KAHN, H., W. BROWN, and L. MARTEL (1976) The Next 200 Years: A Scenario for America and the World. New York: William Morrow.

Kaiser Aluminum & Chemical Corporation (1980, August) At issue: Access to Television. Oakland, CA: Author.

KAMM, T. (1984) "French town with Union Carbide Corp. plant has dual concerns: safety and unemployment." Wall Street Journal (December 26), p. 15.

KATZ, B. (1981) "The light TV viewer." Journal of Advertising 10, 2: 37-40.

KATZ, D. and R. L. KAHN (1978) The Social Psychology of Organizations (2nd ed.). New York: John Wiley.

KELLEY, D. (1982) "Critical issues for issue ads." Harvard Business Review 60 (July-August): 80-87.

———(1983) "Sons of Wall Street Week: viewing the boom in TV business shows." Barron's (September 5): 14, 32-33.

——— and R. DONWAY (1983) Laissez Parler: Freedom in the Electronic Media. Bowling Green, KY: Social Philosophy and Policy Center, Bowling Green State University.

KELLY, O. (1982) "Corporate crime: the untold story." U. S. News & World Report 93 (September 6): 25-29.

KLEIN, W. J. (1983) "Sponsored films." Public Relations Journal 39 (September): 20-21.

KOLKO, G. (1967) The Triumph of Conservatism: A Reinterpretation of American History, 1900-1916. Chicago: Quadrangle.

KRAUSKOPF, A. M. (1979) "Influencing the public: policy considerations defining the tax status of corporate grassroots lobbying." Catholic University Law Review 28: 313-357.

KREBS, F. J. (1978) "Grassroots lobbying defined: the scope of IRC Section 162 (e) (2) (B)." Taxes—The Tax Magazine 56: 516-520.

KRISTOL, I. (1976) "How business should use ads to reply to 'distortion by media.'" Advertising Age 47 (March 1): 51.

LACAYO, R. (1984) "Special-interest groups are using the power of TV." New York Times (March 11), pp. 25, 34 (section 2).

LAGERFELD, S. (1981) "An anti-business business magazine." Policy Review 17 (Summer): 59-75.

LANGLEY, E. (1978) "The CEO and the practitioner." Public Relations Journal 34 (March): 28-33.

LASSWELL, H. D. (1972) "Communications research and public policy." Public Opinion Quarterly 36: 301-310.

"The last word in business communication." (1982) Nation's Business 70 (October): 34-36.

LATAMORE, G. B. (1985) "The business connection." Popular Computing 4 (March): 75-80.

LATSHAW, W. A. (1977) "Target group research: new tool for advocacy advertising." Public Relations Journal 33 (November): 28-33.

LeBART, F. T. (1982) "Campaigning on the issues." Public Relations Journal 38: (November): 30-33.

LeBON, G. (1925) The Crowd: A Study of the Popular Mind. New York: Macmillan.

———(1968) Psychologie des Foules. Dunwoody, GA: N. S. Berg.

LEE, I. L. (1907) "Indirect service of railroads." Moody's Magazine 2: 580-584.

LEON, M. (1983) "Tylenol fights back." Public Relations Journal 39 (March): 10-14.

LERBINGER, O. (1977) "Corporate use of research in public relations." Public Relations Review 3 (Winter): 11-19.

LEVEY, R. N. (1976-77) "Association public relations—today." Public Relations Quarterly 21 (Winter): 13-16.

LICHTER, L. S., S. R. LICHTER, and S. ROTHMAN (1982) "How show business shows business." Public Opinion 5 (October/November): 10-12.

———(1983) "Hollywood and America: the odd couple." Public Opinion 5 (December/January): 54-58.

LINDENMANN, W. K. (1977) "Opinion research: how it works; how to use it." Public Relations Journal 33 (January): 12-14.

———(1983) "Dealing with the major obstacles to implementing public relations research." Public Relations Quarterly 28 (Fall): 12-16.

——— and A. LAPETINA (1981) "Management's view of the future of public relations." Public Relations Review 7 (Fall): 3-13.

LINNEMAN, R. E. and H. E. KLEIN (1985) "Using scenarios in strategic decision making." Business Horizons 28 (January-February): 64-74.

LINSLEY, W. A. (1981) "The supreme court and the First Amendment: 1979-1980." Free Speech Yearbook 1980 19: 67-76.

LIPPMANN, W. (1961) Drift and Mastery: An Attempt to Diagnose the Current Unrest. Englewood Cliffs, NJ: Prentice-Hall.

LODDEKE, L. (1984) "Legislative work under way in aftermath of India tragedy." Houston Post (December 16), p. 8B.

LOWRY, D. T. (1973) "Demographic similarity, attitudinal similarity, and attitude change." Public Opinion Quarterly 37: 192-208.

LUDLAM, C. E. (1974) "Abatement of corporate image environmental advertising." Ecology Law Quarterly 4: 247-278.

LUDLUM, S. (1978) "Remarks," pp. 38-44 in Proceedings of the Third Annual Hopkins/Vansant Dugdale Symposium, presented under the auspices of The Johns Hopkins University Evening College, Baltimore, MD, December 7.

LUKASIK, S. J. (1981) "Information for decision making." Public Relations Quarterly 26 (Fall): 19-22.

LUNDEEN, R. W. (1983) "The media and industry: two different worlds." Presented at the Interstate National Gas Association, Columbia, Missouri, October 28.

LUTTBEG, N. R. [ed.] (1981) Public Opinion and Public Policy: Models of Political Linkage. Itasca, IL: Peacock.

MacDOUGALL, A. K. (1981) "The credibility gap—business blitzes the media." Washington Journalism Review 3 (July/August): 20-25.

Magazine Publishers Association (1985) "New product success begins with the super innovators." AMA Newsletter of Research 49 (March).

MAHER, P. (1982) "Network TV warms up to issue advertisers." Industrial Marketing 67 (August): 33-39.

MAPES, L. V. (1984) "For PACs it's the gift, not the thought, that counts." Wall Street Journal (November 1), p. 28.

MANDESE, J. (1983) "Satellite net tunes in for inter-firm ads." Adweek (October 10): 8.

MARBACH, W. D., F. GIBNEY, Jr., M. GANDER, D. TSURUOKA, and N. F. GREENBURG (1984) "A company in shock." Newsweek 104 (December 17): 37.

MARCH, A. W. (1971) "Public concern for environmental pollution." Public Opinion Quarterly 35: 102-108.

MARKER, R. K. (1977) "The Armstrong/PR data management system." Public Relations Review 3 (Winter): 51-59.

MARSH, W. W. (1978) "So you want to be a futurist." Public Relations Journal 34 (October): 18-20.

MAYER, R. N. and D. L. SCAMMON (1983) "Intervenor funding at the FTC: biopsy or autopsy?" Policy Studies Review 2: 506-515.

MAZUR, A. (1981) "Media coverage and public opinion on scientific controversies." Journal of Communication 31 (Spring): 106-115.

McADAMS, T. P., Jr. (1981) "How fair is broadcast news?" Presented at the annual Texas UPI Broadcasters Meeting, San Antonio, June 20.

McBEE, S. (1983) "Reagan's regulators—their fire is flickering," U.S. News & World Report 95 (September 26): 51-53.

McCOMBS, M. (1977) "Agenda setting function of mass media." Public Relations Review 3 (Winter): 89-95.

McCONNELL, D. (comp.) (1983) Issues Management Bibliography. Stamford, CT: Issues Management Association. (September)

McELREATH, M. P. (1977) "Public relations evaluative research: summary statement." Public Relations Review 3 (Winter): 129-136.

———(1980) "Priority research questions in public relations for the 1980s." New York: Foundation for Public Relations Research and Education.

McGINNIS, M. A. (1984) "The key to strategic planning: integrating analysis and intuition." Sloan Management Review 26 (Fall): 45-52.

McKENZIE, R. B. (1983) Using Government Power: Business Against Free Enterprise. Washington, DC: Competitive Economy Foundation.

McLAUGHLIN, B. [ed.] (1969) Studies in Social Movements: A Social Psychological Perspective. New York: Free Press.

McLEOD, J. M. and S. H. CHAFEE (1973) "Interpersonal approaches to communication research." American Behavioral Scientist 16 (March/April): 469-500.

McLUHAN, M. (1969) The Gutenberg Galaxy. New York: Signet.

McNABB, D. E. (1982) "Future-based budgeting." Public Relations Journal 38 (October): 24.

MEADOW, R. G. (1981) "The political dimensions of nonproduct advertising." Journal of Communication 31 (Summer): 69-82.

MEIER, B. (1985) "Study by EPA finds laws may be insufficient to protect the public against toxic chemicals." Wall Street Journal (February 8), p. 4.

MENDELSOHN, (1973) "Some reasons why information campaigns can succeed." Public Opinion Quarterly 37: 50-61.

MEYER, T. P. and A. HEXAMER (1981) "Perceived truth and trust in television advertising among Mexican-American adolescents: socialization and development considerations." Journal of Broadcasting 25: 139-153.

MEYERS, R. A., T. L. NEWHOUSE, and D. E. GARRETT (1978) "Political momentum: television news treatment." Communication Monographs 45: 382-388.

MICHAEL, K. V. (1983) Marketing representative, BizNet. Letter to R. A. Nelson.

MILLER, W. H. (1981) "Fighting TV hatchet jobs." Industry Week 208 (January 12): 61-64.

MONSEN, R. J. (1973) Business and the Changing Environment. New York: McGraw-Hill.

MOORE, H. F. and F. B. KALUPA (1985) Public Relations Principles, Cases, and Problems (9th ed.). Homewood, IL: Irwin

MOORE, R. H. (1979) "Research by the Conference Board sheds light on problems of semantics, issue identification and classification—and some likely issues for the '80s." Public Relations Journal 35 (November): 43-46.

MORGAN, B. S. and W. A. SCHIEMANN (1983) "Why international communication is failing." Public Relations Journal 39 (March): 15-17.

MORIARTY, S. E. (1983) "New technology: a review of what's up, what's in and what's out." Public Relations Quarterly 28 (Winter): 15-18.

MOSKOWITZ, M. (1985) "Shareholder protests not going to fade away." Houston Post (January 28), p. F4.
MUCH, M. (1980) "Fighting back with issue ads." Industry Week 206 (July 21): 45-50.
MUFSON, S. and A. PASZTOR (1983) "Door-to-door drive to stop decontrol bill attracts wide support." Wall Street Journal (August 22), pp. 1, 7.
MURRAY, L. (1976) "Corporate communications: management's newest marketing skill." Public Relations Quarterly 21 (Spring): 18-28.
NAGELSCHMIDT, J. S. [ed.] (1982) The Public Affairs Handbook. New York: AMACOM.
NAGER, N. R. and T. H. ALLEN (1984) Public Relations Management by Objectives. New York: Longman.
NAISBITT, J. (1982) Megratrends: Ten New Directions Transforming Our Lives. New York: Warner.
National Association of Broadcasters (1984) "Comments of the National Association of Broadcasters before the Federal Communications Commission in the matter of inquiry into section 73.1910 of the Commission's rules and regulations concerning the general fairness doctrine obligations of broadcast licensees." Gen. Docket No. 84-282 (September 6).
National Wildlife (1985) "Is the nation losing its impetus to conserve energy?" (February-March): 35.
NAVARRO, P. (1984) The Policy Game: How Special Interests and Ideologues are Stealing America. New York: John Wiley.
NELSON, H. L. and D. L. TEETER, Jr. (1982) Law of Mass Communications: Freedom and Control of Print and Broadcast Media (4th ed.). Mineola, NY: Foundation Press.
NELSON, R. A. (1981) "Propaganda," pp. 321-383 in M. T. Inge (ed.) Handbook of American Popular Culture, Vol. 3. Westport, CT: Greenwood Press.
———(1983) "Entering a brave new world: the impact of the new information and telecommunications technologies." Journal of the University Film and Video Association 35 (Fall): 23-33.
——— and R. L. HEATH (1984) "Corporate public relations and new media technology." Public Relations Review 10 (Fall): 27-38.
NELSON-HORCHLER, J. (1982) "Why TV hates business." Industry Week 213 (May 17): 38-43.
The New Technologies: Changes and Challenges in Public Relations, A Sourcebook of General Information (1983) Washington, DC: The Media Institute.
NIMMO, D. D. (1974) Popular Images of Politics: A Taxonomy. Englewood Cliffs, NJ: Prentice-Hall.
———and J. E. COMBS, (1981) "'The horror tonight': network television news and Three Mile Island." Journal of Broadcasting 25: 289-293.
NOELLE-NEUMANN, E. (1983) "The effect of media on media effects research." Journal of Communication 33 (Summer): 157-165.
NORRIS, F. (1903) The Pit: A Story of Chicago. New York: Doubleday.
NORTHART, L. J. (1976) "More clout for corporate ads." Public Relations Journal 32 (November): 12.
NOVAK, M. [ed.] (1979) The Denigration of Capitalism. Washington, DC: American Enterprise Institute.
NOWLAN, S. E. and D. R. SHAYON (1984) Leveraging the Impact of Public Affairs: A Guidebook Based on Practical Experience for Corporate Public Affairs Executives. Philadelphia: HRN.

———(1984) "Reviewing your relationship with executive management." Public Relations Quarterly 29 (Spring): 5-11.

NOWLING, J. R. (1977) "Trans Alaska pipeline: classic PR dilemma." Public Relations Journal 33 (March): 9-11.

OBERSCHALL, A. (1973) Social Conflict and Social Movements. Englewood Cliffs, NJ: Prentice-Hall.

———(1978) "The decline of the 1960s social movements," pp. 257-289 in L. Kriegsberg (ed.) Research in Social Movements, Conflict, and Change: An Annual Compilation of Research, Vol. 1. Greenwich, CT: JAI Press.

Opinion Research Corporation (1981a) "The business climate." Public Opinion Index 39 (March).

———(1981b) "Priority analysis of 45 national issues." Public Opinion Index 39 (June).

O'SHEA J. (1983) "Drive to kill withholding bill shows power of banking lobby." Houston Post (April 25), p. 4C.

O'TOOLE, J. E. (1975a) "Advocacy advertising act II." Cross Currents in Corporate Communications 2: 33-37.

———(1975b) "Advocacy advertising shows the flag." Public Relations Journal 31 (November): 14-16.

OTTEN, A. L. (1984) "States begin to protect employees who blow whistle on their firms." Wall Street Journal (December 31), p. 11.

PAGAN, R. D., Jr. (1983) "Issue management: no set path." Presented at the annual meeting of the Issues Management Association, New York City, November 7.

PASKOWSKI, M. and B. DONATH (1981) "Focus—telling the corporate story." Industrial Marketing 66 (March): 43-44, 46, 48.

PEDERSEN, J. T. (1976) "Age and change in public opinion: the case of California, 1960-1970." Public Opinion Quarterly 40: 143-153.

PERKINS, D. J. (1982) "The sponsored film: a new dimension in American film research?" Historical Journal of Film, Radio & Television 2 (October): 133-140.

PETERFREUND, S. (1974) "Employee publications: deadly but not dead yet." Public Relations Journal 30 (January): 20-23.

PETZINGER, T., Jr. and B. BURROUGH (1984) "U.S. cities and towns ponder the potential for chemical calamity." Wall Street Journal (December 14), pp. 1, 6.

PHILLIPS, K. (1981) "Business and the media." Public Affairs Review 2: 53-60

PINCUS, J. D. (1980) "Taking a stand on the issues through advertising." Association Management 32 (December): 58-63.

PIRES, M. A. (1983) "Texaco: working with public interest groups." Public Relations Journal 39 (April): 16-19.

POOL, I. DE SOLA (1983) Technologies of Freedom. Cambridge, MA: Harvard University Press.

POST, J. E. (1978) Corporate Behavior and Social Change. Reston, VA: Reston.

———(1979) "Corporate response models and public affairs management." Public Relations Quarterly 24 (Winter): 27-32.

———(1980) "Public affairs and management policy in the 1980's." Public Affairs Review 1: 3-12.

———(1985) "Assessing the Nestle boycott: corporate accountability and human rights." California Management Review 27: 113-131.

———E. A. MURRAY, Jr., R. B. DICKIE, and J. F. MAHON (1983) "Managing public affairs: the public affairs function." California Management Review 26: 135-150.

Prentice-Hall Federal Taxes (1982) Vol. 2. Englewood Cliffs, NJ: Prentice-Hall.

PRESTON, I. L. (1975) The Great American Blow-Up: Puffery in Advertising and Selling. Madison: University of Wisconsin Press.

"Private enterprise and public values" (1979) Society 16 (March/April): 18-19.

Public Affairs Council (1978) The Fundamentals of Issue Management. Washington, DC: Author.

"Public relations' role in corporate advertising." (1977) Public Relations Journal 33 (November): 34-35.

"Pubsat: a world-wide radio-TV satellite network." (1983) Information sheet, Public Affairs Satellite System, Inc., Washington, DC.

RAUCHER, A. R. (1968) Public Relations and Business: 1900-1929. Baltimore, MD: Johns Hopkins University Press.

Regulation: AEI Journal of Government and Society (1983) "Perspectives on current developments: Truth vs. provability at the FTC." (February): 7: 4-6.

RENFRO, W. L. (1982) "Managing the issues of the 1980s." The Futurist 16 (August): 61-66.

REUSS, C. and D. E. SILVIS [eds.] (1981) Inside Organizational Communication. New York: Longman.

RESSLER, J. A. (1982) "Crisis communications." Public Relations Quarterly 27 (Fall): 8-10.

RHODY, R. (1983) "The public's right to know." IPRA Review 7 (November): 46-47.

RICE, R. D. (1976) "The role of television in corporate advertising." Public Relations Journal 32 (November): 18.

ROBERTS, D. F., P. CHRISTENSON, W. A. GIBSON, L. MOOSER, and M. E. GOLDBERG (1980) "Developing discriminating consumers." Journal of Communication 30 (Summer): 94-105.

ROBERSTON, T. S. and J. R. ROSSITER (1977) "Children's responsiveness to commercials." Journal of Communication 27 (Winter): 101-106.

ROBINSON, E. J. (1969) Public Relations and Survey Research: Achieving Organizational Goals in a Corporate Context. New York: Appleton-Century-Crofts.

ROKEACH, M. (1968) "The role of values in public opinion research." Public Opinion Quarterly 32: 547-559.

———(1974) "Change and stability in American value systems, 1968-1971." Public Opinion Quarterly 38: 222-238.

ROMAN, J. W. (1983) Cablemania: The Cable Television Sourcebook. Englewood Cliffs, NJ: Prentice-Hall.

RONICK, H. R. (1983) "The F.T.C.: an overview." Cases & Comment 88 (July/ August): 35-38.

ROSS, I. (1976) "Public relations isn't kid glove stuff at Mobil." Fortune 94 (September): 106-111, 196-202.

ROTFELD, H. J. (1983) "Regulation of the free—advertising and the first amendment." Policy Studies Review 2: 474-483.

ROTH, T. (1984) "Chemical firms may be facing new regulations." Wall Street Journal (December 17), p. 4.

ROWAN, F. (1984) Broadcast Fairness: Doctrine, Practice, Prospects. New York: Longman.

ROWE, K. and J. SCHLACTER (1978) "Integrating social responsibility into the corporate structure." Public Relations Quarterly 23 (Fall): 7-12.

RUBIN, A. (1985) "Video news releases: whose news is it?" Public Relations Journal 41: 18-23.

SADDLER, J. (1983a) "FTC alters its policy on deceptive ads by 3-2 vote, sparks congressional outcry." Wall Street Journal (October 24), p. 41.

———(1983b) "FTC easing rules requiring firms to support ad claims." Wall Street Journal (July 21), p. 29.

SALAMON, J. (1983) "Fight over withholding splits banks." Wall Street Journal (March 28), p. 21.

SALVAGGIO, J. L. [ed.] (1983) Telecommunications, Issues and Choices for Society. New York: Longman.

SAMBUL, N. J. [ed.] (1982a) The Handbook of Private Television: A Complete Guide for Video Facilities and Networks within Corporations, Nonprofit Institutions, and Government Agencies. New York: McGraw-Hill.

———(1982b) "A new outlet for corporation video?" Video User 5 (August): 1, 25.

SCHELLHARDT, T. D. (1975) "More regulations by government gets 56% backing in poll." Wall Street Journal (May 14): 27.

SCHMERTZ, H. [ed.] (1983a) The Energy Crisis and the Media: Ten Case Histories. New York: Mobil Corporation.

———(1983b) "The press and the public." Address before the Annual Review Meeting, Gannett News Service, Washington, D.C., December 13.

SCHORR, B. and C. CONTE (1984) "Public-interest groups achieve higher status and some permanence." Wall Street Journal (August 27), pp. 1, 8.

SCHULTZE, Q. J. (1981) "Advertising and public utilities 1900-1917." Journal of Advertising 10, 4: 41-44, 48.

SCHUMAN, H. and S. PRESSER (1977-1978) "Attitude measurement and the gun control paradox." Public Opinion Quarterly 41: 427-438.

SCHWENK, C. R. (1984) "Cognitive simplification processes in strategic decision-making." Strategic Management Journal 5: 111-128.

SCOTT, R. L. and D. K. SMITH (1969) "The rhetoric of confrontation." Quarterly Journal of Speech 55: 1-8.

SEIFERT, W. (1977) "Our highest court: public opinion." Public Relations Journal 33 (December): 24-25.

SETHI, S. P. [ed.] (1974) The Unstable Ground: Corporate Social Policy in a Dynamic Society. Los Angeles: Melville.

———(1976a) "Dangers of advocacy advertising." Public Relations Journal 32 (November): 42, 46-47.

———(1976b) "Management fiddles while public affairs flops." Business and Society Review 18 (Summer): 9-11.

———(1977) Advocacy Advertising and Large Corporations: Social Conflict, Big Business Image, the News Media, and Public Policy. Lexington, MA: D.C. Heath.

———(1979a) "Grassroots lobbying and the corporation." Business and Society Review 29: 8-14.

———(1979b) "Institutional/image advertising and idea/issue advertising as marketing tools: Some public policy issues." Journal of Marketing 43: 68-78.

———(1981) "Advocacy advertising in America." Presented at the Advocacy Advertising Conference, Canada, Nov. 25.

———(1982) "Moving social responsibility down a peg." Public Relations Journal 38 (August): 25-27.

SHANTS, F. B. (1978) "Countering the anti-nuclear activists." Public Relations Journal 34 (October): 10.

SHELBY, A. N. (1985) "A typology of communication strategies for corporate advocacy." Journal of Business Strategies 2 (Spring): 33-38.

SHELER, J. L. (1983) "Unions' big push to be heard—again." U.S. News & World Report 95 (July 25): 75-76.

SHERIF, C., M. SHERIF, and R. NEBERGALL (1965) Attitude and Attitude Change: The Social Judgment-Involvement Approach. Philadelphia: W. B. Saunders.

SHERIF, M. and C. I. HOVLAND (1961) Social Judgment: Assimilation and Contrast Effects in Communication and Attitude Change. New Haven, CT: Yale University Press.

SHERIF, M. and C. SHERIF (1969) Social Psychology. New York: Harper & Row.

SHIM, J. K. and R. McGLADE (1984) "Current trends in the use of corporate planning models." Journal of Systems Management 35 (September): 24-31.

SIMMONS, S. J. (1978) The Fairness Doctrine and the Media. Berkeley: University of California Press.

SIMON, R. J. (1971) "Public attitudes toward population and pollution." Public Opinion Quarterly 35: 95-99.

SIMONS, H. W. (1970) "Requirements, problems, and strategies: a theory of persuasion for social movements." Quarterly Journal of Speech 56: 1-11.

———(1972) "Persuasion in social conflicts: a critique of prevailing conceptions and a framework for future research." Speech Monographs 39: 229-247.

———(1974) "The carrot and stick as handmaidens of persuasion in conflict situations," pp. 172-205 in G. R. Miller and H. W. Simons (eds.) Perspectives on Communication in Social Conflict. Englewood Cliffs, NJ: Prentice-Hall.

———(1976) "Changing notions about social movements." Quarterly Journal of Speech 62: 425-430.

———(1983) "Mobil's system-oriented conflict rhetoric: a generic analysis." Southern Speech Communication Journal 48: 243-254.

SINCLAIR, U. (1906) The Jungle. New York: Doubleday.

SKELLY, F. R. (1976) "The changing attitudes of public opinion." Public Relations Journal 32 (November): 15-17.

SMELSER, N. J. (1963) Theory of Collective Behavior. New York: Free Press.

SMITH, T. W. (1980) "America's most important problem—a trend analysis, 1946-1976." Public Opinion Quarterly 44: 164-180.

SNYDER, L. (1983) "An anniversary review and critique: the Tylenol case." Public Relations Review 9 (Fall): 24-34.

SOLOMON, J. B. and M. RUSSELL (1984) "U.S. chemical disclosure—law efforts getting boost from tragedy in Bhopal." Wall Street Journal (December 14), p. 18.

SPITZER, C. E. (1979) "Where are we getting all this information and what are we doing with it?" Public Relations Journal 35 (February): 8-11.

———(1982) "Lobbying, ethics, and common sense." Public Relations Journal 38 (February): 34-36.

STAMM, K. R. (1977) "Strategies for evaluating public relations." Public Relations Review 3 (Winter): 120-128.

——— and J. E. BOWES (1972) "Communication during an environmental decision." Journal of Environmental Education 3 (Spring): 49-56.

STECKMEST, F. W. (1982) Corporate Performance: The Key to Public Trust. New York: McGraw-Hill.

STEFFENS, L. (1904) The Shame of the Cities. New York: McClure, Phillips.

STEIN, S. (1983) "Companies using advocacy to get their points across." Houston Post (October 16), p. 5E.

STEPHENSON, D. R. (1982) "How to turn pitfalls into opportunities in crisis situations." Public Relations Quarterly 27 (Fall): 11-15.

———(1983) "Internal PR efforts further corporate responsibility: a report from Dow Canada." Public Relations Quarterly 28 (Summer): 7-10.

STEWART, C., C. SMITH, and R. E. DENTON, Jr. (1984) Persuasion and Social Movements. Prospect Heights, IL: Waveland Press.

STIPAK, B. (1977) "Attitudes and belief systems concerning urban services." Public Relations Quarterly 23 (Winter): 17-18.

———(1982) "Budgeting." Public Relations Journal 38 (October): 20-23.

———(1984) "The communications audit—basic to business development." Public Relations Quarterly 29 (Spring): 14-17.

STRENSKI, J. B. (1978) "The communications audit: primary PR measurement tool." Public Relations Quarterly 23: 17-18.

STRIDSBERG, A. B. (1977) Controversy Advertising: How Advertisers Present Points of View in Public Affairs. New York: Hastings House.

"Study sees too much emphasis on bad business news." (1984) Broadcasting 106 (March 19): 74-75.

TAN, A. S. (1980) "Mass media use, issue knowledge and political involvement." Public Opinion Quarterly 44: 241-248.

TARBELL, I. (1904) The History of the Standard Oil Company. New York: McClure, Phillips.

TARDE, G. (1922) L'Opinion et la Foule. Paris: Alcan.

———(1969) On Communication and Social Influence: Selected Papers (T. N. Clark, ed., intro.). Chicago: University of Chicago Press.

THEBERGE, L. J. [ed.] (1981) Crooks, Conmen, and Clowns: Businessmen in TV Entertainment. Washington, DC: The Media Institute.

———and T. W. HAZLETT (1982) TV Coverage of the Oil Crises: How Well Was the Public Served? Washington, DC: The Media Institute.

THOMAS, H. (1984) "Mapping strategic management research." Journal of General Management 9 (Summer): 55-72.

——— and C. R. SCHWENK (1984) "Decision analysis as an aid to strategy." Management Decision 22, 2: 50-60.

THOMPSON, D. B. (1981) "Issue management: new key to corporate survival." Industry Week 208 (February 23): 77-80.

TICHENOR, P. J., G. A. DONOHUE, and C. H. OLIEN (1977) "Community research and evaluating community relations." Public Relations Review 3 (Winter): 96-109.

TIRONE, J. F. (1977) "Measuring the Bell System's public relations." Public Relations Review 3 (Winter): 21-38.

TOCH, H. (1965) The Social Psychology of Social Movements. Indianapolis: Bobbs-Merrill.

TROST, C. (1985) "Bhopal disaster spurs debate over usefulness of criminal sanctions in industrial accidents." Wall Street Journal (January 7), p. 14.

"TV outpolls newspapers as business news source." (1982) Adweek (October 18): 28.

U.S. Congress (1962) Senate, Congressional Record, Vol. 108. 87th Congress, 2nd session. Washington, DC: Government Printing Office.

U.S. Congress (1978a) House of Representatives, Committee on Government Operations. IRS Administration of Tax Laws Relating to Lobbying. 95th Congress, 2nd session. Washington, DC: Government Printing Office.

U.S. Congress (1978b) Senate, Committee on the Judiciary, Subcommittee on Administrative Practice and Procedure. Sourcebook on Corporate Image and Corporate Advocacy Advertising. 95th Congress, 2nd session. Washington, DC: Government Printing Office.

USEEM, M. (1985) "Beyond the corporation: who represents business to the government and public." Business Horizons 28 (May/June): 21-26.

VAN DEN HAAG, E. (1979) Capitalism: Sources of Hostility. New Rochelle, NY: Epoch Books.

VAN METER, J. R. (1983) "TV didn't invent evil businessmen." Wall Street Journal (October 28), p. 28.

VAN RIPER, R. (1976) "The uses of research in public relations." Public Relations Journal 32 (February) 18-19.

WADE, S. and W. SCHRAMM (1969) "The mass media as sources of public affairs, science, and health knowledge." Public Opinion Quarterly 33: 197-209.

WADEMAN, V. (1975) "Ten questions to ask your advertising agency." Public Relations Quarterly 20 (Summer): 26-29.

WALTY, W. (1981) "Is issue advertising working?" Public Relations Journal 37 (November): 29.

Washington Broadcast News advertisement (1984) Public Relations Journal 40 (February): 15.

WAZ, J. (1983) "Fighting the fair fight." Channels 2 (March/April): 66-69.

WEINSTEIN, A. K. (1979) "Management issues for the coming decade." University of Michigan Business Review 31 (September): 29-32.

WEISSMAN, G. (1984) "Social responsibility and corporate success." Business and Society Review 51: 67-68.

WESSEL, M. R. (1976) The Rule of Reason: A New Approach to Corporate Litigation. Reading, MA: Addison-Wesley.

WHITAKER, M., S. MAZUMDAR, F. GIBNEY, Jr., and E. BEHR (1984) " 'It was like breathing fire . . . ' " Newsweek 104 (December 17): 26-32.

WIEBE, R. H. (1967) The Search for Order: 1877-1920. New York: Hill & Wang.

———(1968) Businessmen and Reform: A Study of the Progressive Movement. Chicago: Quadrangle Books.

WILLIAMS, L. C., Jr. (1978) "What 50 presidents and chief executive officers think about employee communication." Public Relations Quarterly 23 (Winter): 6-11.

WILLIAMS, P. R. (1982) "The new technology and its implications for organizational communicators." Public Relations Quarterly 27 (Spring): 15-16.

WINSLOW, R. (1984) "Woman helps sink nuclear power plant that cost $4 billion." Wall Street Journal (July 18), pp. 1, 19.

———(1985a) "Union Carbide moved to bar accident at U. S. plant before Bhopal tragedy." Wall Street Journal (January 28), p. 6.

———(1985b) "Union Carbide plans to resume making methyl isocynanate at its U. S. facility." Wall Street Journal (February 13), p. 2.

WISEMAN, P. R. (1982) "The new technology and its implications for organizational communicators." Public Relations Quarterly 27 (Spring): 15-16.

WISEMAN, F., M. MORIARTY and M. SCHAFER (1975-76) "Estimating public opinion with the randomized response model." Public Opinion Quarterly 39: 507-513.

WOOLWARD, I. (1982) "Rethinking corporate advocacy media strategy." Industrial Marketing 67 (May): 75-78.

YANKELOVITCH, SKELLY and WHITE, Inc. (1979) Corporate Advertising/Phase II: An Expanded Study of Corporate Advertising Effectiveness. New York: Author.

YOUNG, L. H. (1981) "The media's view of corporate communications in the '80's." Public Relations Quarterly 26 (Fall): 9-11.

ZENTNER, R. D. (1978) "Measuring the effectiveness of corporate advertising." Public Relations Journal 34 (November): 24-25.

ZRAKET, C. A. (1981) "New challenges of the information society." Public Relations Quarterly 26 (Fall): 12-15.

LEGAL CASES AND REGULATORY RULINGS

Accuracy in Media, Inc. (1973) 28 RR 2d 1371.
American B/casting Co. (1969) 15 RR 2d 791.
American B/casting Co., Inc. (1975) 33 RR 2d 305.
American Security Council Education Foundation (1977) 39 2d 1635.
American Security Council Education Foundation v. FCC (1979) 45 RR 2d 1433, US App DC.
Arkansas Cable Television Association (1976) 33 RR 2d 1545.
Banzhaf ruling: *WCBS-TV* (1967) 8 FCC 2d 381; *Banzhaf v. FCC* (1968) 405 F.2d 1082 DC Cir.; certiorari denied (1969) 396 U. S. 842, 90 S.Ct. 50.
Big Bend B/casting Corp. (1970) 20 RR 2d 93.
Bigelow v. Virginia (1975) 421 U. S. 809, 95 S. Ct. 2222, 2227.
Bolger et al. v. Young Drug Products Corp. (1981) USDC DistCol, 526 F. Supp. 823.
Brandywine-Main Line Radio, Inc. (1968) 14 RR 2d 1051 Init. Dec.
Buckley v. Valeo (1976) 424 U. S. 1.
Business Executives Move for Vietnam Peace v. FCC, and *Democratic National Committee v. FCC* (1973) 414 U. S. 94, 93 S. Ct. 2080.
Central Hudson Gas & Electric Corp. v. Public Service Commission of New York (1980) 447 U.S. 557, 100 S. Ct. 2343.
Citizens Communications Center (1971) 21 RR 2d 1222n.
Columbia Broadcasting System, Inc. v. Democratic National Committee; Federal Communications Commission v. Business Executives' Move for Vietnam Peace; Post-Newsweek Stations, Capital Area, Inc., v. Business Executives' Move for Vietnam Peace; and *American Broadcasting Companies v. Democratic National Committee* (1973) 41 LW 4688.
Commarano v. United States (1957) 246 F.2d 751 9th Cir.
Conservative Caucus, Inc. v. CBS, Inc. (1983) 54 RR 2d 61.
Consolidated Edison of New York v. Public Service Commission of New York (1980) 447 U.S. 530.
Consumers Power Co. (1969) 299 F. Supp. 1181 DC Mich.; rev'd on other grounds, 427 F.2d 78 CA-6 (1970), certiorari denied.
Council on Religion and the Homosexual, Inc. (1978) 43 RR 2d 1580.
Saul David (1976) 38 RR 2d 1349.
Energy Action Committee, Inc. (1976) 40 RR 2d 511.
Environmental Defense Fund v. KERO-TV (1982) 51 R R 2d 1445.
Fairness Doctrine (1974) 30 RR 2d 1261.

FCC Public Notice (1974). "Fairness doctrine and the public interest standards," 39 FR 26372; *Report on the Handling of Public Issues Under the Fairness Doctrine and the Public Interest Standards of the Communication Act,* 48 FCC 2d 1.
FCC v. League of Women Voters of California (1984) 104 S. Ct. 3106.
First National Bank of Boston v. Bellotti (1978) 435 U. S. 765.
Friends of the Earth (1970) 24 FCC 2d 743.
Friends of the Earth v. FCC (1971) 449 F2d 1164 D.C. Cir.
Georgia Power Project v. FCC (1977) 41 RR 2d 803, CA 5th.
Green v. FCC (1971) 22 RR 2d 2022, US App. DC.
Grocery Manufacturers of America Inc. (1977) 41 RR 2d 787.
Grosjean v. American Press Co. (1936) 297 U. S. 233; 41 LW 4697.
Iowa Beef Processors, Inc. v. Station WCCO-TV (1982) 51 RR 2d 1225.
Donald A. Jelinek (1970) 19 RR 2d 501.
Joint Council of Allergy and Immunology (1983) 54 RR 2d 396.
Richard Kates (1972) 24 RR 2d 117.
Albert A. Kramer (1970) 19 RR 2d 498.
Roger Langley (1978) 44 RR 2d 506.
Larus & Brother Co. v. FCC (1971) 447 F.2d 876, 4th Cir.
Harry Lerner (1969) 17 RR 2d 173.
Thomas V. Lippitt (1975) 34 RR 2d 141.
Miami Herald Publishing Company v. Pat L. Tornillo (1974) 418 U. S. 241-62.
Muller v. Oregon (1908) 208 U.S. 412.
Munn v. Illinois (1877) 94 U.S. 113.
National Association of Government Employees (1973) 27 RR 2d 1309.
National Association of Manufacturers v. Blumethal (1979) 466 F. Supp. 905 DC-DC, aff'd without issuance of an opinion, CA-DC (1980).
National B/casting Co., Inc. (1975) 33 RR 2d 244.
National Football League Players Association (1973) 27 RR 2d 179.
National Oil Jobbers Council (1980) 47 RR 2d 202.
National Organization for Women v. FCC (1977) 40 RR 2d 679, US App DC.
Alan F. Neckritz (1970) 19 RR 2d 497.
New York Times Co. v. Sullivan (1964) 376 U. S. 254, 265-266, 84 S. Ct. 710, 718.
Terrence Olesen (1976) 38 RR 2d 559.
Police Department of Chicago v. Mosley (1972) 408 U. S. 92, 95.
Public Communications, Inc. (1974) 31 RR 2d 849.
Public Media Center (1976) 37 RR 2d 263.
Radio Station KKHI (1980) 47 RR 2d 839.
Radioactive Waste Policy (1982) 52 RR 2d 481.
Red Lion Broadcasting Co. v. FCC (1969) 395 U. S. 367, 89 S. Ct 1794.
John Roscoe (1978) 42 RR 2d 99.
Scripps-Howard B/casting Co. (1978) 42 RR 2d 851.
Security World Publishing Co. (1976) 38 RR 2d 705.
Lyn A. Sherwood (1971) 21 RR 2d 553.
Mary Sinclair (1970) 20 RR 2d 1226.
Storer Broadcasting Co. (1968) 12 RR 2d 184.
Tri-State B/casting Co., Inc. (1962) 3 RR 2d 175, Staff Letter.
George R. Walker (1970) 20 RR 2d 264.
WCMP B/casting Co. (1973) 27 RR 2d 1000.
Wilderness Society and Friends of the Earth (1971) 23 RR 2d 431.
Yellow Freight System, Inc. (1979) 46 RR 2d 531.

INDEX

ABOUT THE AUTHORS

ROBERT L. HEATH is an associate professor and Director, Graduate Study, School of Communication, University of Houston-University Park. He received his Ph.D from the University of Illinois in 1971. Since then he has published regularly in journals such as *Public Relations Review, Public Affairs Review, Journal of Communication, Communication Yearbook,* and *Journal of Marketing* in the areas of corporate communication, social movements, and rhetorical theory. He is founder of Communication Management, a Houston-based consulting firm specializing in business communication, and a member of the American Society for Training and Development, as well as other professional and scholarly organizations.

RICHARD ALAN NELSON is associate professor of communication and Associate Director, International Telecommunications Research Institute, School of Communication, University of Houston-University Park. A former trade journalist, technical editor, and public information coordinator, he is professionally accredited by the Public Relations Society of America. A business communication consultant, he is a member of the Issues Management Association. He is a graduate of Stanford University (A.B., political science) and Brigham Young University (M. A., communication). He received his Ph.D. from Florida State University and authored the business history *Florida and the American Motion Picture Industry, 1898-1980* (Garland, 1983) and the forthcoming *Propaganda: A Reference Guide* (Greenwood).